Ethereum Smart Contract Development

Build blockchain-based decentralized applications
using solidity

Mayukh Mukhopadhyay

BIRMINGHAM - MUMBAI

Ethereum Smart Contract Development

Commissioning Editor: Sunith Shetty
Acquisition Editor: Chandan Kumar
Content Development Editor: Amrita Noronha
Technical Editor: Sayali Thanekar
Copy Editor: Safis Editing, Vikrant Phadke
Project Coordinator: Shweta H Birwatkar
Proofreader: Safis Editing
Indexer: Pratik Shirodkar
Graphics: Jisha Chirayil
Production Coordinator: Aparna Bhagat

First published: February 2018

Production reference: 1210218

Published by Packt Publishing Ltd.
Livery Place
35 Livery Street
Birmingham
B3 2PB, UK.

ISBN 978-1-78847-304-0

www.packtpub.com

*Dedicated to my wife, **Mrittika**, for loaning me her ACER laptop to complete this book.*

*And my daughter, **Abriti**, for keeping her mom super busy while
I was crashing it by mining ethers.*

`mapt.io`

Mapt is an online digital library that gives you full access to over 5,000 books and videos, as well as industry leading tools to help you plan your personal development and advance your career. For more information, please visit our website.

Why subscribe?

- Spend less time learning and more time coding with practical eBooks and Videos from over 4,000 industry professionals

- Improve your learning with Skill Plans built especially for you

- Get a free eBook or video every month

- Mapt is fully searchable

- Copy and paste, print, and bookmark content

PacktPub.com

Did you know that Packt offers eBook versions of every book published, with PDF and ePub files available? You can upgrade to the eBook version at `www.PacktPub.com` and as a print book customer, you are entitled to a discount on the eBook copy. Get in touch with us at `service@packtpub.com` for more details.

At `www.PacktPub.com`, you can also read a collection of free technical articles, sign up for a range of free newsletters, and receive exclusive discounts and offers on Packt books and eBooks.

Contributors

About the author

Mayukh Mukhopadhyay started his career as a BI developer. After the 2008-09 financial crisis, he was at Tata Consultancy Services for one of their Fortune 500 clients in the telecom sector. Holding a master's in software engineering from Jadavpur University, he is presently working as a data insight developer, where he focuses on applying data science and machine learning to raw telecom equipment logs to generate business insights. He has a varied list of academic interests, ranging from audio signal processing, structural bioinformatics, and bio-inspired algorithms to consciousness engineering. Apart from being an Oracle Certified Specialist, he is a Certified Bitcoin Professional, recognized by C4 (Crypto Currency Certification Consortium). He tries to apply blockchain as a technology to different business domains.

To my guide @JU Dr Parama Bhaumik —your lectures on distributed systems were my main inspiration while writing this book.

To my professional network connections Ivan Liljeqvist, Dug Campbell, Mahesh Murthy, Kaushik Sathupadi, Ravinder Deol, Narayan Prusty, and Thomas Wiesner—thanks for your blogs and vlogs. This book is as much your creation as it is mine.

About the reviewer

Daniel Kraft studied applied mathematics and theoretical physics in Graz, Austria, where he obtained his PhD from the University of Graz in 2015. After that, he started as a software engineer in Zurich, Switzerland. He has been very interested in Bitcoin and cryptocurrencies since 2011 and involved in Bitcoin development since 2013. Since 2014, he has been the main developer for Namecoin and Huntercoin, and has successfully reimplemented both on top of the modern Bitcoin Core code base. Wherever possible, Daniel also contributed improvements to the upstream Bitcoin Core. He has published multiple research articles in peer-reviewed journals, two of them directly related to cryptocurrency.

Packt is searching for authors like you

If you're interested in becoming an author for Packt, please visit `authors.packtpub.com` and apply today. We have worked with thousands of developers and tech professionals, just like you, to help them share their insight with the global tech community. You can make a general application, apply for a specific hot topic that we are recruiting an author for, or submit your own idea.

Table of Contents

Preface

If you are reading this line, I want to congratulate you because you have already overcome the most difficult hurdle in the pursuit of the understanding blockchain, and specifically, Ethereum smart contracts. This hurdle is the overwhelming hype surrounding this promising yet premature technology and trying to know what is really going on under the hood.

I am a software developer, and through my book, which you are viewing in your electronic device or physically holding in your hand, we will together embark on a fascinating journey through this enigmatic and revolutionary technology.

The chapters in this book have been arranged in an incremental fashion. We start with a gentle introduction to blockchain using the familiar bitcoin, and quickly dive into the world of Ethereum and the major players in its ecosystem.

Then we proceed to do some hands-on coding of a typical "Hello World" smart contract. We then take on the subject of decentralized autonomous organizations, decentralized applications, and smart contract optimization. We also analyze two famous multi-million-dollar hacks that recently occurred in the Ethereum community, along with the preventive measures employed to avoid them in future.

We then move on to the intricacies of the solidity programming language and web3.js library.

The final chapters mainly deal with the development of standardized tokens, the concept of initial coin offering, potential enterprise use cases of smart contracts, designing a decentralized micro-blogging platform, and surfing the dark web marketplace.

We conclude the book by providing primers on advanced topics with promising future prospects such as graph-based DLTs and quantum secured blockchains.

At the onset, I want to have a clear understanding between us. Even though I am the author of this book and it is my sole responsibility to present the facts as accurately as possible in this book, in no possible way do I consider myself as the sole authority on this subject.

As my reader, I want you to realize that I am just another overenthusiastic fellow learner who will try to assist you with your pursuit of knowledge by introducing the optimal amount of information required to kick-start your journey. And I will make you aware of the hurdles and pitfalls I faced along the way so that you can learn from my mistakes.

Enough said. Let's start our journey to blockchain and get our hands dirty with *Ethereum Smart Contract Development*.

Happy reading!

Who this book is for

This book is dedicated to novice programmers, solution architects, and blockchain enthusiasts who want to build powerful, robust, and optimized smart contracts using solidity from scratch and in combination with other open source JavaScript libraries. If you want to build your own extensive, decentralized applications that can smartly execute on a blockchain, then this book is what you need! An open and inquisitive mind is a necessary and sufficient prerequisite. Some preliminary knowledge of data structures, object-oriented programming, networking concepts, and cryptography is a plus and will help the reader to understand the concepts presented in this book.

What this book covers

Chapter 1, *Blockchain Basics*, will serve as a warm-up session about blockchain before we deep dive into Ethereum and smart contract development. To really appreciate blockchain, we must understand the two founding pillars on which blockchain as a technology is firmly grounded: distributed systems and cryptography. Once we have covered these two core concepts, we try to understand a blockchain from two different perspectives: as a software developer and as a trader of financial instruments. Then we probe into the internal logical architecture of a block in the blockchain, focusing the bitcoin block structure, and get a gentle introduction to the mining and forking process. We conclude the chapter by discussing how blockchain has evolved in recent years and clearly marking out its current position in the technological hype cycle.

Chapter 2, *Grokking Ethereum*, will help us to understand the meaning of decentralization and whether Ethereum is truly decentralized. We will also cover its core technological stack and get familiarized with various jargon, such as Mist, EVM, Swarm, Whisper, Ether, and Gas. We will briefly discuss the notion of a Turing-complete language. We'll then revisit forking, mining, and block architecture from the perspective of Ethereum. We'll end this chapter by getting a notion of Ethereum wallets and client interfaces, which will serve as a firm base for smart contract development.

Chapter 3, *The Hello World of Ethereum Smart Contract*, provides a hands-on guide to developing our first smart contract. As an unspoken tradition of a software developer, we start with a "Hello World" program. Then we try some basic arithmetic increment and decrement operations using a contract. We then learn how to code a loop inside a smart contract and how to raise an issue in GitHub. We end this chapter by creating our own private blockchain right from the genesis block, attach it with Geth, and use the Mist browser to deploy one of the smart contracts we studied in this chapter, after mining some ethers.

Chapter 4, *A Noob's Guide to DApps and DAOs*, develops our understanding towards decentralized applications from a developer's perspective. We introduce the high-level steps to develop a decentralized application. Then we explore a unique marketplace called ethercast, which serves as an aggregator of several DApps. We then move on to design a decentralized autonomous organization. We conclude this chapter with a retrospection of the infamous DAO hack, which led to the ETH/ETC split, from a purely technical perspective.

Chapter 5, *Deep-Diving into Smart Contracts*, digs deeper into smart contract designs. We start by understanding the textbook definition of a smart contract. Then we move on to understand different smart contract models and the role of code in a smart contract. We go through the basic anatomy of a smart contract and see how a smart contract works. Then we shift our focus to advanced topics such as smart contract optimization, auditing, and ERC20 compliance. We conclude the chapter with a hands-on drill of building a voting DApp.

Chapter 6, *Solidity in Depth*, is all about the Turing complete solidity language on the Ethereum blockchain. We will start by probing into the design decision of why we really need a new language like solidity. The next sections will cover the nuances of the solidity language and the basic syntax used in it. Specifically, we'll cover contract-oriented features, functions and events, inheritance, libraries, expressions, control structures, units, and variables. Then we'll look at the optimizer and debugging options. We will conclude this chapter by analyzing the code flaw that led to the recent parity wallet hack in the Ethereum blockchain, which stole around $30 million worth of ethers.

Chapter 7, *Primer on Web3.js*, introduces a special application programming interface library written in JavaScript. This interface connects our web browser with the Ethereum blockchain node. We will begin this chapter by understanding the difference between Geth, Web3.js, and Mist. Then we will learn how to import this API library and get connected with Geth. We will then explore the API structure inside the web3.js library. We'll conclude the chapter by studying the design of an ownership contract.

Chapter 8, *Developing Cryptocurrency from Scratch*, provides a hands-on tutorial to develop an ERC20 standardized token using the Truffle framework. We then dive in to the concepts of **initial coin offering (ICO)** and how to identify genuine ICOs among fake and Ponzi schemes. The chapter concludes by discussing various token conversion process and pair-trading concepts.

Chapter 9, *Enterprise Use Cases*, provides some exciting and promising use cases of Ethereum smart contracts. We also discuss the design of a decentralized micro-blogging platform using solidity.

Chapter 10, *BaaS and the Dark Web Market*, introduce us to the blockchain framework of Microsoft and IBM. We conclude this chapter by discussing the difference between the Conventional Web and the Dark Web (.onion website and TOR) and how to safely browse the Dark Web to find use cases of cryptocurrencies.

Chapter 11, *Advanced Topics and the Road Ahead*, deals with exciting topics such as graph-based DLTS with a focus on Tangle, quantum secured blockchain, Ethereum improvement protocols, consortium blockchains, distributed autonomous societies, and common design patterns for solidity.

To get the most out of this book

1. Inform the reader of the things that they need to know before they start, and spell out what knowledge you are assuming
2. Some preliminary knowledge of data structures, object-oriented programming, networking concepts, and cryptography is a plus but not mandatory

Download the example code files

You can download the example code files for this book from your account at www.packtpub.com. If you purchased this book elsewhere, you can visit www.packtpub.com/support and register to have the files emailed directly to you.

You can download the code files by following these steps:

1. Log in or register at www.packtpub.com.
2. Select the **SUPPORT** tab.
3. Click on **Code Downloads & Errata**.
4. Enter the name of the book in the **Search** box and follow the onscreen instructions.

Once the file is downloaded, please make sure that you unzip or extract the folder using the latest version of:

- WinRAR/7-Zip for Windows
- Zipeg/iZip/UnRarX for Mac
- 7-Zip/PeaZip for Linux

The code bundle for the book is also hosted on GitHub at https://github.com/ PacktPublishing/Ethereum-Smart-Contract-Development. In case there's an update to the code, it will be updated on the existing GitHub repository.

We also have other code bundles from our rich catalog of books and videos available at https://github.com/PacktPublishing/. Check them out!

Download the color images

We also provide a PDF file that has color images of the screenshots/diagrams used in this book. You can download it here: http://www.packtpub.com/sites/default/files/downloads/EthereumSmartContractDeve lopment_ColorImages.pdf.

Conventions used

There are a number of text conventions used throughout this book.

CodeInText: Indicates code words in text, database table names, folder names, filenames, file extensions, pathnames, dummy URLs, user input, and Twitter handles. Here is an example: "Open your Google Chrome browser and type remix solidity in Google, as shown in *Figure 3.1*."

A block of code is set as follows:

```
{"jsonrpc":"2.0","method":"eth_coinbase","params":[],"id": 67}
```

Any command-line input or output is written as follows:

```
$  geth --datadir=./chaindata/ init genesis.json
```

Bold: Indicates a new term, an important word, or words that you see onscreen. For example, words in menus or dialog boxes appear in the text like this. Here is an example: "Click on the **Create** button as highlighted in *Figure 3.7*. Voila! You just created your smart contract."

Warnings or important notes appear like this.

Tips and tricks appear like this.

Get in touch

Feedback from our readers is always welcome.

General feedback: Email feedback@packtpub.com and mention the book title in the subject of your message. If you have questions about any aspect of this book, please email us at questions@packtpub.com.

Errata: Although we have taken every care to ensure the accuracy of our content, mistakes do happen. If you have found a mistake in this book, we would be grateful if you would report this to us. Please visit www.packtpub.com/submit-errata, selecting your book, clicking on the Errata Submission Form link, and entering the details.

Piracy: If you come across any illegal copies of our works in any form on the Internet, we would be grateful if you would provide us with the location address or website name. Please contact us at copyright@packtpub.com with a link to the material.

If you are interested in becoming an author: If there is a topic that you have expertise in and you are interested in either writing or contributing to a book, please visit authors.packtpub.com.

Reviews

Please leave a review. Once you have read and used this book, why not leave a review on the site that you purchased it from? Potential readers can then see and use your unbiased opinion to make purchase decisions, we at Packt can understand what you think about our products, and our authors can see your feedback on their book. Thank you!

For more information about Packt, please visit packtpub.com.

1
Blockchain Basics

This chapter will serve as a warm-up session about blockchain before we dive into Ethereum and smart contract development. To really appreciate blockchain, we must understand the two pillars on which blockchain, as a technology, is firmly grounded: distributed systems and cryptography. Once we have tackled these two core concepts, we will try to understand blockchain from two different perspectives: one as a software developer and another as a trader of financial instruments. Then, we'll probe into the internal logical architecture of a block in blockchain, focusing on the bitcoin block structure and get a gentle introduction to the mining and forking process.

We conclude the chapter by discussing the evolution of blockchain as a technology in recent years, three generations of blockchain technology, and the current position of blockchain on the gartner hype cycle.

After studying this chapter, you will be able to:

- Understand the foundation of blockchain technology
- Appreciate blockchain as a developer and a trader
- Discuss the basic structure of a bitcoin block
- Know about blockchain mining and forking and understand the evolution, generations, and hype surrounding blockchain

Understanding distributed systems

To understand a distributed system, we need to first distinguish it from traditional centralized systems. Traditional centralized systems consist of two main components: the client and the server. In the simplest setup, the client is the one who makes a request for getting a job done, and a server is the one who gets it done. This was how web 1.0 operated; the one we started calling the World Wide Web. For example, you placed a search request on Google search engine, and it gave you back a set of web links and summarized results.

Now, if two clients want to communicate between each other, they have to place request via the server, which serves as the middleman. A second example might be, for instance, if I send you a message from the client app of my mobile, this message is pushed to the WhatsApp server, which then notifies your client app about my message. Once you see my message, your client app sends back an acknowledgement signal in terms of a blue double tick to my client app, again using the WhatsApp server. This is how the present internet operates and we call it web 2.0, the advent of the social network. In both of these examples, we can see the centralized system works just fine. In *Figure 1.1*, this centralized setup is represented by the left-side lego block setup. The aggregated middle blocks represent the server, whereas the circumferential isolated blocks represent the clients. However, these centralized servers are generally owned by business organizations and can be influenced by a criminal entity or central authority to leak private data while the clients communicate. To overcome this fundamental flaw, peer-to-peer networking (web 3.0) came into practice (for example, BitTorrent). These were distributed systems, as depicted in the right of *Figure 1.1*, where each node can be a client or server or both and are not distinguishable from other nodes. Even though these systems were good at privacy, they faced challenges like the Byzantine Generals' Problem and the CAP theorem, which we will discuss in the subsequent sections.

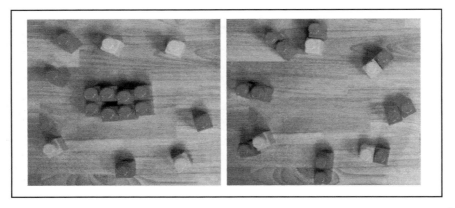

Figure 1.1: Lego block representation of centralized system (left) and distributed system (right)

The Byzantine Generals' Problem

Imagine a time during the dark ages, where a pirate ship is under attack. There are 200 pirates aboard the pirate ship surrounded by six army ships of 50 warriors each, who've anchored, surrounding the pirate ship. Each army ship is commanded by a captain. The 300 warriors can easily overpower the 200 pirates aboard the pirate ship. However, if they don't all attack simultaneously, there is a very real risk that the warriors will be outnumbered by the pirates and they'll go on to lose the battle.

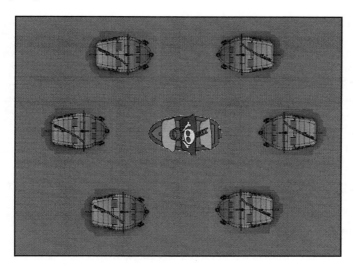

Figure 1.2: Pirate ship (200) surrounded by arm ship (50)

So, how can the captains all agree on the same time to attack the pirate ship? These days, we'd simply need a quick group video-conference call, and the captains would have to agree to attack at 22:00 hours (10 PM).

However, back in the dark ages, things were a little more complicated:

- The 22:00 attack message could only be passed on by a sailor on a small boat. He has to sail around each army ship, visiting each captain in turn to confirm.
- Any captain may be a traitor and in league with the pirates in the pirate ship.

Losing strategy

Captain 1 decides to attack at 22:00. He sends his sailor out with the message (22:00 attack) to deliver to Captain 2. Upon arrival, Captain 2 reads the message, notes the time of the attack, and sends a message that also says 22:00 attack. He sends the sailor on to share the message with Captain 3. However, we have a problem. Captain 3 is a traitor. He wants the attack to fail. So, when he gets the message, he rips it up and replaces it with a new message that says 21:00 attack (9 PM). The sailor continues unaware. Captain 4 now receives a message saying 21:00 attack. He notes the time, signs the message saying 21:00 attack and sends this on to Captain 5, who then sends the same message to Captain 6. Now, the message has gone around everyone, but we have a problem. The dishonest captain has disrupted the result. We now have three captains (4, 5, and 6) with 150 warriors attacking the pirate ship at 21:00. Expecting others to join them, they instead get outnumbered and overpowered by the 200 pirates. The victorious pirates now stream out of the pirate ship and join forces with the treacherous Captain 3. Suddenly, the two remaining captains (1 and 2) have only 100 warriors and find themselves fighting 200 pirates plus 50 traitors. Unfortunately, the pirates and traitors win.

Winning strategy

Captain 1 wants to send the same message (attack at 22:00). However, this time, there are two new rules he must obey:

- He must spend 10 minutes preparing any new message for it to be valid
- He must include the history of every previous message in every new message

So, let's see what happens this time. As before, Captain 1 sends the message (22:00 attack) with the sailor on the boat. This time, however, it is different for Captain 2, because he knows two things for certain:

- The message must have taken 10 minutes to prepare
- There are no previous messages, so it must be the truth (even if Captain 1 is a traitor and put in the wrong time, it doesn't matter; if the majority of captains followed this suggestion and went with a 22:00 attack time, they would still outnumber those in the pirate ship and win the battle)

So, now it is time for Captain 2 to send a message. As required, he spends 10 minutes preparing the new message and he embeds Captain 1's message into his own. The sailor then sets off with this message (now in fact, it is two messages chained together as the second has the first embedded within it). Now it gets to Captain 3.

Remember, he's the traitor. So, what does he do? Last time, he changed the message to 21:00 attack so that captains 4, 5, and 6 would attack early and get overpowered. Now, however, he can't because, under the new rules, he has only 10 minutes to prepare a message for Captain 4. He has two options:

1. Cheat by changing the message to 21:00 attack. To do this, he needs to (a) spend 10 minutes creating his message and then (b) spend an extra 2 x 10 minutes working to create replacement 21:00 attack messages from Captains 1 and 2 to embed these into his message and carry out this 30 minutes of work within the next 10 minutes to avoid the other captains knowing that he's a traitor.
2. Admit defeat and prepare the 22:00 attack message during those 10 minutes.

In other words, every captain has got no more than 10 minutes to provide the next captain with something that would take more than 10 minutes to fake if they were trying to be dishonest. If they can't deliver it within 10 minutes, everyone knows they're dishonest and ignores them, rendering their attempts to mislead others useless.

The CAP theorem

Before stating the CAP theorem, let's try to understand consistency, availability, and partition tolerance using a real-world problem.

As a married person, I know how pathetic a person's life can become if they forget important dates like the birthday and anniversary of their spouse (in most cases, the husband is the culprit, but that is a separate discussion). One of my friends, let's call him Kaushik, saw an opportunity in this and opened up a start-up, HappySpouse.com, to address this issue. During a typical business day, **Kaushik (K)** and his **customer (C)** would have the following conversation:

K: Hello from HappySpouse.com. How may I help you?

C: Hey, I want you to remember my wife's birthday.

K: Sure! When is it?

C: September 3.

K: (Writing it down on a page exclusive for C.) Stored. Call me any time to remind you of your spouse's birthday again!

C: Thank you!

K: No problem! Your credit card has been charged with $0.05.

Kaushik's idea was so simple, needed nothing but a notebook and phone, yet so effective that it rolled off like an avalanche. VC firms started pouring in funds. He also started getting hundreds of calls every day. That's where the problem started. Now, more and more of his customers had to wait in the queue to speak to him. Most of them even hung up, tired of the waiting tone. Besides, when he was sick for a day and could not come to work, he lost a whole day of business. Not to mention all those unsatisfied customers who wanted information on that day. So, Kaushik decided to scale up and bring in his wife to help him.

He started with a simple plan to solve his availability to customers:

1. He and his wife both got an extension phone
2. Customers still dialed the same number
3. A PBX routed the customer calls to whoever was free at that moment

A few weeks went by smoothly. One fine morning, he got a call from one of his old customers, **Joey (J)**:

J: Hello, am I speaking to Kaushik from `HappySpouse.com`?

K: Hi Joey, great you remembered us. What can I do for you?

J: Can you tell me when our anniversary was?

K: Sure. 1 sec, Joey (looking up in his notebook, there was no entry on Joey's page). Joey, I have only your spouse's birthday here.

J: Holy cow! I just called you guys yesterday! (Cuts the call!)

How did that happen? Was Joey lying? Kaushik thought about it for a second and the reason hit him! Yesterday, did Joey's call reach his wife? He goes to his wife's desk and checks her notebook. Sure enough, it's there. He tells this to his wife and she realizes the problem too. What a terrible flaw in this distributed setup! This setup was not consistent!

Now, they decided that whenever either of them got a call to note, they would update each other's notebook. In that way, they would both have the same up-to-date information. Even if one of them was offwork, the other would email the updates so that the person could come the next day and jot down the updates. That way, they would be both consistent and available.

However, fate has its own plans. Due to this hectic schedule, Kaushik himself forgot his wife's birthday. Now his wife was angry with him and would not share any updates, creating a partition. To patch things up, Kaushik had to make himself unavailable to clients and make up to his wife.

Let's look at the CAP theorem now. It states that when we are designing a distributed system, we cannot achieve all three of consistency, availability, and partition tolerance. We can pick only two of CAP and sacrifice the third, that is CA, AP, or CP, where:

- **Consistency**: Once a customer updates information with HappySpouse.com, they will always get the most up-to-date information when they call subsequently, no matter how quickly they call back
- **Availability**: HappySpouse.com will always be available for calls as long as any one of them (Kaushik or his wife) reports to work
- **Partition tolerance**: HappySpouse.com will work even if there is a communication gap/couple-fight between Kaushik and his wife!

Consensus in distributed systems

Consensus is a problem that arises in distributed systems that are replicating a common state, such as data in a database. It is the task of getting all processes in a group to agree on some specific value based on the votes of each process. The consensus algorithm cannot just invent a value. All processes must agree upon the same value and it must be a value that was submitted by at least one of the processes.

In the previous example of HappySpouse.com, to prevent the consistency problem, we can have a run-around clerk, who will update the other notebook when one of the notebooks is updated. The greatest benefit of this is that he can work in the background, and an update doesn't have to wait for the other person to update. Formally speaking, in such distributed systems, one node updates itself locally, and a background process synchronizes all the other nodes accordingly. The only problem is that we will lose consistency for some time.

For example, a customer's call reaches Kaushik's wife first, and before the clerk has a chance to update his notebook, the customer calls back and it reaches him. Then, the customer won't get a consistent reply. So, we have to safely assume a customer won't forget things so quickly that he calls back in a few minutes in order for this eventually consistent solution to work.

Also, if we look back into the winning strategy of the Byzantine Generals' Problem, we see that a consensus among various captains needs to be achieved in order to distinguish a true message from a lie.

Later in this chapter, we will get back to this with the proof-of-work algorithm employed by bitcoin on a blockchain. As for now, it is good enough to be aware of two facts on consensus:

- Raft and Paxos algorithms were some early attempts to solve the consensus problem. Both Paxos and Raft managed to solve the consensus problem using majority votes in a cluster. They differed mostly by their focus. Raft aimed to provide a complete practical algorithm, whereas Paxos provided the building blocks of a consensus algorithm.
- There are two main ways of finding consensus in a distributed ledger system: the **practical byzantine fault tolerance** algorithm (**PBFT**) and algorithms for blockchains. Blockchain algorithms can be further classified into the **proof-of-stake** algorithm (**PoS**) and the **proof-of-work** algorithm (**PoW**). The PoS also has a special form called the **delegated proof-of-stake** algorithm (**DPoS**).

Understanding the hash function and the Merkle tree

Cryptography is the art and science of hiding a message. It is more of an art than a science. Science here just acts as a mere tool to transform an artistic imagination into a mathematical algorithm.

In this section, we will concentrate only on two specific concepts from this immensely vast subject, which will help us to understand the true essence of a blockchain. These are the hash function and Merkle tree. Please note that these are used for verifying integrity, rather than hiding anything.

Let's now understand what a hash function is and how it works. *Figure 1.3* illustrates a hash function. As we can see in this figure, a hash function is a one-way mapping:

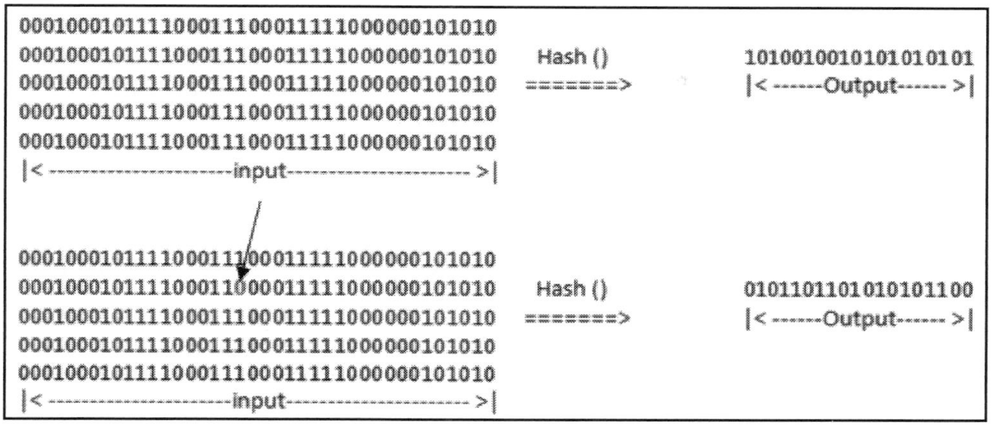

```
00010001011110001110001111100000101010
00010001011110001110001111100000101010    Hash ()        1010010010101010101
00010001011110001110001111100000101010    =======>       |< ------Output------ >|
00010001011110001110001111100000101010
00010001011110001110001111100000101010
|< ----------------------input---------------------- >|


00010001011110001110001111100000101010
00010001011110001100001111100000101010    Hash ()        01011011010101011100
00010001011110001110001111100000101010    =======>       |< ------Output------ >|
00010001011110001110001111100000101010
00010001011110001110001111100000101010
|< ----------------------input---------------------- >|
```

Figure 1.3: Hash function with input and output

That means that it can take an input (the input is usually a large sequence of bits; it can be a movie, a song, an e-book, a picture, or any digital data) and produce a fixed-size value as output, often much smaller than the input size. However, if I change only one bit in this input, the output will be completely different. This is property number one of the hash function and makes the hash function very much collision resistant. The second property is that there is no way to figure out the input if I only have the output. So, if I have the input to a hash function I can always get an output, no matter how big the input is. However, if I only have an output of a hash function, there is no way to reconstruct the input from it, because hash functions are unidirectional. Also note that the output hash is a fixed-length random bit sequence but, when it gets displayed on the terminals, it gets converted to a hexadecimal format and looks alphanumeric.

You might wonder what happens if I take the output of a hash function and feed it back into its input. Nice try! We still get a completely different sequence of fixed-length bits. And guess what, now we cannot even reconstruct the original output. This new output is not just a hash. It is a hash of a hash. It is called a hash chain and is denoted by $h(h(x))$ or $h2(x)$, where x is the original string of bits.

The next thing we need to understand is what a Merkle tree is. A Merkle tree is a data structure where each layer is a combination of hashes from its child layer. Generally, a Merkle tree is represented using a binary hash tree, where each node has at most two children. The branches are the hash of the combined hashes of the two children. This process of re-hashing the concatenation of the child nodes to create the parent node is performed until the top of the tree is reached, called the root hash or the Merkle root. Let me show you how it works with *Figure 1.4*:

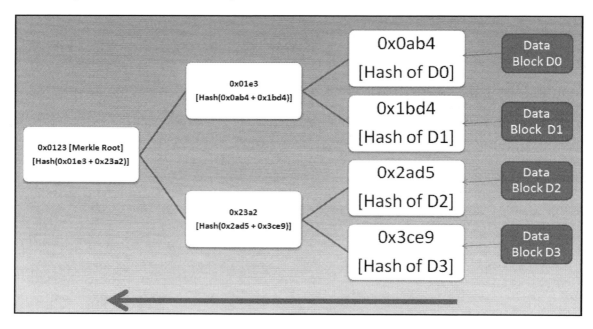

Figure 1.4: Merkle tree using four data blocks D0, D1, D2, and D3

Let's say we have two hash values (**2ad5** and **3ce9**). Please note that **0x** represents a hexadecimal notation, but I will omit the prefix for simplicity. To get the next value in the tree, I combine them to a single hash and get the value **23a2**. As I told you before, this hash is a one-way function. So, by combining **2ad5** and **3ce9** we can always get the hash value **23a2**, but if we only have **23a2** there is no way to figure out the original values. I now do the same hashing with **0ab4** and **1bd4** and combine them to get the value **01e3** and then hashing **01e3** and **23a2** to get the root value **0123**. So, this root value will be a representation of this data structure, but there would be no way for me to go back and figure out all the individual values in the tree, let alone the original data blocks **D0**, **D1**, **D2**, and **D3**. That would be very difficult.

Let's say I am the owner of the data block **D2** in the preceding diagram. I also acquire, from the distributed consensus, the root hash, which in our situation is **0123**. I ask the distributed system to prove to me that my record **D2** is in the tree. What the server returns to me are the hashes **3ce9**, **01e3**, and **0123**. Using this information, the proof is somewhat as follows (please note that, here, the + sign denotes a combiner, and not addition, and that the proof is basically a verification process):

1. Hash of **D2**, which we compute to get **2ad5**
2. Hash of [**2ad5** + **3ce9**] from which we compute **23a2**
3. Hash of [**01e3** + **23a2**] from which we compute **0123**

Since we know the root hash from our distributed consensus, the proof validates that **2ad5** exists in the tree. So does our record **D2**. Furthermore, the system from which you have obtained the proof is proving to you that it is an authority because it is able to provide valid hashes so that you can get from **D2** to your known root hash **0123**. Any system pretending to validate your request would not be able to provide you with the intermediate hashes. Since you're not giving the system the root hash, you're just telling it to give you the proof, the distributed consensus just can't invent the proof because it doesn't know your root hash; only you know that. Moreover, in order to verify the proof, very little information about the tree is revealed to you. Furthermore, the data packet that is needed for this proof is very small, making it efficient to send over a network and to make the proof computation. Now, if I claimed that I had **D4** in place of **D2**, I could not have proved it with the data **3ce9**, **01e3**, and **0123** because the hash of the hash of **D4** combining **3ce9** would have been a completely different number, that is, not **23a2** as we got in *Step 2*. We would have eventually got a different root hash, which would contradict the consensus root hash value of **0123**.

Now that we understand what a hash, a hash chain, and a Merkle tree are and how they work, we can proceed to understand a blockchain which will be discussed in the next section.

Understanding a blockchain–a developer and trader's perspective

From a software developer's perspective, a blockchain is just a giant Merkle tree. Take a moment now, pause your reading. Let this information sink in. I repeat with another layer of clarity.

A blockchain is a giant Merkle tree, where each new block embeds the hash of the previous block as well as the root hash of the present block-action, eventually forming a chain of hash-blocks. It might be not very obvious, but such a Merkle tree structure does not require a central server; each block can come from physically separate clients. Hence, a blockchain is also a distributed system. I can feel you are starting to feel confused right now. Just look at *Figure 1.5* to mitigate some of your confusion. We will discuss timestamp and nonce later, when we explore inside a block.

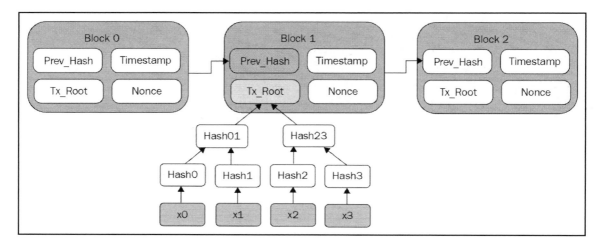

Figure 1.5: Blockchain as a giant Merkle tree

You might argue that blockchain looks more like a linked list with a Merkle tree hanging on each block, but it would be a fundamentally wrong perception because here we cannot backpropagate to the original data value. A more appropriate statement would be that it is very difficult to backpropagate to get back the actual values $x0$, $x1$, $x2$, and $x3$, using the root hash of the block. Yet the advantage lies in the fact that these hashes are immutable. You cannot revert a blockchain, in principle, once it is formed.

Before discussing the trader's perspective of a blockchain, it would be a good time to realize what a bitcoin blockchain is and what an Ethereum blockchain is and how they are different in principle and practice. For beginners who are reading the preceding lines, I would like to state that, in blockchain community, it is an agreed standard to represent a cryptocurrency with small cap while representing the technology, protocol, and ecosystem of that currency with large cap. So, bitcoin or Ethereum represents the virtual cryptocurrency, while bitcoin or Ethereum represents the tech stack, protocol, and ecosystem surrounding the respective virtual cryptocurrency.

Let's look at the over-simplified diagram of blockchains in *Figure 1.6*. All blockchains have some kind of root value **R**. So, when I send 2 bitcoins (BTC) to a friend, I actually do a transaction. Let's call it **T1**.

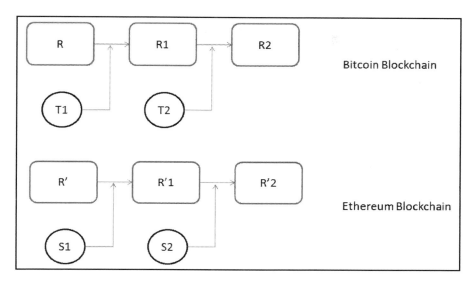

Figure 1.6: Bitcoin and Ethereum blockchains

This transaction, **T1**, a transfer of value, will be hashed together with the previous root **R** and create a new root, **R1**. So, this is almost like a Merkle tree (in fact, it is a Merkle tree) where the data blocks, that is, the leaves of the Merkle tree, are storing bits of data representing a transaction, which in turn get hashed into a new root hash. Then, another transaction **T2** comes in and it gets hashed with root **R1** to form yet another new root **R2**. This is how a bitcoin blockchain works, keeping a permanent store of all transactions which have taken place since the start of the original hash root (also called the genesis block). Now, if we try to cheat the system by stating that my transaction **T1** was of 100 BTC (in reality, we sent only 2 BTC), the fake transaction will be checked by blockchain community, by hashing it with **R** that will generate an entirely new root hash value **R'1**, completely different from **R1**. This rise in contradiction will falsify our 100 BTC claim. This is what makes bitcoin as a cryptocurrency so elegant in preventing the double-spend problem.

An interesting aspect that now arises is how an Ethereum blockchain works. We saw that a bitcoin blockchain is a decentralized application for transferring value and verifying transactions. An Ethereum blockchain, on the other hand, can even execute codes. As software developers, most of you might be familiar with states of a code in runtime.

In simple terms, it is the configuration of a piece of code at any given instant of time. An Ethereum blockchain acts as a decentralized application platform, which stores each state of a code while in execution (that is, during runtime) and creates a hash chain out of it. Again, take a moment to let this concept sink in. So, when we execute a code on an Ethereum blockchain, each and every state (**S1**, **S2**) of the executed code will merge with the roots **R'** and **R'1** respectively and will be publicly visible. Any type of code glitches will be captured and stored on the public blockchain and will remain there for eternity. In the future, we could see all the previous states of all the codes that ever got executed on the Ethereum blockchain. An obvious question arises about how such blockchains can ever scale, with the exponential growth of runtime logs when many such codes will run across the world over the Ethereum platform. Think about it.

Meanwhile, we move on to understand a blockchain from a trader's perspective. A trader of financial instruments or a banker views currency as something which serves the three key functions:

- Medium of exchange
- Store of value
- Unit of account

Cryptocurrency for a trader is no different from physical currencies, even though it has only a virtual presence and has no central authority of control. Blockchain, from a trader's perspective, is viewed as a distributed ledger, where the distributed consensus serves as the apparent central authority for such virtual currencies.

A Blockchain being immutable serves as a permanent record of any transfer of value that has ever taken place in the past, while cryptographically preserving the privacy of the identity of clients at both ends of any transaction.

It needs to be emphasized that both of these perspectives of a blockchain are not mutually exclusive. These apparently different perspectives are not like comparing apples with oranges. They both exist in unison and synergize to give rise to a decentralized economy, which we will explore in later chapters. Now, you can refer to *Figure 1.7*, to understand how a blockchain can be positioned within the financial-technological ecosystem:

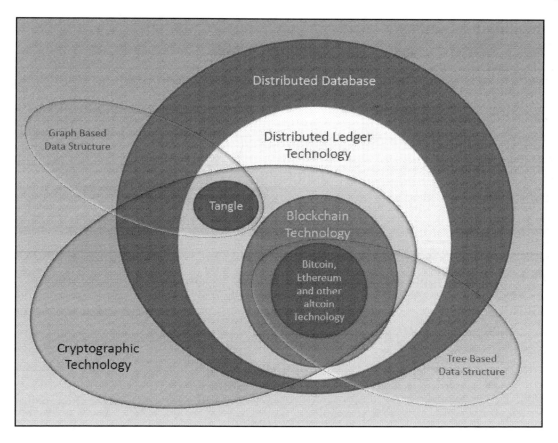

Figure 1.7: Blockchain in fin-tech ecosystem

Inside a block

Let's now discuss the contents of a block of bitcoin blockchain. This will help us in understanding and comparing Ethereum, which we will take up in `Chapter 2`, *Grokking Ethereum*. A block is a very interesting concept, because a block gives blockchain its properties. It is the basic element of a blockchain.

Therefore, it is important to know what a block consists of. *Figure 1.8* lists the basic parts of a bitcoin block. First of all, we have a magic number, also called bitcoin network ID.

Field	Description	Size
Magic no	value always 0xD9B4BEF9	4 bytes
Block size	number of bytes following up to end of block	4 bytes
Block header	consists of 6 items	80 bytes
Transaction counter	positive integer VI = VarInt	1 - 9 bytes
Transactions	the (non empty) list of transactions	<Transaction counter>-many transactions

Figure 1.8: Parts of a bitcoin block (Bitcoin wiki)

It is four bytes long and is an arbitrary number that signals that this is a bitcoin block. The magic number is not something specific to bitcoin. All nodes communicate using transmission control protocol.

In TCP, different types of data packets use different magic numbers to identify themselves. It is like declaring our gender while filling out a passport to identify ourselves as male, female, or transgender. In our context, a block is actually a sequence of 0 and 1. When any machine reads such a data sequence and it encounters the binary version of 0xD9B4BEF9, it will identify the data as a bitcoin block. So, this number is the same for all bitcoin blocks. Now, why was 0xD9B4BEF9 chosen for bitcoin blocks?

As per the comments found in the bitcoin main.cpp files (bitcoin implementations were written in C++ language), the magic number was chosen in such a way that the characters are rarely used in upper ASCII, not valid as UTF-8, and produce a large four-byte integer at any alignment.

Next, we have the block size which is also four bytes and tells us how long this block is with all of its transactions. As of July 2017, the size of an entire bitcoin block can be a maximum of 1 MB. We then have the block header, which is 80 bytes and it is the most interesting part; we will talk about its contents in a short while. The next one is the transaction counter, which is an integer that tells us how many transactions this block has and next we have a list of transactions, which simply contains all the transactions that are in this block.

For example, if we have the transaction counter as 20, we have 20 transactions in the block. The transaction counter is one to nine bytes. So, these were the basic parts of the block.

So, let's go ahead and look up what the bitcoin block header consists of. Here, in *Figure 1.9,* we have the header parts. The header has a version that simply tells us which version of the format we are on currently.

For example, the current bitcoin version is 2.

Field	Purpose	Updated when...	Size (Bytes)
Version	Block version number	You upgrade the software and it specifies a new version	4
hashPrevBlock	256-bit hash of the previous block header	A new block comes in	32
hashMerkleRoot	256-bit hash based on all of the transactions in the block	A transaction is accepted	32
Time	Current timestamp as seconds since 1970-01-01T00:00 UTC	Every few seconds	4
Bits	Current target in compact format	The difficulty is adjusted	4
Nonce	32-bit number (starts at 0)	A hash is tried (increments)	4

Figure 1.9 Bitcoin block header (Bitcoin wiki)

Now, if for some reason a bitcoin block from the version 1 client comes, it will be ignored by blockchain. In the future, there might be a change in the size and format of a bitcoin block. Then, we would have to change this version in each block to keep them relevant in blockchain. The version number is four bytes. Next, we have 32 bytes of hash of the previous block. This represents the hash of the previous block header. This field is very powerful because, in case of any unforeseen catastrophic hack that breaks away blockchain, we can generate the entire blockchain if even one single block remains preserved. Next, we have the hash of the Merkle root. These 32 bytes store the hash of the Merkle root of all the transactions associated with the present block as depicted earlier in *Figure 1.5* as Tx_Root. We saw that the body of the block contains transactions. These are indirectly hashed through the Merkle root. So, hashing a block with one transaction takes exactly the same amount of effort as hashing a block with 10,000 transactions. Next, we have a four-byte timestamp field, which updates every few seconds to keep the current timestamp. The next field of four bytes, called the target, is another interesting field. This field tells us the level of difficulty of this current block. To understand how the target field works, we need to understand how the four-byte nonce field works, where the word **nonce** stands for nonsensical incrementer, which leads us to our next section on mining and forking.

Blockchain mining and forking

When a miner mines a block, what does the miner actually do? What the miner does is take the hash Merkle root of the current block and then append a nonce which they guess by starting the increment from zero. They will hash this concatenated data to get a new hash and compare this result with the target. If this new hash is less than the target, which is basically a 256-bit number specified by bitcoin protocol, then they are done solving the puzzle and get the mining reward. However, if the new hash value is higher than the target value, they have to increase the nonce; that is, increase the nonce from zero to one, and append this one with the hash of the Merkle root, take the hash again to get another completely different new hash value and compare it with the target to check whether this new hash value is lower than the target value. If the new hash is now lower, then, again, they have solved this puzzle; otherwise, they keep repeating this entire process by incrementing the nonce value. So, it is important to realize that the lower the target is, the more difficult it is to find a hash value lower than the target value.

The bitcoin network automatically adjusts this target so that each 10 minutes we get a new block (recall the 10 minute puzzle from the pirate ship captains, this is what the puzzle means here). So, if the bitcoin network notices that it takes 5 minutes for blockchain to mine a new block, it will decrease the target value until it becomes difficult enough to take 10 minutes to solve. Conversely, if, for some reason, it takes 1 hour to mine a new block, the target value will be increased to make the mining easy enough to solve in 10 minutes. This is what the PoW algorithm does. So, what we understand is that mining is nothing but a dumb puzzle and a nonce is a possible solution to this dumb puzzle, while the target field is a benchmark value to check whether I have solved the dumb puzzle with optimal PoW; otherwise, my target benchmark gets changed. Also, it is very important to note that this process is entirely a hit or miss process with the gradual increment of the nonce. In computer science parlance, we call this process a brute force attack, where we try every possible combination to crack a code in shortest amount of time. This is the very reason we require high-performance devices like **application-specific integrated circuit (ASIC)** chips to mine bitcoins rather than normal **central processing unit (CPU)**, **graphics processing unit (GPU)**, or even **field-programmable gate arrays (FPGAs)**. The reward amount for one such mining puzzle is presently 12.5 BTC for solving one block. Earlier, it was 50 BTC, and then it came down to 25 BTC and again down to what we have in the present. The mining of bitcoin will continue with degraded mining reward till all of the 21 million bitcoins have been mined.

Forking, on the other hand, is an entirely different phenomenon that causes a split on blockchain due to a change in the protocol or due to a requirement for reorganization. A blockchain fork splits a single chain of blocks into two. The new forks are the same till the point of forking and behave differently in terms of principles and technicalities post a forking event.

There are two types of fork (hard and soft), which occur in blockchain community. Each of them can be activated by the users or miners as depicted in *Figure 1.10*:

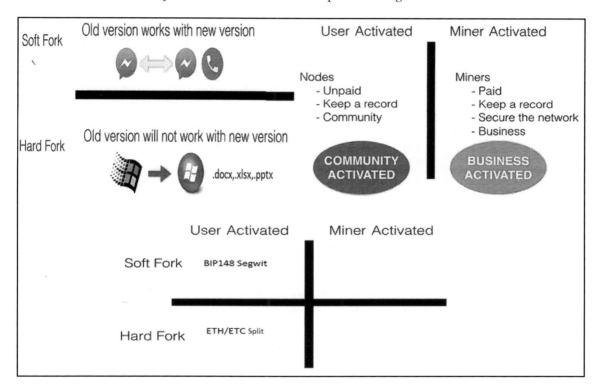

Figure 1.10: Types of forking

For example, in the bitcoin blockchain community, **BIP148 from Segwit** that occurred on August 01, 2017, was actually an **user-activated soft fork** (**UASF**); whereas, in the Ethereum blockchain community, the **ETH/ETC Split** post DAO tragedy was a **user-activated hard fork** (**UAHF**). To summarize, soft forks are backward compatible, while hard forks are not. In hard forks, the community has to choose only one of the forking paths and cannot go back to the other later with the changed specifications. A hard fork is like the red/blue pill of Morpheus from the movie *The Matrix*.

Blockchains – evolution, generations, and hype

We live in exponential times. As mere mortals, we normally perceive time in a linear way.

For example, one of the greatest inventions of mankind, the landline telephone, took about half a century to establish itself as a mainstream consumer appliance from a symbol of luxury, whereas smart phones crossed that barrier within a decade.

Blockchain is a disruptive computing paradigm. It has been positioned as fifth after mainframes, personal computers, the World Wide Web, and social networking. Melanie Swan, a blockchain educator and visionary, has segregated the existing and potential activities in blockchain evolution into three phases: blockchain 1.0, 2.0, and 3.0:

- **Blockchain 1.0**: It includes currency, the deployment of cryptocurrencies in applications related to cash, such as currency transfer, remittance, and digital payment systems.
- **Blockchain 2.0**: It includes contracts (the entire slate of economic, market, and financial applications using blockchain) that are more extensive than simple cash transactions: stocks, mortgages, titles, bonds, futures, loans, smart property, and the Internet of Things.
- **Blockchain 3.0**: It includes blockchain applications beyond currency, finance, and markets. This includes the areas of government, health, science, literacy, culture, and art.

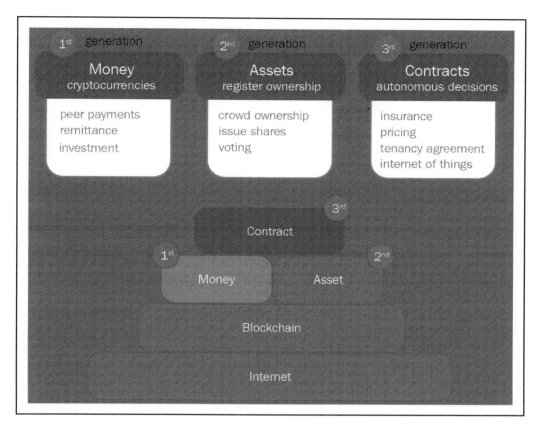

Figure 1.11 Three generations of blockchain - money, assets, contracts. Source: biccur.com

Interestingly, Robert-Reinder Nederhoed, an industry practitioner and grass-roots level blockchain implementer, has classified blockchain technology into three distinct generations. *Figure 1.11* summarizes the three generations the blockchain has experienced since its inception in 2009 by Satoshi Nakamoto (an unknown entity; the word Satoshi translates as wisdom, Naka as central and Moto as origin, so it roughly translates to central intelligence). These are money, assets, and contracts.

As linear thinkers, we must accept the bitter truth that technology life cycles are becoming shorter. Gartner, a market research group, traces this using a famous graph called the hype cycle.

A generic representation of such a graph is shown in *Figure 1.12*:

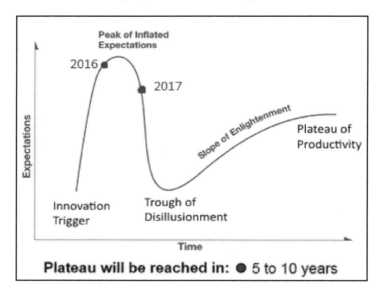

Figure 1.12 Blockchain on gartner hype cycle

As of July 2017, the blockchain has entered the trough of the disillusionment phase. This is the reality check phase for any innovative technology, when the general interest wanes as experiments and implementations fail to deliver. Producers of the technology shake out or fail. Investments continue only if the surviving providers improve their products to the satisfaction of early adopters. Smart contract technology is one such hope which can take the blockchain out of this trough into enlightenment.

Summary

This chapter introduced us to the important challenges and limitations of distributed systems, such as the Byzantine Generals' Problem and the CAP theorem. Then, we moved on to understand the one-way hash function and generating a hash chain and a Merkle tree. We realized how a blockchain is a giant Merkle tree and that the subtle difference between a bitcoin and an Ethereum blockchain lies in representing the leaf nodes of such a tree as a transaction or a state of execution, respectively. We took a deep dive into the bitcoin block structure to demystify mining as an incentivized brute force attack. Forking, on the other hand, signified a change of protocol on blockchain. Lastly, we identified the three types of blockchain generation as money, assets, and contracts, and we contemplated how blockchain is going through its reality check phase, as per Gartner's hype cycle.

In Chapter 2, *Grokking Ethereum*, we will have a gentle introduction to Ethereum as a platform, which has its own Turing complete programming language and has the ability to deploy smart contracts in a decentralized manner.

2
Grokking Ethereum

In this chapter, we will try to understand Ethereum. We will study what decentralization means and whether Ethereum is truly decentralized. We will also cover its core technological stack and get familiar with various jargon such as mist, **Ethereum Virtual Machine** (**EVM**), swarm, whisper, ether, and gas. We will briefly discuss solidity and the notion of a Turing complete language. We'll then revisit forking, mining, and block architecture from the perspective of Ethereum. We'll end this chapter by getting an understanding of Ethereum wallets and client interfaces, which will serve as a firm base for smart contract development.

After studying this chapter, you will be able to:

- Understand the concept of Ethereum
- Appreciate the notion of decentralization
- Be familiar with Ethereum related jargon
- Know about solidity and Turing complete languages
- Comprehend Ethereum mining, forking, and block architecture
- Recognize various Ethereum wallets and client interfaces

Understanding Ethereum

What does Ethereum really mean to us? Is it just another cryptocurrency imitating bitcoin or is it just a distributed software platform that can run various applications on a public blockchain? As a software developer, I can assure you that Ethereum is much bigger than how it is currently defined in the standard Wikipedia article.

Take your time to read the following definition. Pause, close your eyes, and think about it. The following definition broadcasts a subtle but very powerful message. It says to us:

Here is a 24/7 computing system, which you can have with zero upfront cost. You can copy it, use it, imitate it, tinker with it, play with it, and tweak it to meet your needs. Not only that, you can invent your own personalized currency with it and offer it whoever is willing to own it. In return, you will provide them with some service, which is permanently defined via a contract on a public ledger, so neither you nor your clients can cheat. Depending on your service, your value will grow, and so will the value of your currency. You, along with your group of clients, will create a mini ecosystem with its own personalized economy independent of any central authority of control. Efficiency will get rewarded, and complacency penalized. So, are you ready?

The preceding interpretation might sound highly audacious and ambitious, but, in reality, this is orders of magnitude less imaginary than sitting during the 1990s and thinking how the internet will disrupt the taxi industry, which apps such as Uber and Ola shoved in our faces two decades later, as shown humorously in *Figure 2.1*:

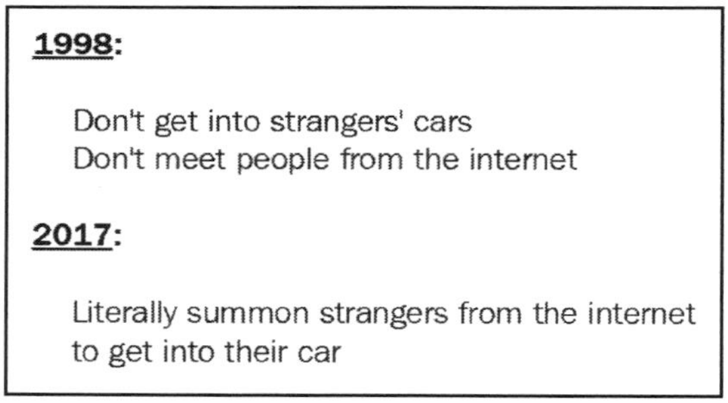

1998:

Don't get into strangers' cars
Don't meet people from the internet

2017:

Literally summon strangers from the internet
to get into their car

Figure 2.1: Meme. Source: StareCat.com

So, rather than opposing such disruptive paradigms, we need to embrace the changes. A positive step toward it would be to understand the notion of decentralization and how this applies to Ethereum, which we will tackle in the next section.

The notion of decentralization

Why do we need to build something that is decentralized by nature at all?

To understand this, let me walk you through a real-world use case based on a centralized economy with a central authority of control.

Sofia is the owner of a pub in Cardiff, UK. To penetrate the liquor market, she decides to allow her loyal consumers—most of whom are heavy drinkers—to **drink now but pay later (DNPL)**. She keeps track of the pints consumed on a ledger. Sofia's DNPL business model gets rave reviews from her clients, new consumers flood into Sofia's pub, and soon she has the largest sales, volume of any pub in Cardiff.

By providing her clients with freedom from immediate payment, Sofia gets no resistance when she substantially increases her prices for whisky and rum, the most consumed beverages. Her sales, volume increases massively.

A young and dynamic vice president at the local bank recognizes these client debts as valuable future assets and increases Sofia's borrowing limit. He sees no reason for undue concern, since he has the debts of the patrons as collateral. At the bank's headquarters, quantitative traders transform these liquor loans into **neatbonds**, **pintbonds**, and **hangoverbonds**. These securities are then traded on security markets worldwide. Rookie investors didn't really understand that the securities being sold to them as AAA-rating bonds were really the debt loans of heavy drinkers without an income. Nevertheless, the bond prices continuously rose and the securities became the top-selling items for some of the nation's leading brokerage firms.

One day, although the bond prices are still rising, a risk manager at the local bank decides that the time has arrived to demand payment on the debts incurred by the customers at Sofia's pub. Sofia demands payment from her patrons, but, being unemployed, they cannot pay back their drinking debts. So, Sofia cannot meet her loan obligations and claims bankruptcy. Neatbonds and pintbonds drop in price by 95%. Hangoverbonds perform better, stabilizing in price after dropping by 75%. The decreased bond asset value destroys the local bank's liquidity and prevents it from issuing new loans. The suppliers of Sofia's pub, having granted her generous payment extensions and having invested in the securities, are faced with writing off her debt and losing over 80% on her bonds. Her whisky supplier files for bankruptcy and her rum supplier is taken over by a competitor, who immediately closes the local plant and lays off 40 workers. The bank and brokerage firms are saved by the government, following dramatic round-the-clock negotiations by leaders from both major political parties. The funds required for this bailout are obtained by either introducing a new social welfare tax levied on employed middle-class non-drinkers or by infusing new funds in to the economy by passing an amendment or a new bill, adding to the inflation caused by the money supply, resulting in the debasement of the currency.

Note here that if Sofia had not been approached by the local bank's vice president in the first place, her business model would have failed due to lack of funds much earlier, with much less impact, rather than a catastrophic magnitude due to valueless fund pumping. We also observe that, in such a centralized economy, the intermediaries and central authorities have nothing to lose due to their discretionary power, whereas the real burden is passed onto the general working class. This is one of the prime reasons the notion of decentralization came into existence.

Ideally, we can either have a fully centralized system, generally represented by a star topology, also called a client server architecture, or we can have a fully distributed system, represented by a mesh or grid topology. However, in the real world, due to various practical constraints like logistic and financial barriers, we end up, somewhere in between, with a network that is partially centralized and partially distributed. It is a like a grid-of-many-star topology, which we term as a decentralized system. Paul Baran, in his classic text on distributed communication networks (August 1964), distinguished these three kinds of architectures that would be applicable to communication networks as depicted in *Figure 2.2*:

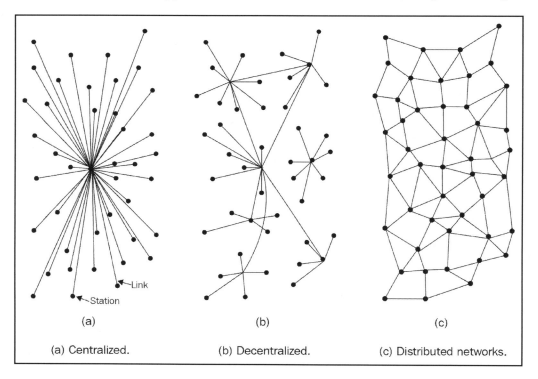

(a) Centralized.   (b) Decentralized.   (c) Distributed networks.

Figure 2.2: Centralized, decentralized, and distributed architecture

Now, we need to discuss whether Ethereum is decentralized. You might have heard someone say that Ethereum is not decentralized. They might be partially correct. Even Vitalik Buterin, one of the founders of Ethereum, says so. You might be thinking that this is completely crazy. Of course, Ethereum ought to be decentralized. It is a blockchain technology, and the whole idea of a blockchain technology is that it should be decentralized.

However, the answer to this is not a simple yes or no. It is a bit more complex than that. Vitalik Buterin has analyzed this notion of decentralization, which we will discuss right now.

Decentralization consists of at least three important axes: the architectural axis, the political axis, and the logical axis. A system such as Ethereum can either be centralized or decentralized along these three orthogonal axes. It can also sometimes be the case that it is hard to draw a line and say that this system is centralized or decentralized as a whole. It is just hard to decide in practical terms.

Let us start with what we mean by the architectural axis. If a system is centralized in the architectural axis and I remove a couple of nodes/computing terminals from the system, it would collapse. Conversely, in a system that is decentralized on the architectural axis, even if I remove the majority of the nodes/computing terminals, the system would still function as intended. So, in that sense, Ethereum is decentralized on the architectural axis, because we can remove many computing nodes from the system but the whole network will still function. However, if you have a website that you host on a server or a network of servers where each one needs all of the others, and you remove one server, the servers and the website will obviously no longer function as this was a centralized system on the architectural axis.

Let us move on. The second axis is the political axis.

For example, a centralized system on the political axis could be a company or an enterprise where we have a CEO and maybe we have a board of directors, and they decide on the course of the company. However, Ethereum is decentralized on the political axis, because even the Ethereum Foundation cannot make everyone use their clients or force everyone to follow a protocol.

Now, the last axis of discussion is the logical axis. So, a system that is centralized on the logical axis acts as a single entity, as a monolithic object, while a system that is decentralized on the logical axis can be divided into several parts, and each of those parts would behave and function as intended.

For example, the BitTorrent protocol and the BitTorrent system is decentralized on the logical axis because we can split the system into several parts, and the computers in those split parts will still be able to use the BitTorrent protocol as intended. However, here is where Ethereum is not decentralized. In fact, Ethereum is centralized when it comes to the logical axis, because Ethereum acts as a single computer. You execute your contracts on Ethereum and on this one huge computer that is running on the blockchain. So, in that sense, Ethereum is centralized. If we split Ethereum into two different parts, then they would no longer function as intended because the whole idea of Ethereum is that it should be a single computer—it should act as a single computer. In that way, Ethereum is not centralized on the logical axis.

Figure 2.3 illustrates all three notions of decentralization for Ethereum:

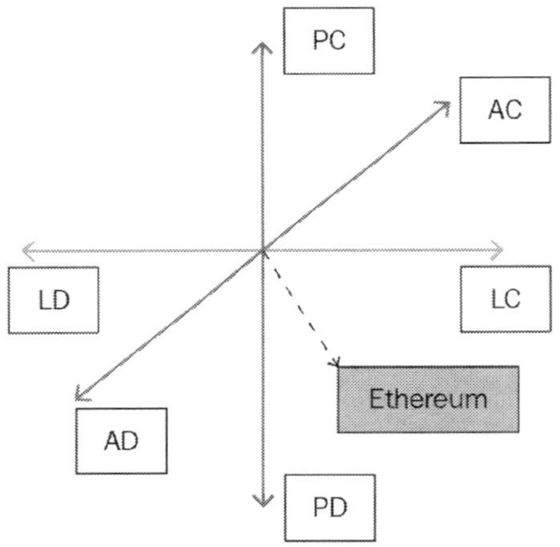

Axis	Decentralized	Centralized
Architectural	Yes	No
Political	Yes	No
Logical	No	Yes

Figure 2.3: Notion of decentralization for Ethereum

The question still remains: how does Ethereum, as a distributed computing platform, achieve such a level of centralized logical abstraction, despite having a fully decentralized architecture? To answer that, we need to get familiar with various components of the Ethereum ecosystem and try to construct its technological stack. The next section does just that. So, let us dive in.

The Ethereum ecosystem

In Chapter 1, *Blockchain Basics*, we studied how an Ethereum blockchain is represented as a giant Merkle tree with the leaves of the tree being the state of execution of a code. We also learned that blockchains are distributed ledgers with a web 3.0 framework.

Figure 2.4 depicts such a framework for an Ethereum technological stack. Things are going to get tricky now, so please pay close attention:

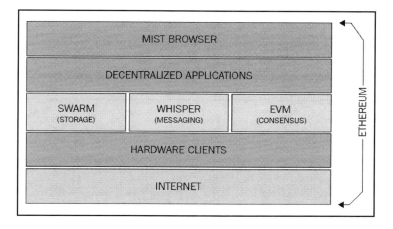

Figure 2.4: Web 3.0 tech stack for Ethereum, Source: Ethereum stack exchange

Mist

Let us start with the mist browser, which will be easiest to understand. This is the user-facing layer of the Ethereum platform. If you are a smartphone user and have used Android or iOS phones, you can think of a mist browser as the web 3.0 equivalent of Google Play Store or Apple App Store. Mist is the tool of choice to browse and use decentralized applications.

The tricky part is that, as of today, this browser has no stable release available for mobile phones.

It is worth mentioning that P-ACS, a team of Java developers, released an unstable version of an Android compatible Ethereum API app for developers (https://goo.gl/ANSRv4) in October 2016. So, technically, this team made a web 3.0 app browser available via a web 2.0 Play Store. Backward compatibility rocks! Don't you think? *Figure 2.5* illustrates the browser analogy for clarity.

However, the desktop version is quite stable and is available for Linux, Mac, and Windows. We will study its installation in `Chapter 3`, *Hello World of Ethereum Smart Contract*:

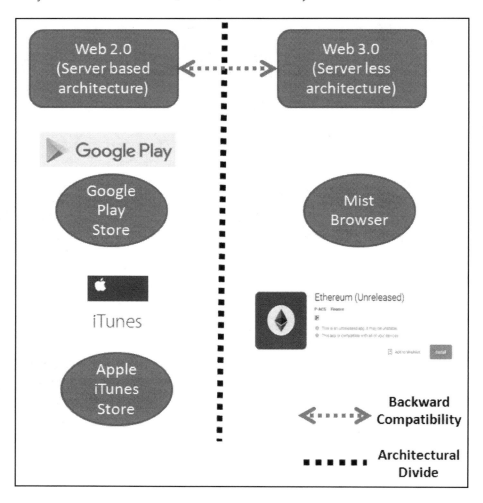

Figure 2.5: Mist browser analogy

Decentralized applications

Now, let us discuss the next layer: **decentralized applications (DApps)**. These are basically applications that get executed over a decentralized peer-to-peer network and have an open source code. It can be a simple logic based program that adds two numbers, or it can be something quite complex, such as a micro blogging service.

Being a foodie, I often imagine a mist browser as a five-star hotel's weekend brunch buffet table (along with gas burners) on which different kinds of DApps are spread out, ready to be devoured by hungry software developers and clients. The only thing is that these DApps, rather than coming from a single centralized kitchen employing many chefs, are procured in a potluck manner by different software developers. They are even made to pay for the gas burner to keep their DApps palatable. The best part is that the developers must share the recipe and ingredients for free. *Figure 2.6* shows such DApps on a mist browser:

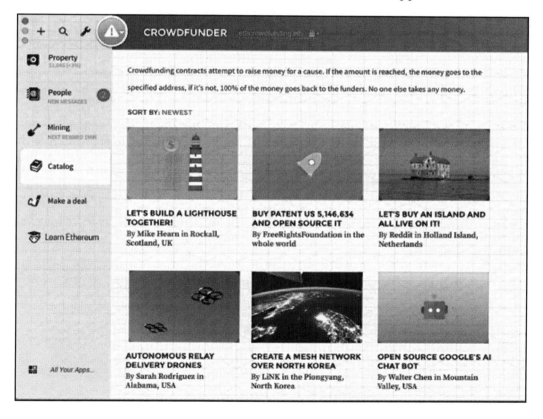

Figure 2.6: Listed DApps on mist browser. Source: ronnierocket.com

Middleware

Mist and DApps are mainly part of the frontend stack of Ethereum. Let us now move into backend mechanisms. First, we start with the **middleware**. The middleware of Ethereum has a flat hierarchy, as there is no central authority, such as a server. It consists of three prime components of equal importance:

- **Swarm**: Ethereum's decentralized storage, mainly for static files
- **Whisper**: The walkie-talkie of DApps, that is an identity based messaging system
- **EVM**: An isolated, on-the-fly, human-to-machine code translator, that is in a sandboxed runtime environment

How does an app run without a server? We can figure this out by understanding that the servers in a web 2.0 framework do quite a lot more than they were intended to do in order to keep the client device light. Not only do they serve static web pages, they store private information, administer user authentication, and compute all the complex analytics. All the client side does is to load and display the message to the user. A server-less architecture in web 3.0, on the other hand, allows a much more modular approach, in which different computing devices and different protocols handle specific tasks; some on the client side and some in specialized nodes deployed on a peer-to-peer network. Therefore, all the data logic comprising logs about what is getting saved, who is saving it and resolving conflicts are handled by smart contracts on the blockchain; static files are served via swarm and real-time communication is taken care of by whisper, as shown in *Figure 2.7*. The client device keeps the user authentication and runs the application interface, that is, the mist wallet plus the browser:

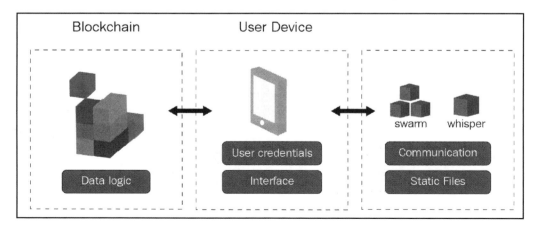

Figure 2.7: Server less architecture. Source: blog.ethereum.org

Figure 2.8 illustrates how these modules work in unison with DApps and the underlying blockchain in a server less architecture. Such a setup also encourages innovation. As the interfaces are detached from the data, anybody can develop a new interface for the same application, creating a more vibrant and competitive ecosystem:

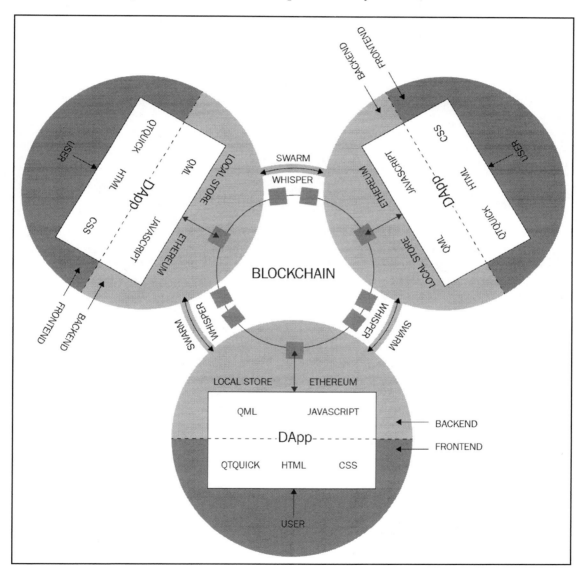

Figure 2.8: Decentralized architecture. Source: Ethereum stack exchange

Swarm

Until now, we have been treating the modules of swarm, whisper, and EVM as a black box, where we are only interested in how these modules interact, rather than what really happens inside them. However, to have a firm base for developing smart contracts, which we will eventually define and take up in `Chapter 3`, *Hello World of Ethereum Smart Contract*, we need to know the bare minimum internal workings of these modules. This will help us in tuning the smart contract code to make its performance better while running on the Ethereum blockchain.

So, how do we measure the performance of our code? The answer is unfortunately not very straightforward, but lies along several axes. Performance is measured along resource consumption, and code consumes a variety of resources. After a certain point, a trade-off among various resources is required. We consume more of one resource and less of another to make a code truly performant in the real world.

Let us now look into the three important resources that measure the performance of a code. They are time, space, and network. Time resource is how long any code needs to run to completely process a set of operations on a given input to generate an output.

Please note that this is not measured in seconds or minutes, but in terms of the number of inputs, also known as the **Big O** notation **O( )**. For example, if a code runs for 1 second for 1 input, 2 seconds for 2 inputs and 100 seconds for 100 inputs, the code is said to be linearly performant in terms of time, that is time complexity of O(n). Space resource, also called **storage**, is how much memory or disk space my code occupies while in execution. In other words, how much extra space the code takes to perform its calculations. Network resource, also called **bandwidth**, is how much data my code transfers across the network while in execution.

The primary objective of swarm is to allow DApps to efficiently share the storage and bandwidth resources of their data in order to provide the necessary services to end users. This is accomplished by three crucial ideas implemented in swarm:

- **Chunks**: It is the basic unit of storage and retrieval in swarm with a maximum size of 4 KB
- **Hash**: It is the cryptographic hash of data chunks with a unique identifier and address
- **Manifest**: It is the path specifier for content retrieval of the hash

When any blob of data, termed as content, is uploaded to swarm, it is chopped up into pieces of data called **chunks**. A unidirectional swarm hash is generated for each chunk with an identifier and address for access. These hash addresses are immutable by nature. In simple words, modifying the content changes the hash address of each chunk. The hashes of these chunks themselves are bundled into another chunk, which in turn has its own hash. In this way, the content gets mapped to a chunk tree, which is basically a Merkle tree. Even for large content files, such as streaming videos, a hierarchical swarm hash prevents any loss of data integrity and allows protected random access.

To access the swarm content, we need the manifest. This file describes a document collection. The document can be a file system directory, a virtual server, or an index of a database. The manifest is like the table of contents of a book, giving the gist of what and where to find content. It is the metadata that allows **uniform resource locator** (**URL**) based content retrieval, by specifying paths and corresponding content hashes.

Swarm node addresses define a location in the same address space as the data. A swarm node participating in the network has its own base address termed as **bzzkey**. This bzzkey is basically derived as the hash of an Ethereum address, the so-called swarm base account of the node. There is no concept of deleting or removal in swarm. Once content is uploaded, there is no way we can initiate swarm to revoke it. Before swarm was released, Ethereum used **interplanetary file system** (**IPFS**).

Whisper

Modern-day hacking and surveillance skills have advanced to such an extent that the hackers do not even need to intercept the actual message while it is travelling through a secured channel. They can guess the information carried by the message by just studying its shadow. By the shadow of a message, we mean the metadata logs and audit trails a message leaves while it is travelling via a channel.

To better understand such attacks, imagine you live in a big city where rents are very high. So, you find an old flat owner downtown who is willing to give you one room for rent, which is within your budget. The only problem is that the rail tracks run too close to your walls. Each night, you can feel the rumbling of your creaky bed when any train passes by. If you are a keen observer and think like a hacker, it would be quite easy for you to get familiar with each kind of train passing you every night, just by knowing the amount of time your cranky bed trembles once a particular train passes. The time band of the bed trembling becomes the signature of a particular train. You might even be able to predict, with a certain level of accuracy, whether the train that passed at a given time was the same train that passed last night or a different train, just by observing this signature property. What if the railway company realizes this and seals the surrounding of the tracks with thick concrete tunnels, which then absorb all the shock and tremors due to trains? Will you be able to identify the signatures even then? Think about it, because light reveals shadow when obstructed, while darkness doesn't.

When Gavin Wood laid down the specifications for whisper as a peer-to-peer communication protocol, in his whitepaper on GitHub (`https://goo.gl/bR5fBZ`), he designed one of the most interesting technologies in the field of cryptography. At a considerable cost of bandwidth and latency, whisper is able to deliver a 100% dark operation. By completely dark operations, we mean that there is zero leakage of metadata during peer-to-peer communication.

By technical definition, whisper is a messaging system with multi **distributed hash table (DHT)**, with routing privacy acting as a companion protocol to the Ethereum blockchain. Any normal communication protocol has a fundamental aim to maximize bandwidth and minimize latency. However, whisper as a communication protocol has only one aim: to nullify leakage of metadata and achieve true darkness, where no third party can eavesdrop while two peers are communicating. For this, whisper is willing to give up on both bandwidth and latency constraints. Whisper operates in a user-configurable manner with regard to how much information the communicating nodes are willing to leak concerning the decentralized application content that ultimately tracks the user activities.

Whisper is based on two key concepts: messages and envelopes. If whisper is considered a datagram messaging service, then an envelope represents an un-encrypted data format, comprehensible by a node, which carries the encrypted message datagram inside it. An envelope consists of original **time to live** (**TTL**, in seconds), the absolute time to expiry (UNIX system time), the encrypted message data field, which is the actual payload, topics (cryptographically secure, probabilistic partial classifications of message), and nonce, an arbitrary value. This nonce is used for the PoW to judge the efforts of a peer. The message has a binary flag for signature with an unfixed payload.

Figure 2.9 illustrates these two concepts for further clarity:

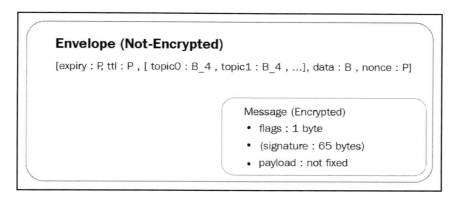

Figure 2.9: Whisper message inside an envelope

EVM

EVM is a stack-based interpreter, which has a memory byte array and key-value storage. To visualize a stack, let us return to our brunch buffet analogy and think about how the clean plates are kept one above another.

Figure 2.10 illustrates such a stack as a **last-in-first-out** (**LIFO**) process with its crucial operations like pop and push:

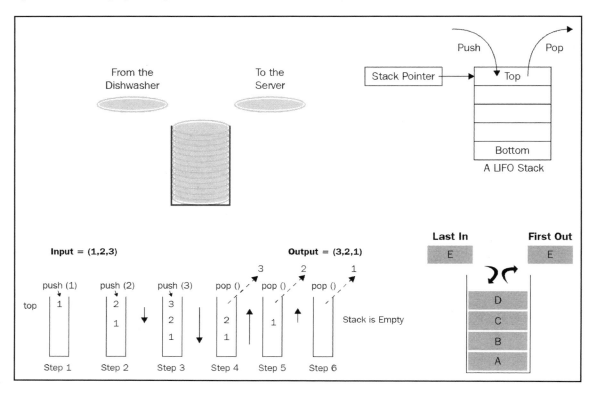

Figure 2.10: Stack operation in nutshell

Elements on the EVM stack are 32 bytes long and all key-value storage are also 32 bytes. Smart contracts, which are coded in high-level languages, run on blockchain through EVM, which generates machine level operational codes (opcodes) during runtime. These opcodes have access to three types of space to store data:

- The stack, a LIFO container to which values can be pushed and popped.
- Memory, an infinitely expandable byte array.
- The contract's long-term storage is a key-value store. Unlike stack and memory, which reset after computation ends, storage persists for the long term.

The code can also access the value, sender, and data of the incoming message, as well as block header data, and the code can also return a byte array of data as an output. There are around 100 opcodes, which are categorized in delineated multiples of 16. The opcodes have a general format as follows:

```
#schema: [opcode, ins, outs, gas]
e.g. #crypto 0x20: ['SHA3', 2, 1, 30]
```

The preceding format tells us how many parameters each `opcode` pops out of the stack and pushes back into the stack, as well as a counter of how much `gas` is consumed. We will discuss `gas` and the meaning of Turing completeness in the upcoming sections.

Figure 2.11 shows how the opcodes are broadly segregated into nine different groups based on their functionality:

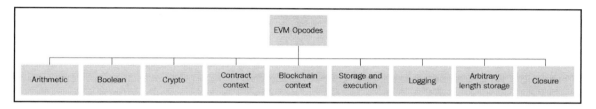

Figure 2.11: EVM opcode categorization for python based Ethereum client

The EVM is designed to permit untrusted code from running over a global public blockchain based operating system.

In order to accomplish this, the following security restrictions are imposed:

- Every computational state of execution in a program is to be paid up front, which in turn prevents denial-of-service attacks.
- Codes only interact with each other by transmitting a single, arbitrary-length byte array. The programs do not have access to each other's execution state.
- Program execution is isolated. A virtual machine program may access and modify only its own internal state and may trigger the execution of other programs on EVM.
- Code execution is fully deterministic in nature and produce identical state transitions for any conforming implementation, which began in an identical state.

The formal execution model of EVM code is surprisingly simple. While the EVM is running, its full computational state can be defined by the tuple (`block_state`, message, code, memory, transaction, stack, gas, and pc), where `block_state` is the global state, containing all accounts with balances and storage.

At the start of every execution round, the current instruction is found by fetching the **program counter** (**pc**) code byte, and each instruction has its own definition in terms of how it affects the tuple.

For example, an ADD operation pops two items from the top of the stack and pushes their sum, reduces gas by one, and increments pc by one; while store pops the top two items off the stack and inserts the second item into the contract's storage at the specified index of the first item. Even though there are many ways to optimize EVM execution via just-in-time compilation, a basic Ethereum implementation can be done in a few hundred lines of code.

Hardware clients and internet

As we have wrapped up our under-the-hood session on swarm, whisper, and EVM, let us move on to the remaining elements of the Ethereum tech stack, which are hardware clients and the internet. The hardware clients will be covered in greater detail in the Ethereum mining section. As of now, it is sufficient to know that normal commodity hardware like CPUs and GPUs are used as hardware clients for Ethereum.

Let us now discuss the internet layer of the Ethereum tech stack, which is basically the Ethereum blockchain. As we have already discussed the blockchain structure for Ethereum in Chapter 1, *Blockchain Basics*, here we will cover only the logical positioning of Ethereum blockchain over the surface web.

We will revisit the blockchain structure when we discuss the Ethereum block architecture, later in this chapter.

The internet as we know is mainly the surface web. There are also the deep web and the dark web, which we discuss in later chapters. The surface web consists of many logical layers, through which a message or data has to pass in order to reach from point **A** to point **B**, which may be geographically and physically separate. Each logical layer has some standard protocol, which a message in transit has to follow or else it would be barred from travelling across the web. These protocols are like the passport and visa rules for an individual when they try to travel from one nation to another. **Internet engineering task force** (**IETF**) is an open community that recommends, in a purely voluntary manner, a common ground of communication on the surface web, by proposing the transmission control protocol/internet protocol suite.

Figure 2.12 represents the TCP/IP and the position of the blockchain as a technology on it. The directed line indicates how a message travels from point **A** to **B**:

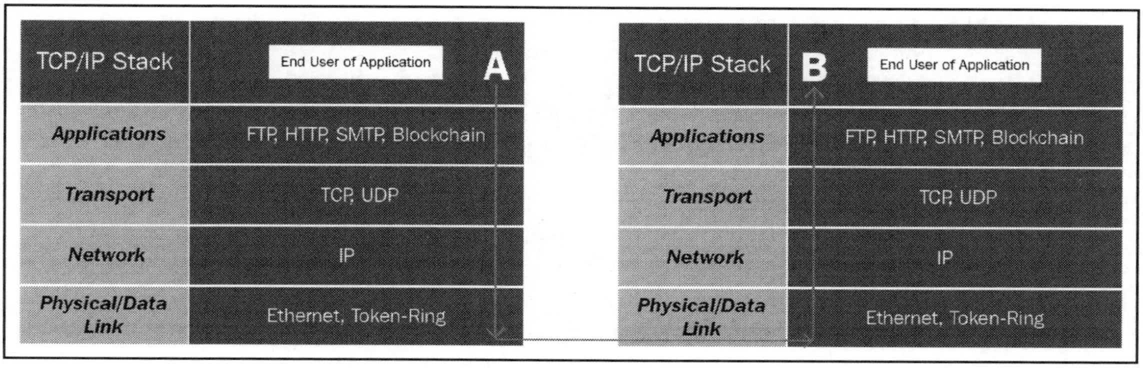

Figure 2.12: Blockchain position on surface web

So, we see that a blockchain is an application layer technology in the TCP/IP stack, which provides a transfer protocol of values. FTP is used to transfer files, HTTP is used to transfer hyperlinked text, SMTP is used to transfer mails, and the blockchain is used for natively digital transfer of values and execution states.

These were the major modules of Ethereum web 3.0 tech stacks, but what makes these modules operate? Is there any magic sauce running inside Ethereum? What is Turing completeness all about? Let us look into them in the next section.

Turing completeness and the magic sauce

As we discussed in the previous section, Ethereum is a platform for decentralized applications. That means that we can write programs that can execute in a decentralized manner, where there is no central server or central entity that is going to execute our programs. The programs are going to be executed on many different computers, and this means that there is no way to take down such a decentralized application. In order to write such applications, we need to develop smart contracts, and smart contracts are written in a programming language called solidity. So, on the Ethereum blockchain, if you want to write a smart contract you need to learn solidity. Solidity is Turing complete. So, what does that mean? To understand this, we need to go back 60 or 70 years.

During that time, people had different calculation machines. The problem was that if you had a machine that could calculate something using one algorithm, then that machine could solve only that problem, and to solve another problem of a slightly different algorithmic construct, you had to build a separate machine from scratch.

So, Alan Turing, one of the greatest mathematicians and computer scientists of the 20th century, developed a logical design of a machine, a theoretical machine. He explained how such a machine could be built so that this machine could run any program.

In his theoretical explanation of this machine, you could build it using a simple tape, made of uniform cells, each storing 0 or 1 and a tape-head that could turn left or right by reading the tape-cells with an ability to store data. Basically he explained how you could build a computer that could run any program and solve any kind of computational problem. That being said, there was no guarantee how long this would take. Some programs could be executed in a minute, but some programs—for example, finding the solution to a problem based on prime numbers-could take thousands or several thousands of years. So, there was a guarantee that, sooner or later, the problem would be solved, but no guarantee how fast this would be. So, in theory, you could solve any computational problem on this Turing machine.

Nowadays, when we say that a particular programming language is Turing complete, we mean that by using that language we could implement any algorithm to solve any kind of computational problem. When a programming language is not Turing complete, it has many logical or syntactical restrictions that prevent it from formulating algorithms to solve certain kinds of computational problems.

For example, the scripting language used in bitcoin is not Turing complete. SQL from SQL92 standard is not Turing complete, whereas from SQL99 standard onwards it became Turing complete. Even big data tools like HiveQL and Pig Latin are not Turing complete. They become Turing complete only when they are supplemented by **user defined functions (UDF)** written in Java. On the other hand, PL/SQL, Java, JavaScript, Python, R, C, and C++ are all examples of Turing complete programming languages.

From a software developer's perspective, there is one important feature of a programming language which can quickly identify with sufficient accuracy whether that language is Turing complete or not. That feature is the ability to construct a programming loop. That means that if you have loops in your programming language, you can tell a program to do a set of instructions over and over again. This is what we have in solidity. Solidity has loops.

Vitalik Buterin usually explains Turing complete language as a programming language which can construct a loop, while scripting language of Bitcoin can only construct simple transaction logic and cannot construct a loop. So, if you want to do something a hundred times in the bitcoin scripting language, you would have to copy and paste the code a hundred times, while in Ethereum you could just write it once and tell the computer to execute it a hundred times.

For example, a simple computing device that has a loop and with an add operation can also be modified to do multiplication by looping a specific add operation; that is, 5 x 3 is equivalent to 5 + 5 + 5, which is equivalent to adding 5 with itself in 3 loops. However, it must be noted that loops are not always good for code performance, as loops within loops can exponentially increase the time complexity of any code. So, loops are good for identifying Turing completeness, but need to be avoided unless completely necessary, as they reduce code performance. We also have another problem of scalability, which will be addressed in later chapters, where we discuss the concept of sharding.

That is one of the prime reasons bitcoin avoided a Turing complete language. It was a decision by choice and not by mistake. You see, the whole idea of a Turing complete language running loops on a blockchain can be dangerous; because if you have a loop that executes some kind of code millions and millions of times, and this code has to be executed on a blockchain, it will really overload the network. That is why the developers of bitcoin decided not to use a Turing complete language. They just wanted a simple mechanism to get the basic job done, that is, to perform the transfer of values across peers. While in Ethereum, the design ideology is completely different with the introduction of complex DApps, which has to be executed using smart contracts on the Ethereum blockchain. Here, we absolutely need a Turing complete language, which must have looping constructs. Again, we cannot overload the Ethereum blockchain by running a million loops. So, we seem to be stuck in a catch-22 situation where loops are a necessary evil, the evil being blockchain overload and spamming other users.

This is the exact situation when we need a magic sauce; we call it gas in the Ethereum blockchain. Each operation done by solidity on the Ethereum blockchain has some fixed amount of gas fee associated with it. Let us go back to our brunch buffet analogy, where we talked about a gas burner for which developers/potluck chefs had to pay some fee to keep their DApps/recipes warm and palatable. You see, if I had to pay for gas burner fuel, I would automatically cook recipes that are good even on low gas usage, rather than recipes that require a lot of flames and constant high gas usage. So, rather than bringing hot kebabs, which need constant flames, I would bring something like a bread or bakery item, which require mild or no gas burner usage, to ensure I am not losing my money while waiting for someone to come and consume what I have cooked.

So, coming back to the Ethereum blockchain, if some rookie developer comes up with a super crazy program with millions of loops that could spam and overload the network, the gas cost will significantly increase for this programmer and his entire code will eventually stop executing once the gas purchased by the developer gets exhausted.

For example, if we run a code with five operations looping a 100 times, the gas fee would be consumed for each of the 500 loops. So, gas is that magic sauce, which needs to be purchased using **ether** (**ETH**) tokens to run a solidity smart contract on an Ethereum blockchain. And yes, it is a prepaid model. You first buy some ether tokens using fiat money then, using these ether tokens you top-up your gas limit. Then, you run your smart contract program, which will continue to eat up gas from your account. The more efficient your code is, the less gas will be consumed by your code, the longer it can run on the blockchain, and the better your DApps will be to your clients.

It is crucial to differentiate between gas and ether in an Ethereum blockchain. As discussed earlier, gas is a sort of fee to run smart contract operations on an Ethereum blockchain, whereas ether is the cryptocurrency token on the Ethereum blockchain. A good real-life analogy would be petrol or diesel for driving a car. To drive a car on the highway, we need to fill it with petrol or diesel. We need plain cash, credit/debit cards, or e-wallet money to buy the petrol or diesel. Now, it really depends on the internal mechanics of the car, the weather conditions, the road and traffic conditions, the way we drive, and many such parameters, which affect the consumption of fuel per unit of miles travelled. We call it the **mileage** and this parameter determines the performance of the car. Again, the fuel price can fluctuate due to a change in international market conditions and its effect on the value of fiat currency. On the same lines, if the car is the solidity smart contract code, gas is the fuel used to fill up the car to make it run on the highway of a blockchain. We purchase this gas using ether, where ether is equivalent to our real-world fiat currency.

Figure 2.13 illustrates the scale of unit on an Ethereum blockchain and the ETH equivalent value in fiat money in present money:

Date	Price (USD)
2017-08-13	297.18211755
2017-08-12	308.41962326
2017-08-11	296.06275828
2017-08-10	295.84876057
2017-08-09	297.56832730
2017-08-08	268.51285398
2017-08-07	263.60533075
2017-08-06	257.20038065
2017-08-05	221.72746126
2017-08-04	225.31148118
2017-08-03	219.91355873

```
 'wei':         '1',
 'kwei':        '1000',
 'ada':         '1000',
 'femtoether':  '1000',
 'mwei':        '1000000',
 'babbage':     '1000000',
 'picoether':   '1000000',
 'gwei':        '1000000000',
 'shannon':     '1000000000',
 'nanoether':   '1000000000',
 'nano':        '1000000000',
 'szabo':       '1000000000000',
 'microether':  '1000000000000',
 'micro':       '1000000000000',
 'finney':      '1000000000000000',
 'milliether':  '1000000000000000',
 'milli':       '1000000000000000',
 'ether':       '1000000000000000000',
 'kether':      '1000000000000000000000',
 'grand':       '1000000000000000000000',
 'einstein':    '1000000000000000000000',
 'mether':      '1000000000000000000000000',
 'gether':      '1000000000000000000000000000',
 'tether':      '1000000000000000000000000000000'
```

ether = main unit
finney = for micropayments
shannon = for gas prices.
wei = for discussion around APIs

Figure 2.13: Ether on money market along with units in an Ethereum blockchain

A genuine concern now arises that we can never know how my smart contract code will perform on a blockchain unless we run it. For that reason, the Ethereum platform has introduced the concept of testnet and mainnet. Once we code our solidity smart contracts, we can run them on testnet and check how much operations are costing in terms of gas fee, but in a virtual setting; that is, we can run the code for free to simulate the gas fee amount. Once we are satisfied with the gas consumption rate and efficiency of our smart contract code, we deploy it as the final code into the mainnet where the code gets engraved permanently into the Ethereum blockchain. The earlier testnet was called the **morden**, and was scrapped due to security issues. The current testnet is called the **Ropsten**.

So, we see that smart contracts are more than mere transactions representing transfer of values. A natural question arises about whether the block architecture of bitcoin is sufficient for Ethereum? Moreover, how do we mine in an Ethereum blockchain? And why do we have two separate cryptocurrency tokens ETH and ETC? Let us find out in the next section.

Ethereum block, mining, and forking

Before we dive into the details of Ethereum block architecture, we need to revisit the blockchain structure of Ethereum. In `Chapter 1`, *Blockchain Basics*, we learned that an Ethereum blockchain is a Merkle tree where the leaves represent execution states of a code. For the sake of simplicity, a finer detail was suppressed. The Merkle tree of Ethereum is not a binary Merkle tree, as we saw for the bitcoin blockchain. You see, binary Merkle trees are great data structures when it comes to authenticating information that is in a list format, that is, a series of data chunks placed one after another. For such a transaction tree, it really doesn't matter how long it takes to edit the tree after it gets created. This is because the transactions remain in a form of one frozen tree which can only keep growing.

Ethereum, on the other hand, is a state tree. Here, the situation is more complex. The state in Ethereum is represented as a key-value map where the key signifies the address and the value signifies the declared amount, balance listing, nonce, code, and account storage. Even the storage is itself a tree.

Here, unlike the transaction history, the states are frequently updated. This happens due to the change in the balance and nonce of accounts, insertion of frequently created new accounts, and frequent insertion and deletion of keys in storage.

A desirable data structure in such cases should be able to quickly calculate the new tree root after an insert, update, edit or delete operation, without re-computing the entire tree. Additionally, the depth of such a tree should be bounded. This prevents any hacker from infinitely deepening the tree and launching a DoS attack on its legitimate users. Also, making updates in a different order or even re-computing the tree from scratch should not change the root; that is, the root should be dependent only on the data.

Donald R. Morrison described such a tree data structure around 1968. It was called the **Practical Algorithm to Retrieve Information Coded in Alphanumeric (PATRICIA)** tree. Basically, it is a Radix tree where Radix equals 2, which means that each bit of the key is compared individually and each node is a two-way branch. In such a tree, searching, inserting, and deleting occur with linear time complexity, even in the worst case scenario.

Figure 2.14 illustrates a how a typical insertion occurs within a Patricia tree:

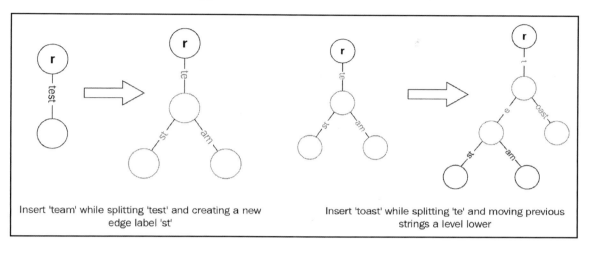

Insert 'team' while splitting 'test' and creating a new edge label 'st'

Insert 'toast' while splitting 'te' and moving previous strings a level lower

Figure 2.14: Patricia tree insertion demo, Source: Wikipedia

Hence, the Ethereum blockchain is technically a Merkle-Patricia tree where each block header in the Ethereum blockchain contains three such trees for representing three kinds of object:

- Transactions (represent transfer of value)
- Receipts (data chunks showing the effect of each transaction)
- State (represents all information of an account)

These three kinds of objects are used by a miner to answer the following five queries, which is essentially the mining activity on an Ethereum blockchain:

1. Has a transaction been included in a particular block?
2. What are all instances of an event emitted by this address in the past 30 days?
3. What is my account's current balance?
4. Does this account even exist?
5. What would the output be if I simulate execution of this transaction on this contract?

The first query is handled by the transaction tree, the second by the receipt tree, and the third and fourth by the state tree. The first four are fairly straightforward to compute. The miner simply finds the object, fetches the Merkle branch where the list of hashes goes up from the object to the tree root and replies back to the light client with the branch. The fifth query is also handled by the state tree, but the way it is computed is more complex. Here, we need to construct the Merkle state transition proof. Basically, this proof makes the following claim: if we run transaction **T** on the state with root **R**, the result will be a state with root **R'**, with log **L** and output **O**. Although not theoretically necessary, the concept of an output exists in Ethereum, because every transaction is a function call. In order to compute the proof, the miner locally creates a fake block, sets the state to **S**, and pretends to be a light client while applying the transaction. That is, if the process of applying the transaction requires the client to determine the balance of an account, the light client makes a balance query. If the light client needs to check a particular item in the storage of a particular contract, the light client makes a query for that, and so on. The miner responds to all of its own queries correctly, but keeps track of all the data that it sends back. The miner then sends the client the combined data from all of these requests as a proof. The client then undertakes the exact same procedure, but using the provided proof as its database; if its result is the same as what the miner claims, then the client accepts the proof.

So, how is the proof accepted? This is done using a consensus algorithm, which compares PoW from different miners .This algorithm is called ETH hash. Even though the future versions of the Ethereum framework might switch to PoS, PoW is currently in use. We will cover this algorithm in detail in the later chapters. As of now, remember the fact that this algorithm combines the nonce with a DAG to generate a new hash and check whether it is less than the target threshold to solve the dumb puzzle of mining, as discussed in `Chapter 1`, *Blockchain Basics*. The problem is that the DAG, which is essentially a direct acyclic graph of a huge dataset (more than 2 GB), takes a lot of **random access memory (RAM)** to process. This memory hardness is the main reason why we cannot use an ASIC miner to mine Ethereum blocks, as ASICs are very low in memory caches. The best hardware clients to mine Ethereum are GPU miners.

Here are the listed specifications shown for configuring an Etherum miner using a GPU device:

For example: RX 470 Specs

- **Cost**: ~ $175 (March 2017)
- **Memory**: 8 gigabytes
- **Memory Bandwidth**: 211 gigabyte/sec

Apart from these three tree objects, the block architecture has several other modules which are illustrated in *Figure 2.15* and are defined in the Gavin Wood's yellow paper:

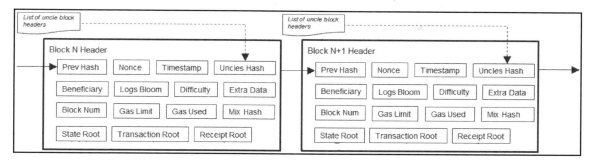

Figure 2.15: Modules inside an Ethereum block

If we study this representation closely, we find that, apart from the **parent hash** (**prev hash**), we also have an uncle hash or ommers hash. So, what is an uncle doing in an Ethereum blockchain? If I am a block and the blockchain is my family tree, my uncle would be very close to my dad. Yet, it would have been quite different if I had been born from the genes of my uncle. In that case, my dad would have been my uncle. So, the parent hash is my dad and is the correct previous hash from which I have come. Uncle hashes represent those blocks that were very close to being my correct previous block, but could not make it, as it suffered a blow from my dad. By a blow, I mean that my dad had done more PoW than my uncle; hence, the mining consensus chose him and not my uncle. So now, what happens to my uncle? He has now become a **miner activated hard fork** (**MAHF**) with respect to my blockchain, hence, is not accessible to me as I lie on my parent blockchain just after my dad, that is, the prev hash.

In somewhat similar lines, we can discuss the difference between Ethereum and Ethereum classic. If you are new to cryptocurrency and new to Ethereum, you might have noticed that you can buy two different types of Ethereum. So, you can buy Ethereum that is ETH but you can also buy Ethereum classic that is ETC. So, what are the technical and ideological differences between these two? At the beginning of the Ethereum genesis block in the blockchain, there was only ETH and there was no Ethereum classic. So, how did the ETC get created? Everything started with the DAO project on Ethereum. **Decentralized autonomous organization** (**DAO**) was a project built on top of Ethereum. This project was basically an application which could act as a self-steering organization and it had the biggest crowd sale in the history of cryptocurrency. People invested their own fiat money into this project and they received ETH tokens for their investment.

However, there was a flaw in the smart contracts, which this decentralized organization consisted of. This flaw or exploit made it possible for a group of hackers to take 50 million worth of ether from the crowd sale. Note that these hackers were technically exploiters, because it wasn't really a hack due to a bug but an exploitation of a flaw in the smart contract design logic of the DAO. So, by using this flaw the exploiters were able to steal 50 million USD worth of ethers. This caused a lot of discussions and the majority of the Ethereum community wanted to do a hard fork and reverse this theft, so that investors could get their money back and the hackers would lose their money. However, to do that, they needed to make alterations to the blockchain and this is where the whole ideological debate started within the Ethereum community. While the majority of the community agreed on the alterations and hard fork, a smaller but vocal minority opposed this notion of mutating the blockchain because the whole idea of a blockchain is that it should be immutable. Code once engraved in the blockchain should be treated as law, so if an exploit does occur, we may amend it from happening again, but we can't just go back and reverse what has happened, however unfortunate. So, at this point of the debate, the community was standing on a juncture where one portion wanted the blockchain to mutate, while another wanted to keep going as if nothing happened. So, this vocal minority kept continuing in the old blockchain, which became the Ethereum classic as a result of user/community activated hard fork. Meanwhile, the ETH was eventually mutated to return the money to investors as the stakes were high. This is why we have both ETH and ETC as cryptocurrencies.

Now, if you bought some ETH or ETC, where would you store it? For fiat money, we generally store them in bank accounts or in our wallet. Now, in a decentralized setup we do not have a bank. However, we do have wallets and clients, which we will discuss in the next section.

The Ethereum wallet and client interface

An Ethereum client refers to any node which can parse and verify the Ethereum blockchain and execute smart contracts on top of it. As we have seen in the early sections of this chapter, the main purpose of user-faced clients is to authorize user credentials and provide an interface to conduct various operations. They also provide interfaces to create transactions and mine blocks, which is crucial for blockchain interaction. *Figure 2.16* illustrates the classification of Ethereum client interfaces:

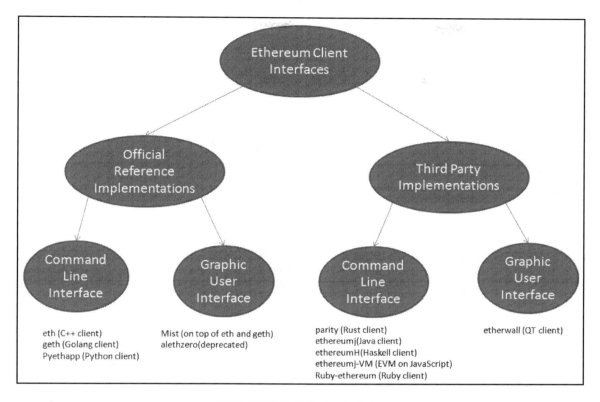

Figure 2.16: Ethereum client interface classification

A wallet provides a service of sending, storing, and receiving funds. The main parameters of a good wallet service are security and trust. Users must feel that their funds are secure and the administrator of the wallet will not steal the funds. Such wallets are known as hot wallets, because they are always connected to the network and are often vulnerable to hacks and exploits. More secure wallets include paper wallets and hardware wallets, which are often called cold wallets. These basically store the tokens in offline mode. A paper wallet is stored as scanned QR codes representing the receiving address, along with a passcode, which must be remembered. In simple words, you print your keys on a paper so that they do not get hacked. Hardware wallets have hardwired encryption over a USB enabled device, which opens only with a passcode.

Figure 2.17 represents a classification of wallets for clarity:

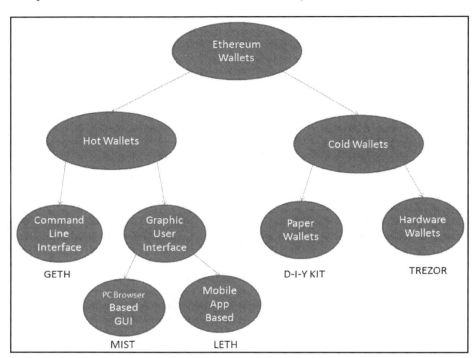

Figure 2.17: Ethereum wallet classification

Among all these Ethereum clients, **light Ethereum mobile wallet (LETH)** by Inzhoop deserves a special mention, because it not only has a wallet service but also a DApps browser store hosting quite a few working DApps. The Android-based alpha release also has a group chat, as well as personal chat tabs, which are entirely based on whisper. The chat history persists for 24 hours. As of now, picture files can be sent with generated bzzkey. It is presently hosted on the testnet Ropsten with the wallet on mainnet. So, to chat or play games or even open an account after installation, you do not have to spend any valuable ether. You need zero programming knowledge to operate this app, and it is available on the Google Play Store. Beginners are very much encouraged to try this mobile-based app to get a feel of how DApps, whisper, and swarm work together to create a good browser plus wallet platform. They also have a full working app for desktop.

Figure 2.18 shows a few snapshots on LETH (alpha release):

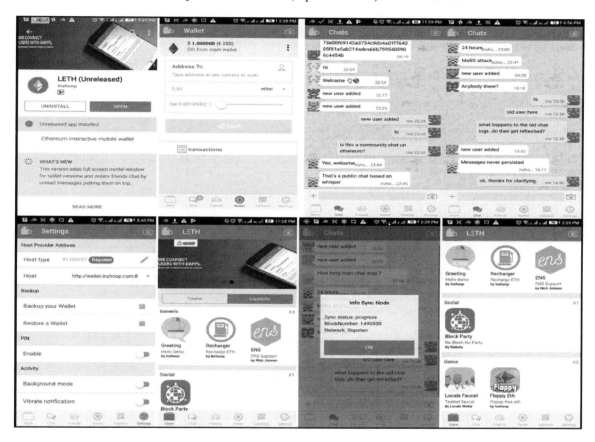

Figure 2.18: Light Ethereum mobile wallet (Android release)

This brings us to the end of our chapter. I hope this chapter helped you to gain the necessary theoretical base to embark on the journey of Ethereum blockchain and smart contract development in the later sections.

Roll up your sleeves, grab some hot coffee, and put your device on charge. We are going to get our hands dirty soon with some solidity smart contracts. See you in Chapter 3, *Hello World of Ethereum Smart Contract*.

Summary

We started this chapter with an understanding of the Ethereum platform as a way to achieve a decentralized economy. We explored the meaning of decentralization over political, logical, and architectural axes. Ethereum was found to be centralized about the logical axis. We dived deep into the web 3.0 technological stack of Ethereum and saw how swarm stores data, how whisper communicates, and how EVM interacts with blockchain, using smart contracts and a stack-based machine code. We identified that loops are a good rule-of-thumb for a language being Turing complete. We saw how gas is the magic sauce to curb performance related problems on Ethereum and how we need ether to top up our gas limit to run smart contract codes on the blockchain. We introduced the notion of uncle hash in the Ethereum blockchain. Also, we distinguished between ETH and ETC as a community activated hard fork. Mining requires huge memory access and hence prevents ASIC miners but encourages GPU miners. Finally, we concluded by classifying various wallets and client interfaces for Ethereum, and we had a quick tour of Android-based LETH.

In Chapter 3, *Hello World of Ethereum Smart Contract*, put on your developer hat. It's time for some fun ways of coding your first smart contract.

3

Hello World of Smart Contracts

This chapter is a hands-on guide for developing our first smart contract. As an unspoken tradition of software developers since the days of Dennis Ritchie, the creator of C language, we will start with a Hello World program. We will then introduce some basic increment, decrement, and loop operations using smart contracts. We walk through the process of creating our own private blockchain, right from the genesis block, and mining our own ethers. After studying this chapter, you will be able to:

- Write your first Hello World smart contract
- Code a contract with basic increment and decrement operation
- Code a loop
- Raise an issue on GitHub
- Create a private blockchain and mine ethers to run a smart contract

A smart contract in seven lines of code

In this section you will learn to code your first smart contract in just seven **lines of code** (**Loc**), no hidden terms and conditions. And did I say that you do not need any special software, apart from your web browser, or to spend any real ethers from your pocket? Let's see. I am using Windows 7 (64 bit OS) and a Google Chrome browser:

1. Open your Google Chrome browser and type `remix solidity` in Google, as show in *Figure 3.1*:

Figure 3.1: Google search for remix solidity online compiler

2. Click the highlighted link in *Figure 3.2*. You can also type the following in your browser URL box to get to the website directly: `http://remix.ethereum.org`:

The present remix ethereum webpage is going through rapid changes and version increments. Meanwhile, and older yet stable version is provided to Solidity users for practice in the following link:

`https://yann300.github.io/remix04/`

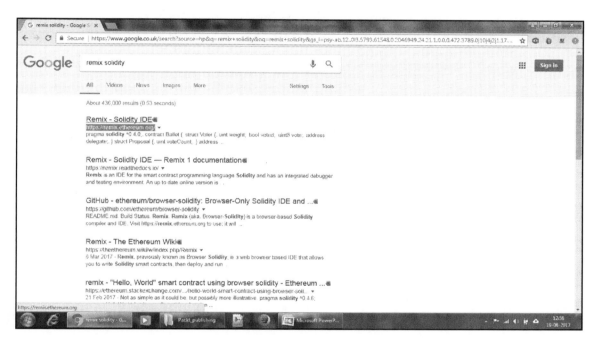

Figure 3.2: Remix—Solidity IDE

3. Click the plus sign as marked in *Figure 3.3* to create a new untitled Solidity (`.sol`) file.

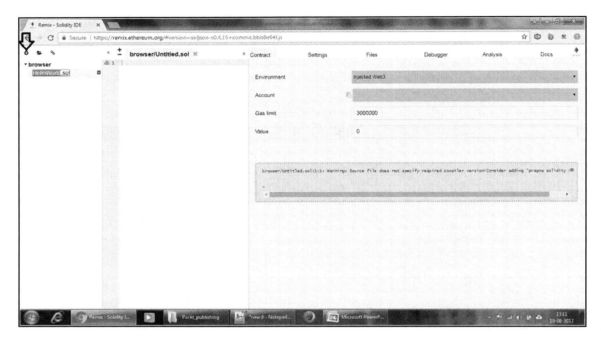

Figure 3.3 Untitled Solidity file in remix IDE

Rename it `HelloWorld.sol` and confirm the renaming, as shown in *Figure 3.4*:

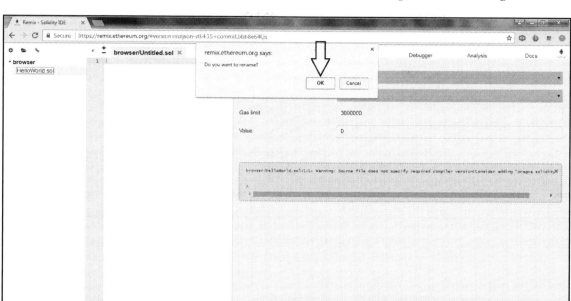

Figure 3.4: Untitled.sol renamed to HelloWorld.sol

4. Write the following seven lines of code in the `HelloWorld.sol` file, as shown in *Figure 3.5*:

```
ContractDefinition HelloWorld
1  pragma solidity ^0.4.11;
2
3  contract HelloWorld{
4      function myFirstHelloWorld() public pure returns (string){
5          return 'Hello World !';
6      }
7  }
```

Figure 3.5: HelloWorld.sol

Choose the JavaScript VM Environment option, as shown in *Figure 3.6*:

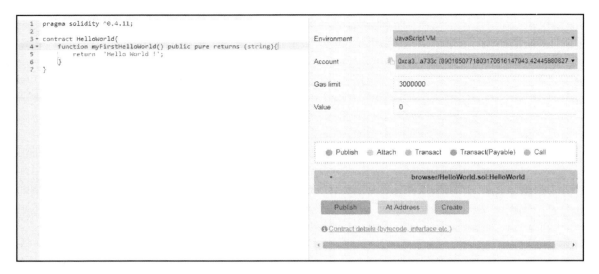

Figure 3.6: JavaScript VM acting as a blockchain simulator

5. Click the **Create** button, as highlighted in *Figure 3.7*. Voila! You just created your smart contract. The only caveat is that we would be simulating it on our local machine using in-memory, which mimics an Ethereum blockchain:

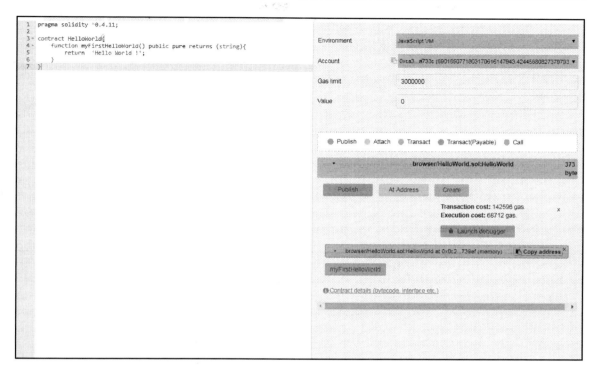

Figure 3.7: Our first smart contract of 368 bytes

6. To execute this contract, we press that **myFirstHelloWorld** button, as shown in *Figure 3.8*. We get the desired output: **Hello World !**

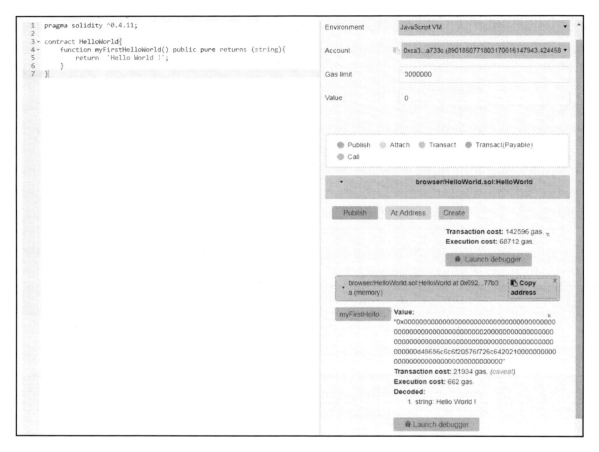

Figure 3.8: Execution of myFirstHelloWorld function using a smart contract

7. We can also explore the byte codes, which are generated as a result of this smart contract execution, by pressing the **Launch debugger | Instructions** or just by clicking the **Contract details (bytecode, interface etc)** link. *Figure 3.9* depicts the 368 bytes of virtual machine code generated by the hello world smart contract execution:

```
000 PUSH1 60        102 DUP1           158 DUP1           213 NOT            300 POP
002 PUSH1 40        103 INVALID        159 DUP3           214 AND            301 JUMPDEST
004 MSTORE          104 JUMPDEST       161 MLOAD          216 DUP2           302 SWAP1
005 CALLVALUE       108 PUSH2 0051     162 DUP2           216 MSTORE         303 JUMP
006 ISZERO          108 PUSH2 00cd     163 DUP5           217 PUSH1 20       304 JUMPDEST
007 PUSH2 000f      111 JUMP           164 ADD            219 ADD            305 PUSH1 20
010 JUMPI           112 JUMPDEST       166 MSTORE         220 SWAP2          307 PUSH1 40
011 PUSH1 00        113 PUSH1 40       166 JUMPDEST       221 POP            309 MLOAD
013 DUP1            115 MLOAD          167 PUSH1 20       222 JUMPDEST       310 SWAP1
014 INVALID         116 DUP1           169 DUP2           223 POP            311 DUP2
015 JUMPDEST        117 DUP1           170 ADD            224 SWAP3          312 ADD
016 JUMPDEST        118 PUSH1 20       171 SWAP1          225 POP            313 PUSH1 40
017 PUSH2 0151      120 ADD            172 POP            226 POP            315 MSTORE
020 DUP1            121 DUP1           173 PUSH2 0076     227 POP            316 DUP1
021 PUSH2 001f      122 DUP2           176 JUMP           228 PUSH1 40       317 PUSH1 00
024 PUSH1 00        123 SUB            177 JUMPDEST       230 MLOAD          319 DUP2
026 CODECOPY        124 DUP3           178 POP            231 DUP1           320 MSTORE
027 PUSH1 00        125 MSTORE         179 POP            232 SWAP2          321 POP
029 RETURN          126 DUP4           180 POP            233 SUB            322 SWAP1
030 STOP            127 DUP2           181 POP            234 SWAP1          324 STOP
031 PUSH1 60        128 DUP2           182 SWAP1          235 RETURN         325 LOG1
033 PUSH1 40        129 MLOAD          183 POP            236 JUMPDEST       326 PUSH6 627a7a723058
036 MSTORE          130 DUP1           184 SWAP1          237 PUSH2 00d5     333 SHA3
036 PUSH1 00        131 MSTORE         186 DUP2           240 PUSH2 0111     334 PUSH31 2f4ec5e9f9703fdff3125147f9f9f8fd200d411f28e1794f050ewfb0f5340fdd340
038 CALLDATALOAD    132 PUSH1 20       187 SWAP1          243 JUMP           365 STOP
039 PUSH29 0100000000000000000000000000000000000000000000000000000000  134 ADD  188 PUSH1 1f  244 JUMPDEST  367 INVALID
069 SWAP1           135 SWAP2          190 AND            245 PUSH1 40
070 DIV             136 POP            191 DUP1           247 POP
071 PUSH4 ffffffff  137 DUP1           192 ISZERO         248 MLOAD
076 AND             138 MLOAD          193 PUSH2 00af     249 SWAP1
077 DUP1            139 SWAP1          196 JUMPI          250 DUP2
078 PUSH4 a60c7b27  140 PUSH1 20       197 DUP1           251 ADD
083 EQ              143 SWAP1          198 DUP3           252 PUSH1 40
084 PUSH2 003a      144 DUP1           199 SUB            254 MSTORE
087 JUMPI           145 DUP4           200 DUP1           255 DUP1
088 JUMPDEST        146 DUP4           201 MLOAD          256 PUSH1 0d
089 PUSH1 08        147 PUSH1 00       202 PUSH1 01       258 DUP2
091 DUP1            149 JUMPDEST       204 DUP4           259 MSTORE
092 INVALID         150 DUP4           205 PUSH1 20       260 PUSH1 20
093 JUMPDEST        151 DUP2           207 SUB            262 ADD
094 CALLVALUE       152 LT             208 PUSH2 0100     263 PUSH32 48654c6c6f20576f726c6421000000000000000000000000000000000000000000
095 ISZERO          153 ISZERO        211 EXP            295 MSTORE
096 PUSH2 0049      154 PUSH2 0092     212 SUB            296 DUP2
099 JUMPI           157 JUMPI                            298 POP
100 PUSH1 00                                             299 SWAP1
```

Figure 3.9: 368 bytes [000 to 367] of machine code for Hello World smart contract

Remix in a nutshell

So, what is this remix? In simple words, it is a browser-based **Integrated Development Environment** (**IDE**) for writing smart contracts in Solidity. It has an integrated compiler, a runtime virtual environment without any server-side component, an integrated debugger, an integrated testing environment, and a static code analysis tool. Previously, it used to be called **Browser-Solidity**. It can not only simulate a blockchain, but also highlights syntax and errors, hosts multiple Solidity files, and deploys contracts along with visible byte codes and **application binary interface** (**ABI**), of which details can be found in later chapters.

However, I promised less theory and more hands-on in this chapter. So, let us now jump into an increment and decrement contract. Please note that there are more professional ways to deploy contracts using geth and MIST, which we will look at in detail in the last section. Right now, we will concentrate more on some quick-and-dirty basic smart contracts using Solidity on remix.

Increment and decrement operations using Solidity

Figure 3.10 shows the code of an increment and decrement operation in Solidity. It also has a function that takes input, and a function, that fetches out this number once the contract gets executed:

```solidity
1   pragma solidity ^0.4.11;
2   // define new contract
3   contract ArithValue{
4       uint number;
5       function ArithValue() public {   //constructor function with default value
6           number = 100;
7       }
8   // constructor function to set new value
9       function setNumber(uint theValue) public {
10          number = theValue;
11      }
12  // constructor function to fetch the new value
13      function fetchNumber() public constant returns (uint) {
14          return number;
15      }
16  // constructor function to increment by one
17      function incrementNumber() public {
18          number=number + 1;
19      }
20  // constructor function to decrement by one
21      function decrementNumber() public {
22          number=number - 1;
23      }
24  }
```

Figure 3.10: Increment and decrement operation using Solidity (ArithValue.sol)

Isn't this code a bit more complex than the hello world contract? Let me walk you through this code. The first line starts with `pragma`. As you have realized already, it just states which version of Solidity we are about to use. In our case, we are using version `0.4.11`. As I type, remix IDE supports versions up to 0.4.16.

To understand pragma, let us go back to our brunch buffet analogy from `Chapter 2`, *Grokking Ethereum*. If I specify during the buffet reservation that I am a strict vegan, I am giving the buffet organizers some sort of directive, in advance, that I do not eat non-vegan dishes like meat, fish, poultry, or eggs. So, I get introduced to only those counters which serve vegan dishes when the gala brunch begins. Most obviously, I will be annoyed and flag it to the organizers if I am mistakenly served tender lamb kebabs in place of broccoli curry. Then, I would get my plates replaced even before touching or eating the food, no questions asked.

In a similar way, pragma is a language construct that gives some sort of directive to the compiler about how to process its inputs. Generally, a pre-processor handles such language constructs and specifies compiler behavior. In our example, our directive is to make the compiler behave as if it is running a smart contract on Solidity version 0.4.11 or lower.

So, what happens if we do not write this line? Well, nothing bad happens. A warning is thrown, as shown in *Figure 3.11,* and the code compiles just fine. However, it now uses the default Solidity version, 0.4.16 in our case. By analogy, we can't get angry at the buffet organizers for serving me lamb kebabs if I forget to tell them that I am a vegan. I then somehow manage to eat the food served to me by avoiding the non-vegan portion and save all from further embarrassment.

So, what is the point I am trying to make here? The point I am trying to make is to stick to good programming practice, so that your codes are readable to other programmers who might debug or enhance it in the distant future. As all of the source codes are open source and hosted on GitHub-like platforms, and developers inherently hate to write explicit documentations, it is a recommended professional etiquette to write clean code with logical inline comments:

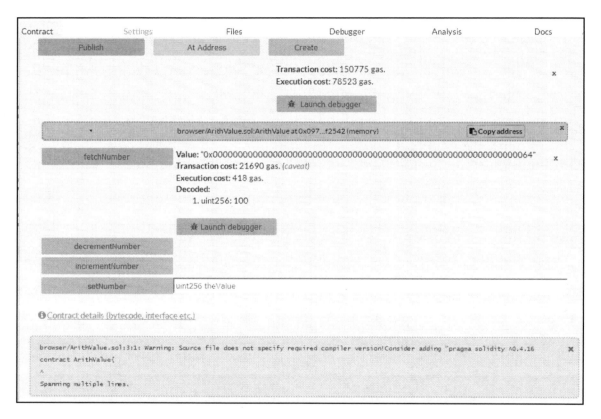

Figure 3.11: ArithValue.sol compiled with warning owing to not mentioning pragma directive

Let us get back to our code:

1. First, we start by defining the contract. We name it `ArithValue`, as we are going to store and manipulate a value using arithmetic operations. There are no hard-and-fast naming rules here. Try to stick to some logical names.

2. Then, we declare an unsigned integer value that will store our default number, which must be a positive integer.

3. Now we need to give our contract a constructor function. So, what is a constructor function? Basically, this is a function that will be called whenever our contract is deployed and initiated for the first time. What's special about this constructor function is that it has the same name as that of the contract, that is, `ArithValue`. Inside the `constructor` function, we assign `100` to the number variable. So, now, whenever the contract gets initiated for the first time, it will set a default value of `100` to our unsigned integer variable number.

4. Now we create four other functions inside the contract that basically set, fetch, increment, and decrement the value we assigned to the variable number. These steps will be shown in *Figure 3.12*, *Figure 3.13*, *Figure 3.14*, and *Figure 3.15*, after we create the contract. Ideally, we must first publish the contract and then create it to instantiate, which will cost us real ethers on a blockchain, but at this point the publishing is of little sense, as we are working on a simulated blockchain environment and will not publish anything on a permanent basis.

5. As we can see in the *Figure 3.12*, once the contract is deployed and instantiated, four functions, namely `fetchNumber`, `decrementNumber`, `incrementNumber`, and `setNumber`, get created. Due to the constructor function, our default value is set to `100` in the contract.

6. As depicted in *Figure 3.13*, if we press the **incrementNumber** button and press the **fetchNumber** button, the value gets incremented to 101.

7. In *Figure 3.14*, we type in a random positive integer `143` and press **setNumber**.

8. We then press **fetchNumber** and our value has changed to `143`.

9. Then, as shown in *Figure 3.15*, we press the **decrementNumber** button, followed by **fetchNumber**; the value `143` is decremented to `142`.

As you try this example on your laptop, keep a watch on the **Account** drop-down tab, which is just below the **Environment** drop-down tab. Did you notice the decreasing value of the ether? Do check it:

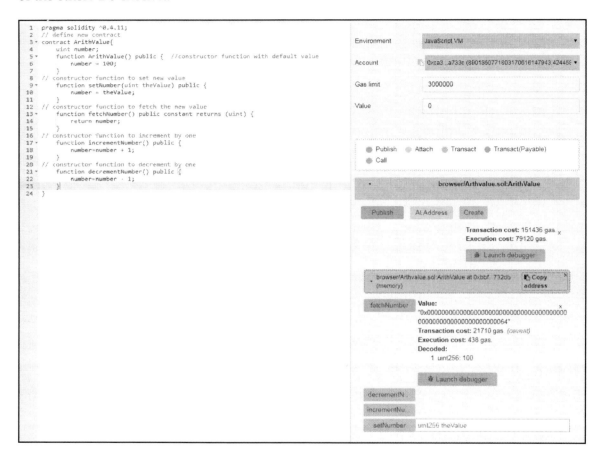

Figure 3.12: Deploy and create ArithValue contract

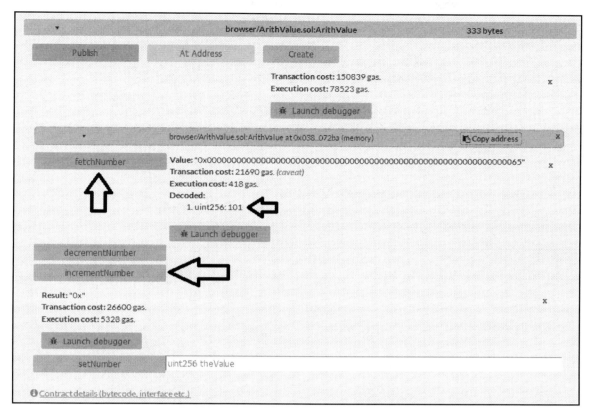

Figure 3.13: Working of incrementNumber function

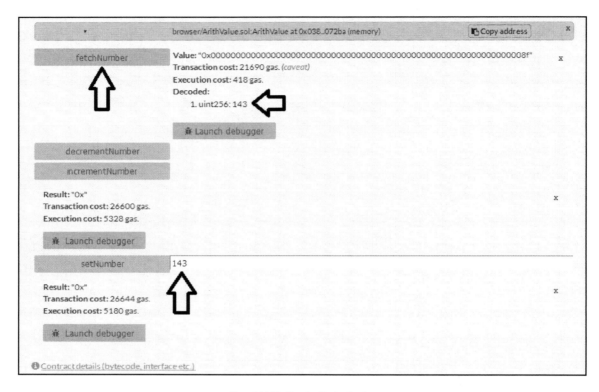

Figure 3.14: Working of setNumber function

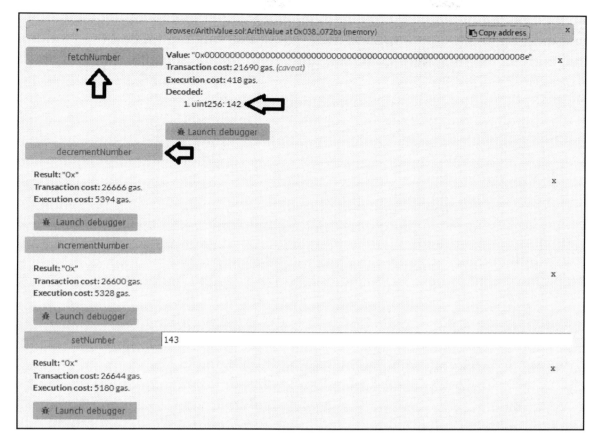

Figure 3.15: Working of decrementNumber function

Coding a loop

Loops are very helpful when we need to repeat the execution of a piece of code a certain number of times. Rather than copying and pasting the same lines of code, making the code block longer, we use this programming construct to add brevity to our code. Loops can be finite or infinite in nature. For the infinite loop, we generally provide a break statement to come out of it.

The smart contract in *Figure 3.16* is using a finite loop to calculate the summation of a finite number of integers:

```
1    pragma solidity ^0.4.11;
2
3 - contract numberLoop {
4        uint number; // unsigned integer is positive integer
5        //constructor function with default value
6 -      function numberLoop() public {
7            number = 100;
8        }
9 -      function myFirstLoop() public returns (uint) {
10 -          for (uint i = 1; i < 10; i++) {
11               number = number + i;
12           }
13           return number;
14       }
15   }
```

Figure 3.16: Loop inside a Solidity smart contract

The output on remix IDE is shown in *Figure 3.17*. As discussed earlier, keep a watch on the amount of ethers that is getting decreased in the **Account** tab for each call of the myFirstLoop function:

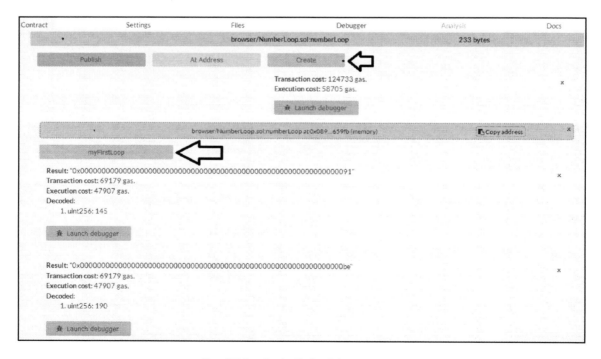

Figure 3.17: Execution of myFirstLoop inside a smart contract

The best way to check the inner working of a loop in runtime is to go to the **Launch debugger** tab and manually push the horizontal scroll bar from left to right, as shown in *Figure 3.18*. Try it! It will be fun:

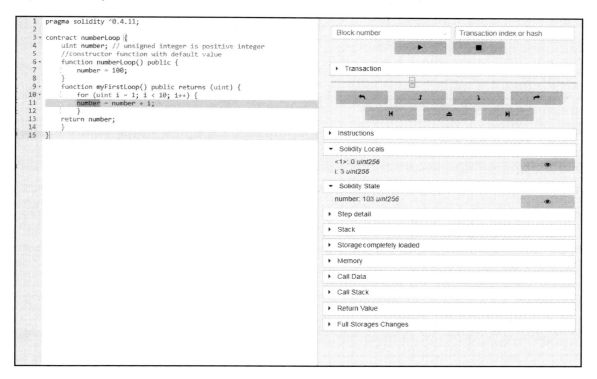

Figure 3.18: Debugging mode to identify states of execution

At this point, I hope you are quite comfortable playing with smart contracts using the remix IDE in your browser. However, what I have shown is just a happy-path scenario. The development community for Ethereum is highly agile and is rolling out newer changes very quickly. By the time you start reading this book, there might be slight or major modifications in the IDE. Once you start coding, you will realize the nuances and even capture many peculiar bugs down the line. The next section is all about what you can do when you are stuck with a problem or a code bug.

Raising an issue on GitHub

When you have a code bug, before raising any issue on GitHub, please have a check on the Ethereum documentations, freely available via any search engine. Then, ask the same in the Ethereum stack exchange. In most of the cases, you will not be the lone person who has faced that bug. So, the solution to your problem might be already out there on the web. The last resort is to raise an issue in the GitHub. GitHub is a code repository with version control freely available to all. Most of the blockchain related source codes are available on GitHub. I will show you how I raised an issue for the LETH wallet app for Android, which was discussed in `Chapter 2`, *Grokking Ethereum*:

- **Identifying issue**: While uploading picture files to the chat window, which uses whisper communication protocol, there is no option to provide a message or caption, as we can do in chat services like WhatsApp.
- **Logging issue**: Create a free GitHub account and log into the LETH GitHub repository page, as shown in *Figure 3.19*. Click the **New issue** button to log in the issue. Once the issue is described with any necessary images and descriptions, click the **Submit new issue** button, as shown in *Figure 3.20,* to generate the new issue, as I had generated in *Figure 3.19*. You can check the issue details in the link, `https://github.com/inzhoop-co/LETH/issues/31`:

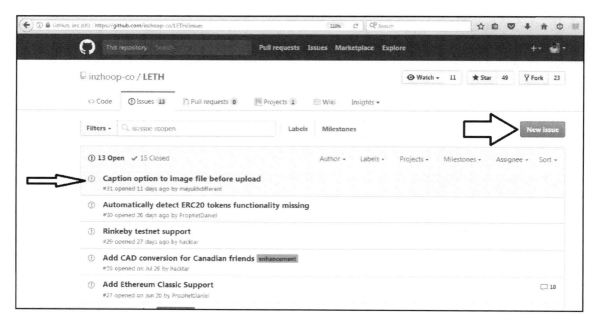

Figure 3.19: Creating new issue on GitHub

Figure 3.20: Describing and submitting new issue on GitHub

Smart contract on a private blockchain

Let us do some grown-up stuff now. Yes, we are still not going to spend any fiat money to buy ethers to code on a blockchain. Rather we will do the following:

1. Write a genesis block file for a private blockchain.
2. Create the private blockchain using geth commands.
3. Link the private blockchain with the MIST browser.
4. Mine the chain to generate our own ethers as rewards.
5. Use those ethers to deploy a smart contract on our very own private blockchain.

The pre-requisite tools to be installed are as follows:

- Windows 7 (64-bit) (Instructions are for Windows user, for Ubuntu/Mac refer appendix)
- Cygwin setup-x86_64 (For Bash-Shell on Windows 7) (https://cygwin.com/install.html)
- geth-windows-amd64-1.6.7-ab5646c5 (https://geth.ethereum.org/downloads/)

- Mist-win64-0-9-0 (`https://github.com/ethereum/mist/releases`)
- Node.js (node-v6.11.2-x64) (`https://nodejs.org/en/download/`)
- .NET framework 4.5
  (`https://www.microsoft.com/en-in/download/details.aspx?id=30653`)

I am not going into the details of the installation. The installations are pretty straightforward, involving the terms and conditions page (which we never read), followed by blind-surfing of **Next** and **I Agree** buttons, and while the installations are going on, watching some random YouTube videos or stand-up comedians to entertain ourselves.

For troubleshooting, Google and the stack exchange are your best friends, ever. *Figure 3.21, Figure 3.22, Figure 3.23, Figure 3.24, Figure 3.25,* and *Figure 3.26* are provided for your reference, to check whether you are on the right track during installation, especially for MIST, geth, Cygwin, and Node.js. The only recommendation is to try to keep all these installation, in one separate folder in a separate drive, apart from .NET framework, so that they do not mess up your main program files. My downloads and installations were inside `F:Ethereum_Environment path:`

Figure 3.21: Mist installer package

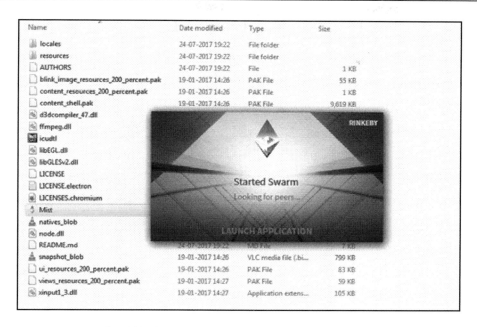

Figure 3.22: Default start of MIST on RINKEBY public blockchain (avoid this step)

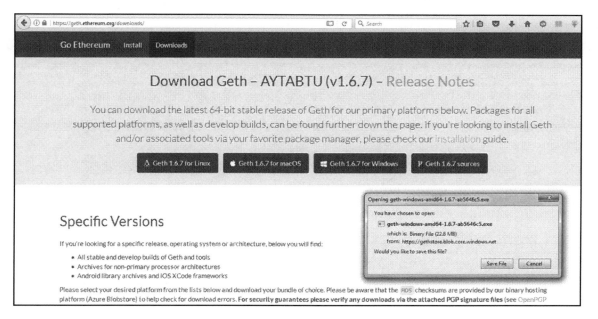

Figure 3.23: Geth download page

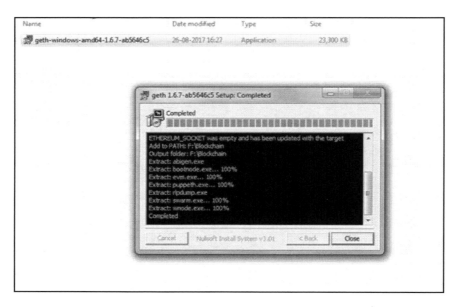

Figure 3.24: Geth Successful Installation page

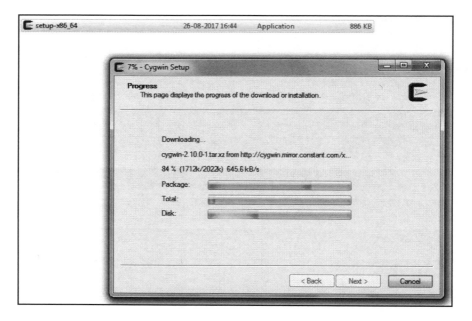

Figure 3.25: Cygwin Setup

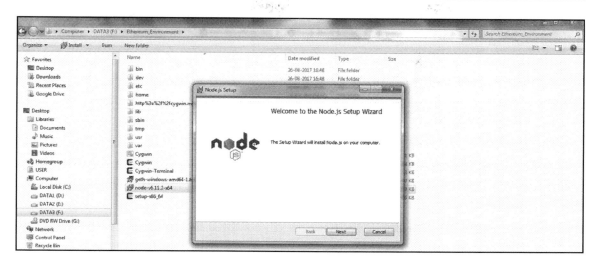

Figure 3.26: Node.js Setup Wizard

Writing the genesis block

The first step for creating a private blockchain is to create a genesis block. It is basically submitting a **JavaScript Object Notation (JSON)** file with the following details. In this chapter, we just lay down the structure, rather than going deep into what the block contents mean. One point to remember is to use a random integer other than 1 for the `chainId` parameter, as shown in *Figure 3.27*:

```
{
    "coinbase"   : "0x0000000000000000000000000000000000000001",
    "difficulty" : "0x20000",
    "extraData"  : "",
    "gasLimit"   : "0x2fefd8",
    "nonce"      : "0x0000000000000042",
    "mixhash"    : "0x0000000000000000000000000000000000000000000000000000000000000000",
    "parentHash" : "0x0000000000000000000000000000000000000000000000000000000000000000",
    "timestamp"  : "0x00",
    "alloc": {},
    "config": {
        "chainId": 15,
        "homesteadBlock": 0,
        "eip155Block": 0,
        "eip158Block": 0
    }
}
```

Figure 3.27: genesis.json

Building a private blockchain

1. In order to create a private blockchain, we first open the Cygwin command line and create a folder and files, using the following commands:

```
$  mkdir Ethereum
$  cd Ethereum
$  mkdir Project
$  cd Project
$  mkdir chaindata
$  vi genesis.json    ## this line opens the vim editor where we paste
the content of genesis file
       ## we save the file content using command [Esc button press] wq
$  ls -lha    ## this command list down the folder structure as shown
in Figure 3.28
```

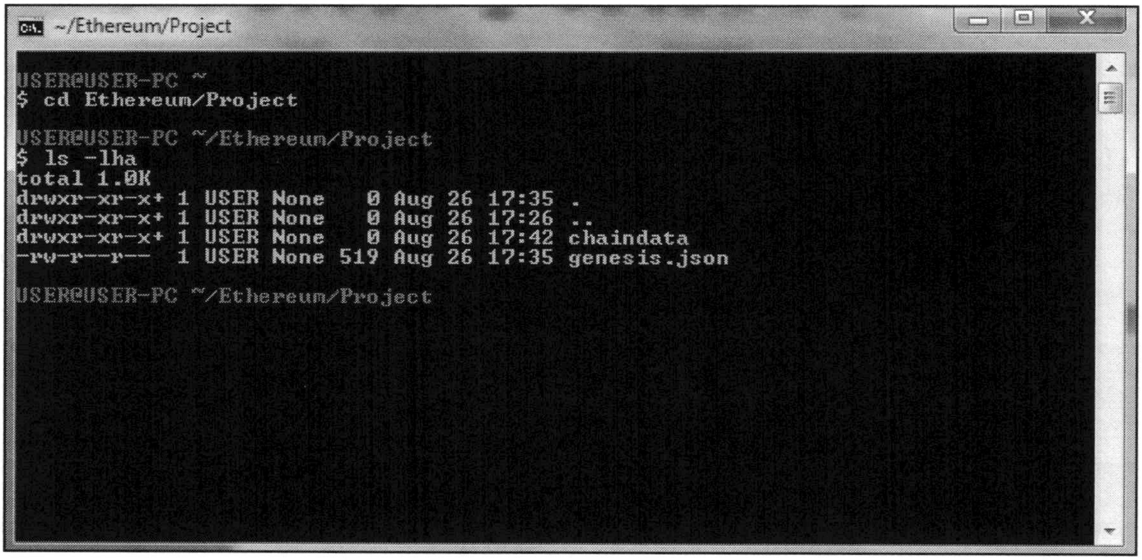

Figure 3.28: genesis.json file always outside chaindata folder

2. Now, in a separate Cygwin command window, we start geth, using the command $ geth. As in *Figure 3.29*, the line IPC endpoint opened ... geth.ipc means we are on the right track. This step is optional and is done to check whether geth is able to open port 30303 for **Inter-Process Communication (IPC)**:

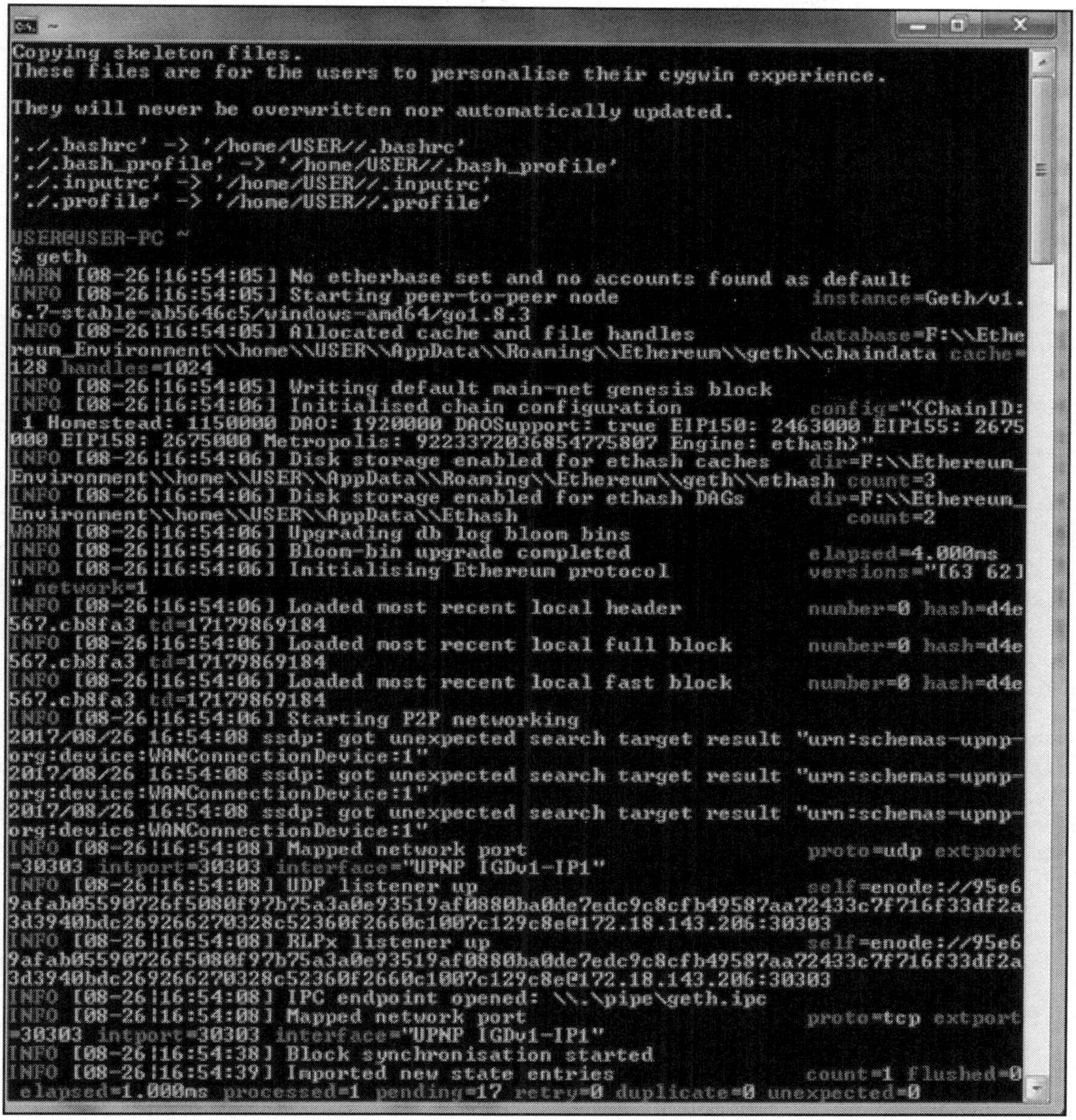

Figure 3.29: Starting geth for the first time

3. Now, in the old Cygwin window, we type the following command, as shown in *Figure 3.30*:

```
$ geth --datadir=./chaindata/ init genesis.json
```

4. This initiates geth's data directory to be assigned by the `chaindata` directory using the genesis state. In simple worlds, we have initiated our private blockchain in the command line:

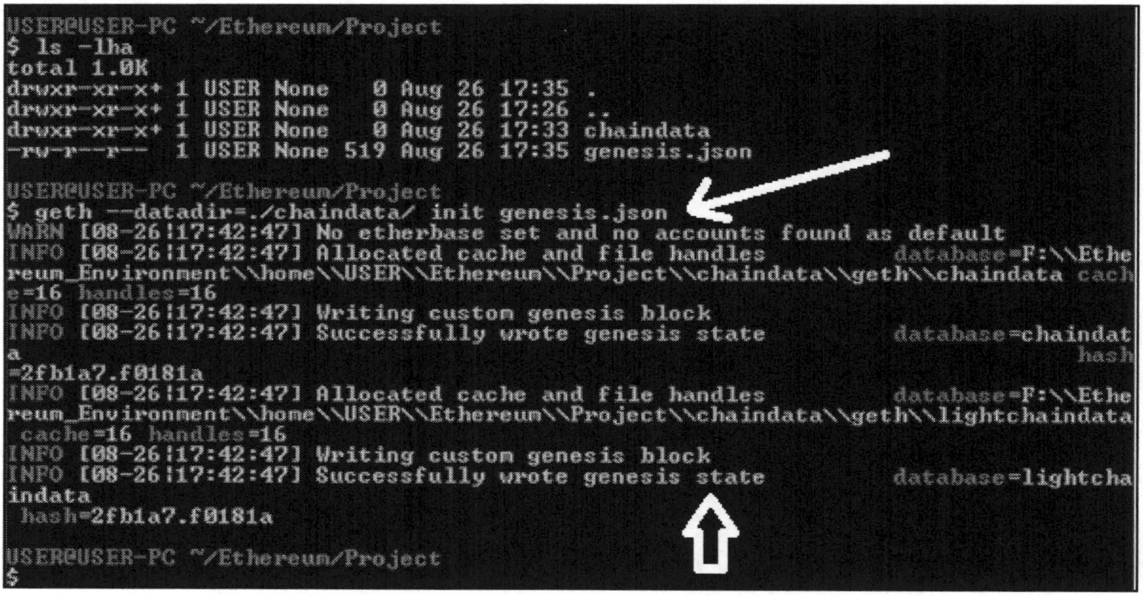

```
USER@USER-PC ~/Ethereum/Project
$ ls -lha
total 1.0K
drwxr-xr-x+  1 USER None    0 Aug 26 17:35 .
drwxr-xr-x+  1 USER None    0 Aug 26 17:26 ..
drwxr-xr-x+  1 USER None    0 Aug 26 17:33 chaindata
-rw-r--r--   1 USER None  519 Aug 26 17:35 genesis.json

USER@USER-PC ~/Ethereum/Project
$ geth --datadir=./chaindata/ init genesis.json
WARN [08-26|17:42:47] No etherbase set and no accounts found as default
INFO [08-26|17:42:47] Allocated cache and file handles         database=F:\\Ethe
reum_Environment\\home\\USER\\Ethereum\\Project\\chaindata\\geth\\chaindata cach
e=16 handles=16
INFO [08-26|17:42:47] Writing custom genesis block
INFO [08-26|17:42:47] Successfully wrote genesis state         database=chaindat
a
                                                                           hash
=2fb1a7.f0181a
INFO [08-26|17:42:47] Allocated cache and file handles         database=F:\\Ethe
reum_Environment\\home\\USER\\Ethereum\\Project\\chaindata\\geth\\lightchaindata
 cache=16 handles=16
INFO [08-26|17:42:47] Writing custom genesis block
INFO [08-26|17:42:47] Successfully wrote genesis state         database=lightcha
indata
 hash=2fb1a7.f0181a

USER@USER-PC ~/Ethereum/Project
$
```

Figure 3.30: Initiating geth with a private blockchain

5. We can now write the command $ `geth --datadir=./chaindata/`, as shown in *Figure 3.31*. This connects the geth to our private blockchain, without explicit initiation to the genesis state:

Figure 3.31: Starting a private blockchain using geth

Connecting MIST browser using geth

After starting geth using `chaindata` directory, if we open the MIST browser, it connects to PRIVATE-NET, depicted in *Figure 3.33*, rather than the public blockchain RINKEBY (refer to *Figure 3.22*):

Figure 3.33: MIST launching in PRIVATE-NET

Now, we create a new wallet account in MIST on top of our private blockchain, as shown in *Figure 3.34* and *Figure 3.35*. In *Figure 3.36*, we assign this new account as our main etherbase account:

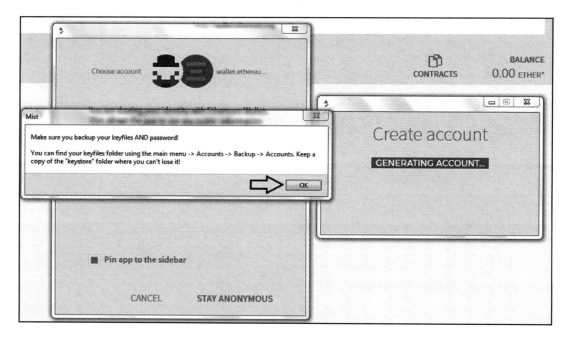

Figure 3.34: Creating a new account on a private blockchain

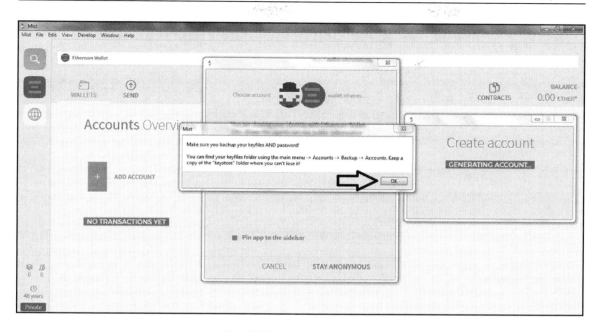

Figure 3.35: Generating the new MIST account

Figure 3.36: Authorize new account as main etherbase account

Mining ethers in a private blockchain

We go back to a new Cygwin command window and type $ `geth attach` to attach the geth to the IPC, as shown in *Figure 3.37*. Then we type $ `miner.start(1);`. Please note that the background geth window, which was started with `datadir`, should be still running. It takes a while to mine the blocks and then we can stop the miner using the command $ `miner.stop();`.To check the intermediate steps, we can have an additional step before we start the miner in geth. The command is $ `debug.verbosity(4);`.

Figure 3.37 also depicts the number of blocks (`100`) we have mined and the ethers (`500.00`) we earned as a reward. Please note that these ethers have no market value, as they are mined on our private blockchain and not on the main public Ethereum blockchain. However, we can use these ethers to deploy smart contracts, which we will illustrate in the next section:

Figure 3.37: Block mining and ether rewards

Deploying smart contracts on our private chain

Now that we have mined quite a few ethers, we can start to deploy our smart contract. *Figure 3.38, Figure 3.39, Figure 3.40, Figure 3.41, Figure 3.42, Figure 3.43, Figure 3.44,* and *Figure 3.45* depicts how to create a smart contract, then deploy it on the private blockchain by spending a few ethers and then executing the contract where each step requires us to spend some ethers. We have kept the miner started in the background so that our account gets filled up with ethers, and we do not exhaust our ethers in the middle of the execution of the smart contract. We also need the mining to deploy the smart contract. The smart contract used is the same increment and decrement operation, we discussed earlier in this chapter, using remix browser IDE:

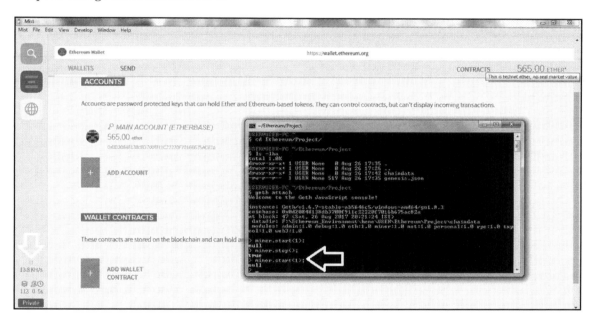

Figure 3.38: Restarting the miner in the background to keep the ether rewards coming

Figure 3.39: Creating a new contract (Click + sign)

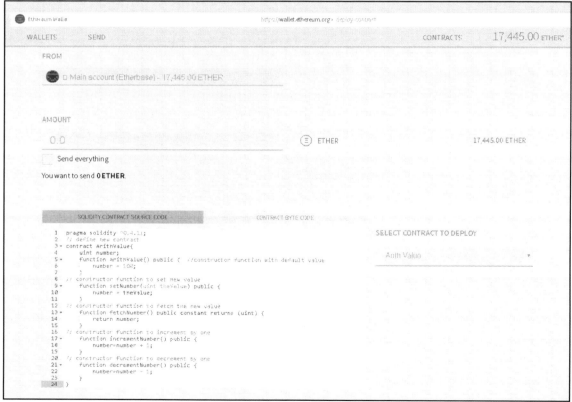

Figure 3.40: Coding the ArithValue.sol

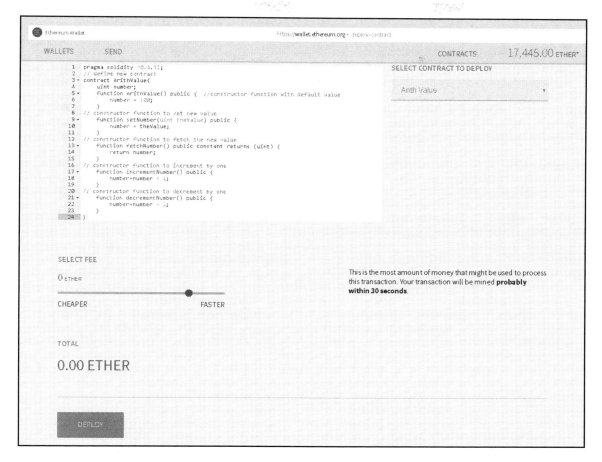

Figure 3.41: Deploy the smart contract after fee selection

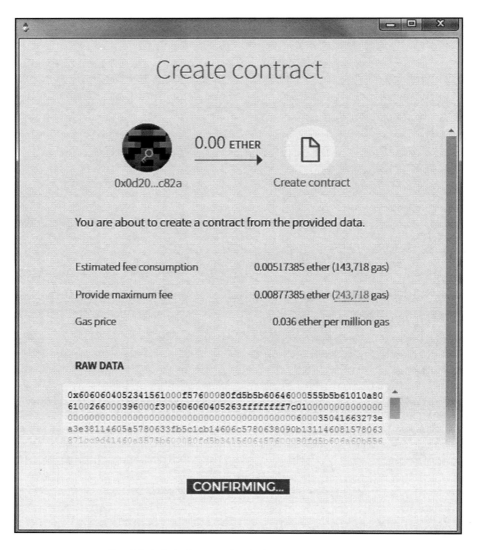

Figure 3.42: Confirming the contract after authorizing with passcode (new123456)

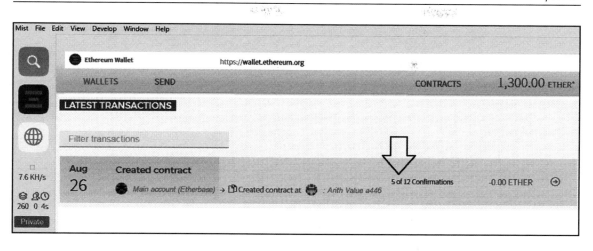

Figure 3.43: Confirmation through miner in progress for the smart contract (12 of 12 means complete)

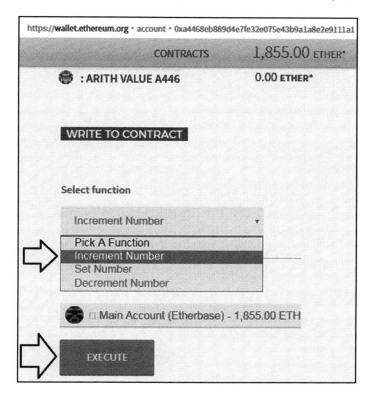

Figure 3.44: Executing the increment number operation in the CONTRACTS tab

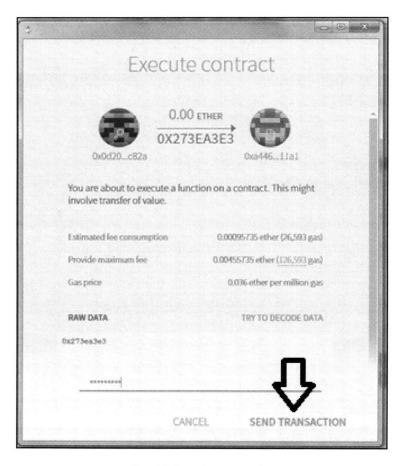

Figure 3.45: Execute the contract operation

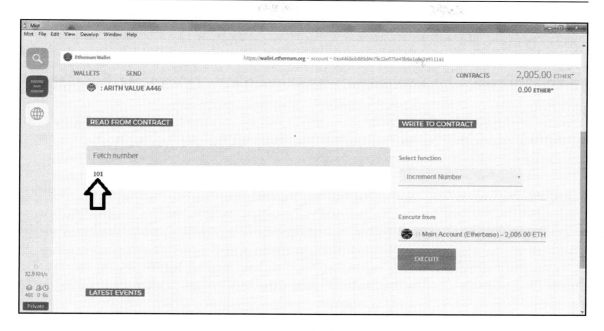

Figure 3.46: The increment operator has increased 100 to 101 (similarly, we try the other operations)

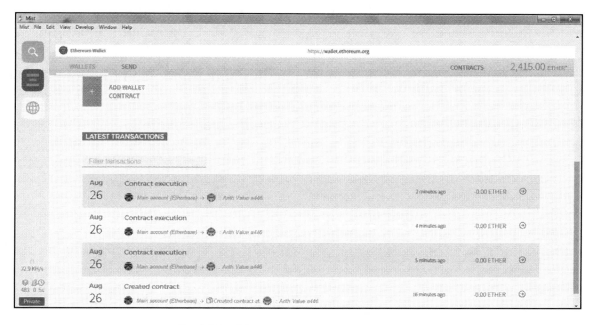

Figure 3.47: Log of all the operations executed after smart contract creation

Summary

This chapter was more of a lab exercise with minimal theoretical backing. We started it with a simple hello world smart contract on remix IDE, using a web browser. We also explored the increment and decrement operation using a contract. We then jumped in to code a quick `for` loop in Solidity and proceeded to learn how to consult while troubleshooting and raise issues on GitHub. We closed the chapter by creating a private blockchain using a geth console, mining blocks, earning rewards in ethers, and using those ethers to deploy and execute smart contracts in the MIST browser.

In `Chapter 4`, *A Noob's Guide to DApps and DAO*, we will take on the topic of decentralized applications and DAOs.

4

A Noob's Guide to DApps and DAO

This chapter develops our understanding of decentralized applications from a developer's perspective. We will introduce the high-level steps to develop a decentralized application. Then we will explore a unique marketplace called ethercast, which serves as an aggregator of several DApps. We will then move on to design a **Decentralized Autonomous Organization (DAO)**. We will conclude this chapter by looking back at the infamous DAO hack, which led to the ETH/ETC split, from a purely technical perspective.

After studying this chapter, you will be able to:

- Identify the generic steps to develop DApps
- Understand DApp architecture
- Achieve basic knowledge about ethercast
- Design a simple DAO from scratch
- Understand the DAO hack

Understanding DApps

Creation of new life always fascinates us, even more so when we are a part of such creation. For instance, consider a zygote cell. Smaller than a tiny speck of sand, it has the ability to grow into a complex biological entity, breathing life into a newborn infant.

But why are we talking about zygotes rather than DApps? Well, a zygote signifies that juncture when one biological cell's generation ends and the next one begins. It acclimates, responding to the outside world without any genetic changes. A zygote cannot be regulated, as it is stuck with its own genes. It can only grow recursively. A zygote is also autonomous. This is because it is still a cell; it's formation is rapidly distributed during the cleavage phase and it is authorized to act as a single entity, apart from other cells. In fact, a zygote is the perfect metaphor of a decentralized application.

An application qualifies as a DApp (pronounced as Dee App, similar to e-book) if it satisfies the following four criteria:

- The application must be open source, that is, source code freely available to the public. In addition to this, the application must operate autonomously with no major entity controlling its tokens, that is, the protocol of the application will be fully regulated by the consensus of users.
- The application must not have a single point of failure, with all its data and operation logs cryptographically stored in a public blockchain.
- The application must use some type of native token for various processes and access, and any contribution of value must be rewarded in terms of such tokens.
- The application should use some standard and well-accepted cryptographic algorithm as proof of value contributed by a node to generate tokens.

In 2014, David Johnston, CEO of Factom Inc., proposed the Johnston's law for DApps:

"Everything that can be decentralized, will be decentralized."

Academically, this law is a morphed version of Murphy's law over Moore's Law, which is a rule of thumb for any innovative technology, stating that the rate of entries occurring on a blockchain per day would double every 2 years in the foreseeable future.

Murphy's law, coined by the US Air Force, states that anything that can go wrong will go wrong. In the UK, an equivalent Sod's law exists, which states that anything that can go wrong will go wrong with the worst possible outcome.

He has also proposed an interesting classification of decentralized applications based on the blockchain the DApp is residing in, of three types:

- **Type I**: DApps have their own blockchain. Bitcoin is the most famous example of a type I decentralized application but Ethereum and other "alt-coins" are of the same type.
- **Type II**: DApps use the blockchain of a type I decentralized application. Type II decentralized applications are protocols and have tokens that are necessary for their function.
- **Type III**: DApps use the protocol of a type II decentralized application. Type III decentralized applications are protocols and have tokens that are necessary for their function.

Steps to develop a DApp

DApps have the potential to become self-sustaining because they empower their stakeholders to invest in the development of the DApp. The development process of DApps generally comprises the following steps, as outlined by *David Johnston et al*:

1. Create a whitepaper that has at least the following sections:
   - Intentions and goals of the DApp
   - Plans for token distribution
   - Mechanism for establishing consensus
   - Structure of the non-profit that oversees the DApp
   - Management of developer bounties
   - Technical description of the DApp

2. Gain community engagement by releasing the plan and by revising it based on feedback
3. Set a date when the community can contribute to the crowdsale
4. Sell the initial tokens based on your whitepaper and establish a non-profit to oversee the development of the DApp
5. Begin executing your idea while the non-profit plans future development

Architecture of a DApp

Figure 4.1 represents an Ethereum DApp at a high level. If you notice, every client browser communicates with its own instance of the application. There is no central server to which all clients connect. This means, every person who wants to interact with a decentralized application will need a full copy of the blockchain running on their computer/phone, and so on. That means, before we can use an application, we have to download the entire blockchain and then start using the application. This might sound ridiculous at first but it has the advantage of not relying on a single central server that might disappear tomorrow, or start charging us third-party commissions.

To build web-based DApps, Ethereum comes with a handy JavaScript library called `web3.js`, which connects to our blockchain node using **remote procedure calls** (**RPCs**). So, we can just include this library in our favorite JavaScript frameworks, such as ReactJS or AngularJS, and start developing our DApp:

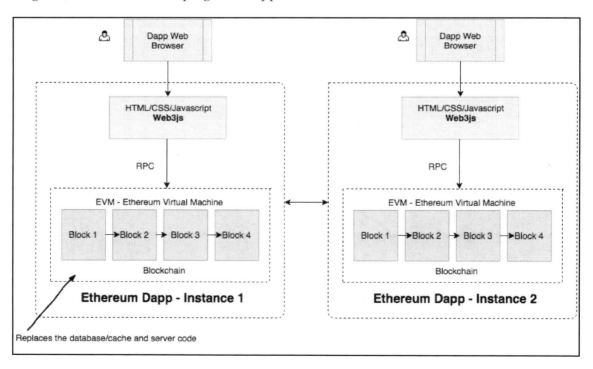

Figure 4.1: High-level DApp architecture. Source: Mahesh Murthy, medium.com

In `Chapter 2`, *Grokking Ethereum,* we discussed how DApps interacted with Swarm, Whisper, and EVM. This described the typical backend interaction of a DApp. Here, in *Figure 4.2,* we show how the frontend of a DApp interacts when creating a smart contract for the first time (steps 1-5) and function call transactions (step 6+) once the contract gets deployed on the blockchain:

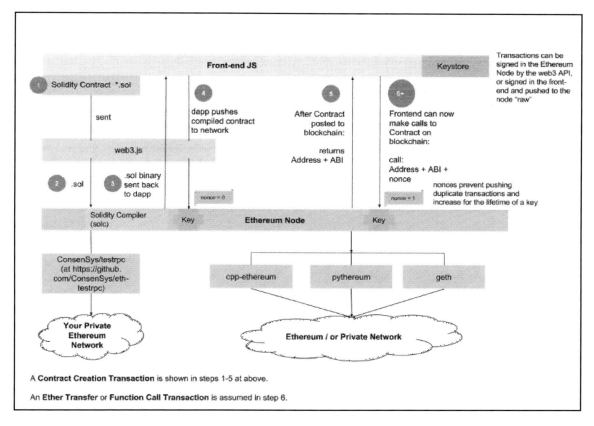

Figure 4.2: DApp frontend steps for smart contract creation, Source: busy.org

What is ethercast?

If you can recall the buffet analogy from `Chapter 2`, *Grokking Ethereum*, ethercast is analogous to the buffet table. It is a website that serves as a platform to freely register DApps at different states of their development life cycle, as depicted in *Figure 4.3*. Once it is registered, a DApp life cycle status can be tracked as progress in development is made. It is a Web 2.0-based app store that links us to progression states of Web 3.0-based DApps.

This app store (`https://dapps.ethercasts.com/`) was founded by Joris Bontje. The site is going through a revamp, which can be reached at: `https://www.stateofthedapps.com/`.

The DApp life cycle status is color-coded according to the legend mentioned in *Figure 4.3*. If we click on any of the DApp tiles, further information and web links are detailed for user convenience, as shown in *Figure 4.4*. This app store can serve as a one-stop guide to developers who are new to the Ethereum DApp developmental workspace:

Figure 4.3: State of DApps on ethercast

Let's now check three DApps on ethercast that have a lot of potential.

btcrelay.org

This is a project that has been recommended by Joris Bontje. It is developed by Joseph Chow and has a live status on ethercast. It is actually the first working side chain for bitcoin.

This DApp serves as a building block that allows Ethereum-based smart contracts to verify bitcoin transactions securely and without any intermediaries. It stores bitcoin blockheaders, which in turn, is used to build a mini-version of the bitcoin blockchain. In simple words, users can pay in bitcoin to use Ethereum DApps.

oraclize.it

This is a DApp that makes it possible for smart contracts to base their business logic on real-time feeds of external data.

It serves as a data carrier between APIs and DApps. It was founded by Thomas Bertani and has a live status on ethercast. We will dive more into oraclize in later chapters on smart contracts.

the-pitts-circus.com

This is the first Ethereum-funded movie. The website suggested that with every ticket they would be provided a paper wallet of five tokens which the user can cash in from the profits for the next 20 years. The story revolves around an Australian family that happens to run a circus. This is a unique venture and gives rise to a whole new perspective to the entertainment industry.

The author is Ken Evil, as depicted in *Figure 4.4*:

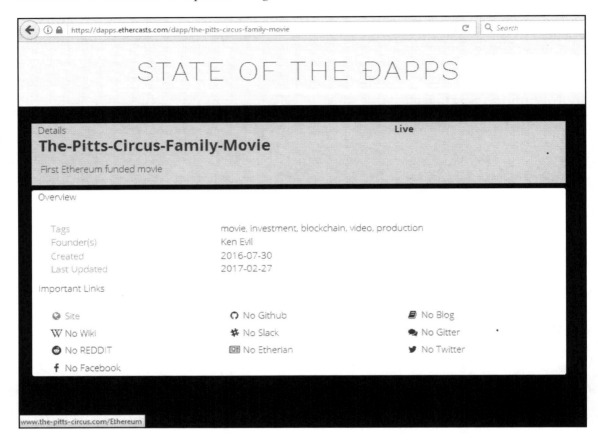

Figure 4.4: Ethereum-funded movie as DApp on ethercast

Understanding the design of DAO

Is a DAO a smart contract? Is a DAO a DApp? Vitalik Buterin has described the decentralized autonomous organization as an entity that lives on the World Wide Web and has its own set of rules. DAO also heavily relies on hiring individuals to perform certain tasks that the automaton itself cannot do.

Grasping the concept of DAO can be bit tricky. From a software developer's perspective, a DAO is just a piece of code, specifically a complex smart contract, or an interacting module comprising many simple smart contracts, which are abstracted as an organization. From a trader's perspective, the closest analogy of DAO is a **Limited Liability Company (LLC)**. Let's try to understand a bit about LLC. Suppose Susan has a great business idea and wants to open a start-up with her life-savings. Rather than going through the venture capitalist route to fund the rest of the money for doing business, she chose to go the LLC route. That way, she invites shareholders to own a piece of her company; whoever is willing to contribute. Again, being an LLC, she is immune to the personal tax axe for any profit generated by the LLC, which is basically a separate entity, coming under the purview of business tax. God forbid, if Susan's business does not take off and suffers losses, she again has immunity by filing for bankruptcy, and she would not be held responsible for losing all the shareholders' money, as it is an LLC. So, an LLC is basically a CAO, centralized autonomous organization. Hence DAO is an LLC over a decentralized network.

Let's now try to decipher what autonomous means. The very word autonomous brings up the memory of Arnold Schwarzenegger's Terminator and Skynet. Yes, robotic autonomy can be quite exciting stuff but let me be quite blunt here. The DAO is autonomous but in a reactive sense. The coding logic for a DAO, at the moment, cannot self-initiate without using a timer and external oracle. A better way to understand autonomy of a DAO is as a programmatic implementation of a set of rules that are instantiated by smart contract codes over a public Ethereum-based blockchain.

The best way to understand DAO would be to just create a simple DAO from scratch. It will serve us the twin purpose of showing how to create a complex DApp, such as a DAO, and make us aware of vulnerabilities in the code logic, which we can miss very easily, leading to a disaster and loss of funds:

```solidity
pragma solidity ^0.4.11;

contract DAOFundraiser {

    mapping(address=>uint) balances;


    function withdrawAllMyCoins() public {

        uint withdrawAmount = balances[msg.sender];
        TypicalWallet wallet = TypicalWallet(msg.sender);
        wallet.payout.value(withdrawAmount)();

        balances[msg.sender] = 0;
    }

    function getBalance() constant public returns (uint){
        return this.balance;
    }

    function contribute() payable public {
        balances[msg.sender] += msg.value;
    }

    function() payable public {

    }
}
```

```solidity
contract TypicalWallet{

    DAOFundraiser fundraiser;
    //uint r = 10;

    function TypicalWallet(address fundraiserAddress) public {
        fundraiser = DAOFundraiser(fundraiserAddress);
    }

    function contribute(uint amount) public {
        fundraiser.contribute.value(amount)();
    }

    function withdraw() public {
        fundraiser.withdrawAllMyCoins();
    }

    function getBalance() constant public returns (uint){
        return this.balance;
    }

    function payout() payable public{

    }

    function() payable public{

    }
}
```

Figure 4.5: Sample DAO fundraiser along with typical wallet

Let's now write our contract, which is basically a fundraiser, the main component of the DAO, because it is basically a decentralized investment fund. We will also write code for a wallet, through which we will be able to contribute and withdraw our funds. For example, if I funded the fundraiser DAO with 10 ethers, then I would be able to withdraw my 10 ethers, whenever required. *Figure 4.6* represents the basic design of the fundraiser DAO, and a typical wallet to fund and retrieve ethers in terms of wei using solidity code:

Figure 4.6: Enter value as 10 ETH, then press fallback, get balance to get the amount in wei (10* 10^18)

As we can see in the code, the DAOFundraiser contract can basically do three things:

- `contribute()` function: Contribute to the fund when someone provides ether to this contract using a wallet
- `withdrawalALLmycoins()` function: Withdraw all funds back to my wallet, if requested by a fellow user
- `getBalance()` function: Returns the final balance in the fund raiser:

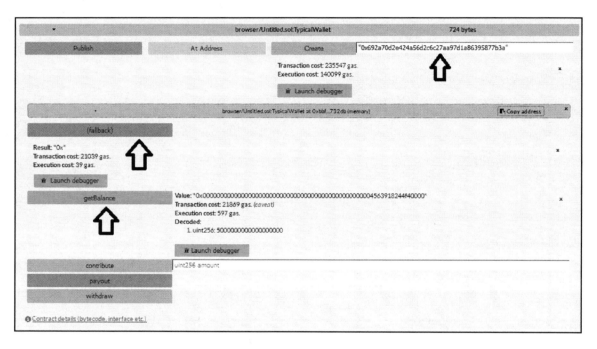

Figure 4.7 Using fallback to get 5 ETH in wei to fill up wallet

We now pictorially show how this simple DAO works in *Figure 4.6*, *Figure 4.7*, *Figure 4.8*, and *Figure 4.9*. We will be using the same remix online IDE as we used while coding `Hello World`:

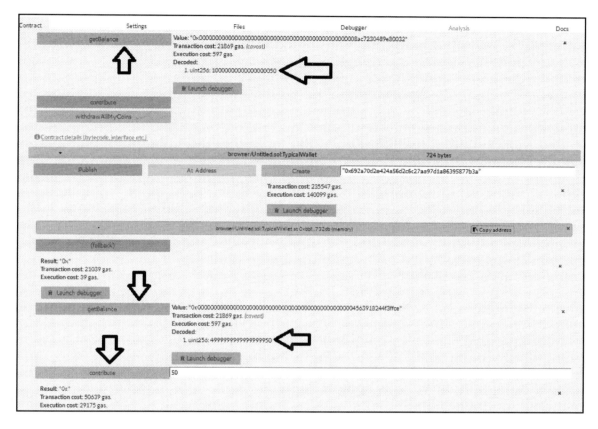

Figure 4.8 Contributing 50 wei from wallet (amount decrease) to DAOFundraiser (amount increase)

A small point that I need to mention is when we copy the DAO address into the wallet contract, as shown in *Figure 4.9*, wrap the address in double quotes to avoid runtime errors while creating the wallet contract just after the creation of the DAO fundraiser contract:

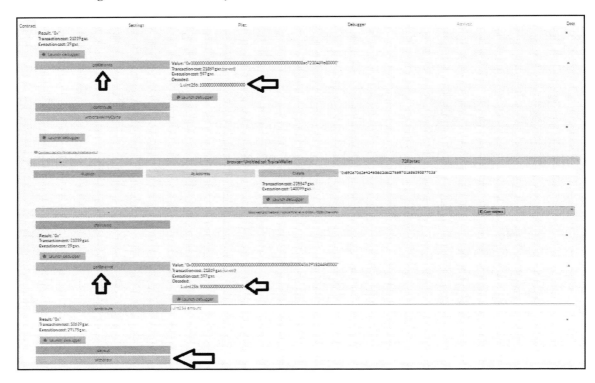

Figure 4.9: Pressing withdraw in wallet contract to withdraw all funds contributed by the wallet to DAO

So, we have created a simple DAO from scratch and it's working just as expected. Feeling empowered, right? But if you are a keen-eyed software developer, you will have already noticed the DAOFundraiser logic has a major flaw, which can be exploited to take money from my wallet using a small tweak in the wallet logic. That was how the 50 million USD-worth of ether hack was done, which we are going to analyze in our final section.

The rise and fall of DAO

The original, vulnerable DAO had many complex contracts but the essence was the same as that of the simple DAO we created in the previous section. In May 2016, DAO was formed by a huge crowdsourcing of funds, where stakeholders bought Initial **coin offers** (**ICO**) worth more than 150 million USD. But in the next month, June 2016, a hacker (one of the users) exploited the vulnerability to siphon out around 50 million to their own wallet. This amount was later taken back by blockchain reorganization but led to the hard fork of ETH/ETC. Calling this a "hack" is technically a misnomer because there was no break-and-enter violation of the fundraiser. It just exploited a vulnerable line of code logic present in the DAOFundraiser contract by changing the wallet logic.

This is quite possible because wallets are normally separate modules and can have any custom logic and interface. *Figure 4.10* represents the function block that is vulnerable to an exploit. Please note, we have not made any changes to the DAO contract apart from comment lines:

```
function withdrawAllMyCoins(){

    uint withdrawAmount = balances[msg.sender];
    TypicalWallet wallet = TypicalWallet(msg.sender);
    wallet.payout.value(withdrawAmount)();
    //vulnerable
    balances[msg.sender] = 0;
}
```

Figure 4.10: Vulnerability in simple DAO

Let's now write a malicious wallet, which is basically the exploit logic inside the old `TypicalWallet`. *Figure 4.11* represents the code logic:

```
contract TypicalWallet{

    DAOFundraiser fundraiser;
    uint r= 10;

    function TypicalWallet(address fundraiserAddress){
        fundraiser = DAOFundraiser(fundraiserAddress);
    }

    function contribute(uint amount){
        fundraiser.contribute.value(amount)();
    }

    function withdraw(){
        fundraiser.withdrawAllMyCoins();
    }

    function getBalance() constant returns (uint){
        return this.balance;
    }

    function payout() payable{
        // exploit
        if(r>0){
            r--;
            fundraiser.withdrawAllMyCoins();
        }
// receive payment
// log or do other activity
// complex codes

    }

    function() payable{

    }
}
```

Figure 4.11. Exploiting the payout function inside TypicalWallet

What does this exploit do exactly? This exploit calls the payout function recursively until the end of the loop when it reaches `balance[msg.sender]=0`. Hence, the wallet ends up siphoning up more tokens back to its wallet. In this case, it is about 10 times more money. *Figure 4.12* and *Figure 4.13* depicts the exploitation:

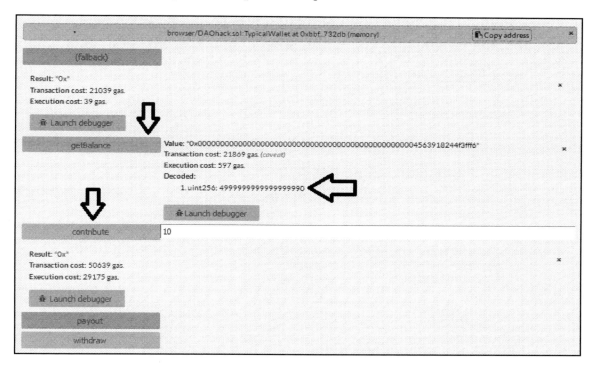

Figure 4.12: Contributing 10 wei from hacker wallet similar to typical wallet

Now, how do we fix this? If we look closely at the vulnerability in *Figure 4.10*, we will see that moving the `balance[msg.sender]=0` line inside, just after the first line of the function as depicted in *Figure 4.14*:

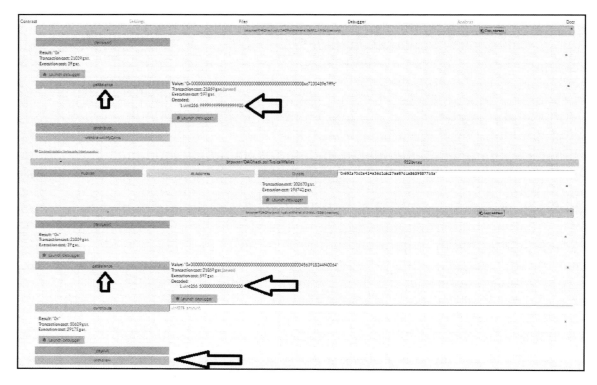

Figure 4.13: For the same 10 wei, when we withdraw we receive 100 wei in the wallet from DAO

Now, even with the malicious logic in the wallet, the code cannot siphon out ethers from the DApp. This is because the recursion path has been modified and the counter is set to zero before the recursive code recalls itself:

```
function withdrawAllMyCoins(){

    uint withdrawAmount = balances[msg.sender];
    //not vulnerable anymore
    balances[msg.sender] = 0;
    TypicalWallet wallet = TypicalWallet(msg.sender);
    wallet.payout.value(withdrawAmount)();

}
```

Figure 4.14. Code fix for DAO

We saw how a single line of code can cause financial catastrophe. We really need to get over the delusion that blockchain coding is fun app development or web programming in general. Here we are dealing with other people's money and the consequences of any mistake are not pretty.

Summary

We started this chapter by defining the four ground rules for a DApp. Those are open source, no single point of failure, presence of native tokens, and algorithm for proof of values. We discussed Johnston's law for DApps along with the three major types of DApps. We then went through the steps to develop a DApp. We discussed the frontend architecture of a DApp, then moved to ethercast and its various status-color mapping. We then got introduced to DAO as a limited liability company on a blockchain. We even coded a simple DAO from scratch and transferred tokens from a wallet. Lastly, we detailed down the recursive step exploit vulnerability, which resulted in a 50 million DAO hack. In Chapter 5, *Deep-Diving into Smart Contracts*, we will take a deep-dive into smart contracts, to learn how to build robust and scalable code.

5

Deep-Diving into Smart Contracts

In this chapter, we take a deep-dive into smart contract designs. We start by understanding the textbook definition of a smart contract. Then we move on to understanding different smart contract models and the role of code in a smart contract. We then go through the basic anatomy of a smart contract and see how a smart contract works. Then we shift our focus to some advanced topics, such as smart contract optimization, auditing, and ERC20 compliance. We conclude the chapter with a hands-on drill of building a voting DApp.

After studying this chapter, you will be able to:

- Define a smart contract and understand various design models
- Appreciate the role of code in a smart contract
- Visualize the basic anatomy of a smart contract
- Understand smart contract optimization, auditing, and compliance
- Understand the design of a voting DApp using smart contracts

What makes a contract "smart"?

Long before blockchains and the internet, in the analog era, we had mechanical devices that basically executed smart contracts. These were vending machines, as depicted in *Figure 5.1*. Once you pay a certain amount in a certain currency, you get to choose the product code. Once the code is confirmed, then the product comes out of the machine. If you do not pay, the product does not come out. If you delay more than the waiting-time threshold after paying, or there is any mechanical malfunction and your session expires, the product does not come out:

Figure 5.1: Vending machine

We can see that the concept of smart contracts existed way before blockchains and the internet. So, even before defining a smart contract, we must address the myths surrounding it. The myth that tops the list is whether a smart contract is intelligent. The answer is no, it is smart and dumb, but not intelligent. To understand this subtle concept, let us use the analogy of a smartphone. Does your smartphone make a call for you even before you think about dialling? For instance, you are stuck in a riot; does the device sense the riot-like situation using the GPS or some other built-in app and call 911 or local police on your behalf? No, right? (Ideally, it shouldn't trigger such calls, as it is very context-dependent. You might actually be in a safe house and the false alarm might cause a nuisance.) However, the smartphone might process information smartly and blink a recommendation. How it manipulates the information in a particular way depends on the instructions (stored in the form of code) given by some specific app. So, apps present on the smartphone that are capable of processing the information in some desired manner, make the smartphone smart. Another myth is that smart contracts are lines of computer code. To understand this, let us go through the definition and design of a smart contract presented in the next section.

Definition and design

The smart contract was formally defined by Nick Szabo in his 1996 paper titled, *Smart Contracts: Building Blocks for Digital Markets*. He described it as follows:

> *"A Smart contract is a set of promises, specified in digital form, including protocols within which the parties perform on these promises."*

Yup, that's it. That's the definition. Duh! What's so exciting about it? Let us spice it up a little bit. If we closely observe the definition, we will see that it consists of four specific elements:

- **A set of promises**: These are basically business conditions. For example, Judy and Ashley are business partners who jointly own an auction company. A simple business condition could be as follows:
    - IF the auction sale results in a profit THEN split the profit amount in a 60:40 ratio
    - ELSE IF the auction sale results in breaking even THEN donate 100 GBP each to welfare fund
    - ELSE IF auction sale results in a loss THEN recover the loss amount in a 70:30 ratio

Such business conditions can be in the form of a contract signed by either the partners or implemented by a rule-based operation applied to their respective business accounts.

- **Specified in digital form**: A smart contract consists of human-readable lines of code, as well as the software that prescribes its conditions and outcomes converted to machine-level binary code of 1s and 0s. Contractual clauses or rule-based lookups are embedded as code within software.
- **Protocols**: A set of rules for how each party should process data in relation to a smart contract. Generally implemented using computer algorithms, these sets of rules are technology-enabled, rule-based operations that enable actions such as the release of payments.
- **Within which the parties perform**: This is the trickiest element of the smart contract definition. Once a smart contract is deployed on a blockchain, it becomes irrevocable. An encoded smart contract cannot typically be stopped from performing. Automated performance is the soul of a smart contract.

Yet code can be flawed, and if a contract inherently reaches an unmet condition, the contract can stop performing. This is why we need smart contract auditing before deploying it over a public or live blockchain. Before that, we need to know various design models of a smart contract.

From the point-of-view of a blockchain, a smart contract is a piece of code that sits within a "block". Once deployed, it becomes part of the consensus state of the network. The block acts as a software generated container that bundles the messages of a smart contract. Such messages can be inputs, outputs, or pointers to other computer code. Regardless of how a smart contract is designed, they involve code. But this give rises to the common misconception that a smart contract consists of just code.

In fact, there is a whole spectrum of smart contract design models, which is illustrated in *Figure 5.2*:

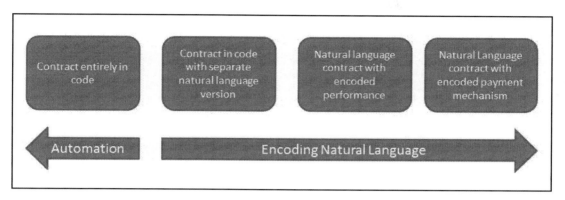

Figure 5.2: Smart contracts lie on a spectrum, Source: Chamber of Digital Commerce, Nov 2016

More variations are likely to emerge as we progress further in developing more smart contract-based DApps. Hence, it becomes really important to study the role of code, which makes up a sizable portion of any smart contract.

Role of code in a smart contract

All smart contracts involve code and all code has bugs. If not, they acquire them eventually. Today's requirement can become tomorrow's bug. Before we stepped into the 21st century, the year format in many computing and database systems was denoted by YY instead of YYYY. That was a requirement to save on the extra bytes.

While approaching the end of the 1990s, programmers realized how messed up this was going to get because once we are past the year 2000, the year format YY will become ambiguous. Will 19-11-17 be known as the 19th of November, 1917 or the 19th of November, 2017? Some were over-smart, they had the luxury of YYYY format but the algorithm just rolled the date back to the initial 1900. History books recorded this as the bug of the millennium, aka the Y2K bug.

Although organizations worldwide checked, fixed, and upgraded their computer systems to address the anticipated problem, it is not known how many problems went unrecorded. The point is that code does not always perform as the parties which implement it intends. Messages get delayed, passphrases get spooled-out, and data can get corrupted during transmission. The liability implications of such incidents needs to be taken into account before a smart contract is up on the blockchain. Such events need to be part of the overall plan of the contract. Otherwise, it just becomes a risky contract, not a smart one.

So, the role of code just does not end at the auditing, but also takes into account the legal aspect of a contract as we progress in time. Once a smart contract is up in the blockchain, it is treated as law. But any sane person will argue that we can always amend laws later on. Why can't this be done for smart contracts? Of course it can, and it is done using oracles. We oraclize a smart contract so that it can amend itself by taking in external feeds from reliable sources, as depicted in *Figure 5.3,* using a simple insurance contract. Such oracle engines feed in an authenticity proof along with the data feed, so that the feed is tamper-proof and independent of the third-party feed API, as well as the oraclize service engines over the blockchain protocol. A related analogy would be buying a certified diamond from a local jewelry store. If a diamond has an external certification of authenticity, such as GIA or AGSL, that specifies its 4Cs (carat, cut, clarity, and color) and that it is conflict-free. Its resale value becomes independent of the store we bought it in:

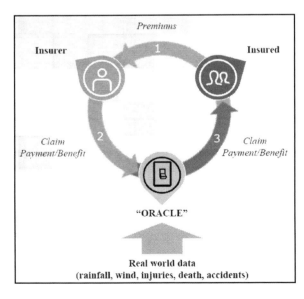

Figure 5.3: Oraclized insurance contract. Source: Digital Chamber of Commerce. Nov 2016

We will look more at the oracle aspect of a smart contract in the *Optimization and audit* section. Before that, we need to know about the basic anatomy of a smart contract; otherwise, we might not be able to get a clear mental image of the oraclize engine and how it fits into the grand scheme of things.

Basic anatomy of a smart contract design

Blockchain technology has become the jet fuel for propelling the concept of the smart contract in the world of business transactions. Large corporate institutions are rapidly adopting this concept to remain ahead of their competitors. This has led to a call for an industry-wide initiative for formalizing the design framework of a smart contract. One of the big four auditing firms, Deloitte, teamed up with the advisory board of the Digital Chambers of Commerce, has come up with a six-point anatomy to formalize a smart contract design, which has been summarized in *Figure 5.4*:

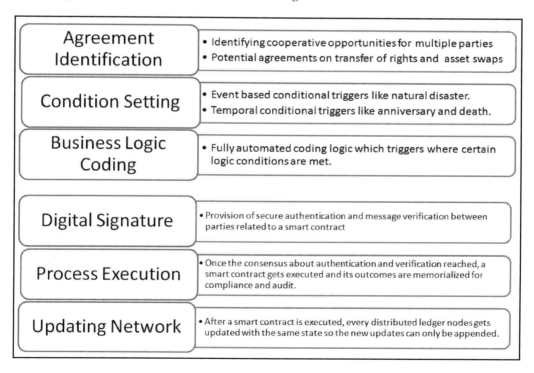

Figure 5.4: Six-point anatomy of smart contract design, Source: Digital Chamber of Commerce, Nov 2016

Smart contract optimization

In `Chapter 2`, *Grokking Ethereum*, we discussed the concept of ether and gas (recall the buffet and car-fuel analogy). Smart contracts that are under-optimized consume more gas than necessary. The creator and user of such smart contracts will always be over-charged while deploying and running them on the blockchain. Xiapu Luo et al, a group of blockchain researchers from the Hong Kong Polytechnic University and UEST China, have identified seven such gas-costly programming patterns that belong to two categories, as illustrated in *Figure 5.5*. The first category, useless code pattern, introduces additional gas cost due to the increase in bytecode size during the deployment and the runtime removal of bytecode. The second category involves expensive operations using a loop:

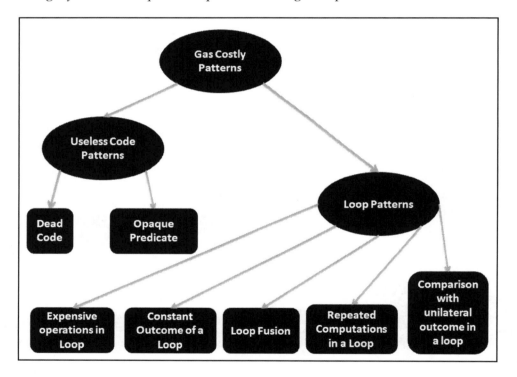

Figure 5.5: Gas-costly programming patterns

Figure 5.6 illustrates pseudo-code representing these entirely under-optimized code patterns. Ideally, this needs to be depicted as bytecode but pseudo-code has been used for ease of understanding. Pattern 1 is an example of dead code because we will never reach the print statement in line 4 due to the `inner-if` condition at line 3 stating y*y <20. If you are still wondering what just happened, then go upward toward the `outer-if` condition at line 2 which states y >5. This means y, which is an unsigned integer, can only have values greater than 5, that is 6 and higher. Hence y*y always returns an integer equal or greater than 36. In other words (36 or more) < 20 always return a `false` condition, so we always ignore any statement that occurs inside this `inner-if` condition.

Interestingly, when the solidity compiler generates the bytecode of this logic, it never removes lines 3 and 4, which are practically ignored at runtime, and this wastes money in terms of gas consumption. Opaque predicate outcomes are identified without any execution. If we look into the pseudo-code of pattern 2, line 3, y>2 is `true` by default; hence it is redundant. It can be removed to save gas. In the second category, we see that moving expensive operations out of the loop can save gas. For example, in the pseudo-code of pattern 3, since the variable `sumout` is stored in the storage, line 4 calls `SLOAD` to load `sumout` on the stack and a `SSTORE` to save the outcome of the `ADD` operation to the storage. Normally, the storage-related operations consume a lot of gas, and hence, are very expensive. An optimized compiler generally assigns `sumout` to a local variable temp that resides in the stack, then adds `j` to temp inside the loop, and finally assigns temp to `sumout` after the loop.

Such optimization reduces the storage-related operations from 2X to just 2, that is, one SLOAD and one SSTORE:

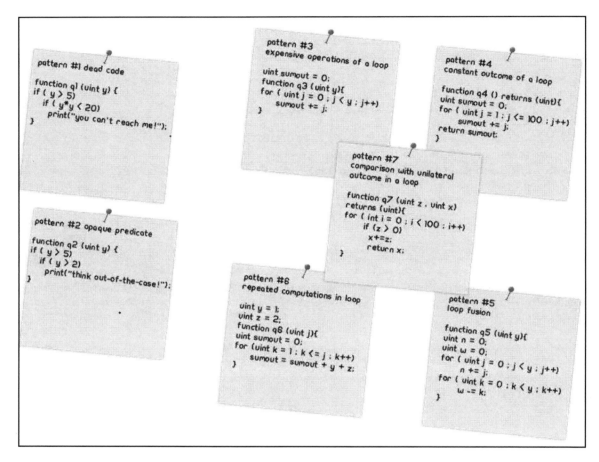

Figure 5.6: Pseudo-code of gas-costly pattern

In pattern 4, the outcome of the loop is a constant value and deterministic in nature. Rather than using a loop, we can just use a statement, such as return 5050, and assign it to sumout, minimizing gas usage. Pattern 5 illustrates the need for a loop fusion where we combine several loops into one to minimize gas usage. We can combine the summation and subtraction step of n and w inside a single loop rather than running them in sequential separate loops. Pattern 6 depicts repeated computation in a loop. The summation of y+z is very expensive due to the use of a SLOAD operation before ADD. This can be avoided by summing up y+z outside the loop and then reusing the result inside the loop.

And, lastly, pattern 7 shows unilateral redundant comparison inside a loop. In simple words, z>0 can safely go outside the loop without loss of functionality and in turn minimize gas cost as we are preventing the same comparison from occurring 100 times, which gives the same result anyway. It is noteworthy, that as we increase the loop counters, the gas cost keeps on multiplying, which can make a smart contract quite expensive to operate.

Apart from changes to the programming pattern, optimization can be achieved at runtime by tinkering with the Ethereum virtual machine. We already saw in Chapter 2, *Grokking Ethereum*, how EVM interacts with swarm and whisper to run DApps on a blockchain using smart contracts. EVM basically allows us to execute arbitrary code in a trustless environment in which the outcome is fully deterministic. EVM operates on 256 bit integers and requires 256 bit arithmetic. Because of the 256 bit nature of the EVM, the gas can theoretically be $2^{256}-1$ but actually never will because the cost incurred by such an execution would be way too much. Instead, there is a cap of using up to 2^{64}, which present processors have native support for and can generally be optimized. Even though 2^{64} is still "too costly", it is a very nice constraint to have and allows us to hard-cap the gas on something the computer can natively understand. The EVM natively uses a quadratic-memory gas calculation, where for each word of 32 bytes there is a cost associated with memory expansion. This capping of 64 bit has also put a limit on the expansion of associated memory with the expansion never going beyond $2^{64}-1$.

Lastly, the performance at blockchain level can be optimized by a process called **sharding**. Currently, all the transactions and calculations that are performed on an Ethereum blockchain need to be run by all of the nodes. So, each node has to perform every calculation. And that is of course inefficient if scaled. That is not a characteristic that is desirable worldwide. If we want to make complex decentralized applications run efficiently on the public blockchain, we need to speed up the execution process compared to the present day's runtimes. What Ethereum performs today in terms of execution speed is comparable to that of what happened in the late 1980's computers. Roughly, this is about 7-15 transactions per second. So it is really too low for practical purposes. Sharding is one of the main proposals for how we can increase in terms of performance at scale, the other two being using different altcoins and increasing the block size. The problem with increasing the block size is that even though we could accomplish more transactions or operations in one go, it will become increasingly difficult for normal computers to act as nodes due to the heavy blocks on the entire chain. General purpose computer hardware wouldn't be enough to act as a node, and the entire ecosystem will tend towards centralization and monopolistic cartel-like behavior, because only those operators that have massive hardware support will be able to act as nodes by downloading the complete blockchain on their machines.

The idea of using different altcoins is not to make the public blockchain overloaded, and use separate blockchains to execute different operations. This is sometimes called **merge-mining** on sidechains. This is good performance-wise, but overall security is low when we have a segregated consensus acting on isolated blockchains, which eventually makes the 51% attack more likely.

Coming back now to the main proposal of sharding. Sharding is a philosophy where we give away the notion of sequential executions of processes on each node of a blockchain. Rather, we split up the entire execution into sizable chunks called shards and many nodes process such shards in parallel. Users of one node computing one shard are not able to communicate with users of another node who are computing another shard. This is one of the main challenges while implementing sharding. For example, consider you live in Dublin but you have to attend an urgent business conference in London. And no, you cannot Skype talk as the session might turn out to be a solid deal. To top it off, the meet-up session might stretch to the entire day. Hence, you have to book a flight and reserve a hotel yet still want to make sure both operations are atomic—either both succeed or neither do. Now, if the flight ticket application and hotel room booking applications are on the same shard, they will be done in a sequential manner, and if one of the bookings fails, the other rolls back before committing. But if these are on different shards, unless we have cross-shard communication, this can land us in a big mess, the worst being that the hotel gets booked but the flight remains unreserved. One way to solve it is by using asynchronous, cross-shard communication. In simple words, one shard books the flight, and another shard books the hotel room. Then the shards message each other to acknowledge each other. Finally, the shards send us a confirmation. This is what we discussed in Chapter 1, *Blockchain Basics*, as eventual consistency (recall the CAP theorem). Vitalik Buterin and other co-founders of Ethereum have a better plan regarding sharding. This is to abstract this entire sharding activity from the smart contract and DApp developers and handle it internally at runtime. This is somewhat analogous to the map-reduce framework on top of HDFS for HIVE QL developers in the big data industry. This will allow the developers to concentrate more on DApp and smart contract functionality rather than performance-level sharding operations. Imagine having a coupon with a flight ticket that includes a pre-booked hotel room. Sharding is a very hard, if not impossible, mission to solve in the blockchain community, which is still under development. A strong auditing and strict compliance is required for such complex mechanisms to stand the test of time, which will be our next topic of discussion.

Smart contract auditing and compliance

Presently, audits of a smart contract are limited to peer-reviewing by a senior developer. Although a well-documented framework is yet to come out for auditing smart contract code in the blockchain community, there has been a lot of noteworthy, tangible progress in the research community:

- XiapuLuo et al. have come out with a proprietary tool named **GAS-costly pattern checker** (**GASPER**), using which they have identified public smart contracts with many types of gas-costly patterns discussed in the earlier section

- Juels et al. diagnosed that smart contracts can facilitate crimes and showed how criminal smart contracts can be facilitated to leak confidential information, theft of cryptographic keys, and various real-world crimes

- Atzei et al. studied a series of attacks that exploit the vulnerabilities of contracts to steal or tamper with assets

- Zhang et al. developed TOWN CRIER, which aims to provide trustworthy data to smart contracts, as many applications of smart contracts need data from outside the blockchain

- Kosba et al. have developed HAWK, which is a decentralized smart contract system that enables developers to code privacy-reserved smart contracts

- Luu et al. have developed OYENTE, a novel, symbolic, execution-based tool, which discovers security bugs in Ethereum smart contracts

- Bhargavan et al. use formal verification to analyze smart contracts

Let us now get back to the oraclize engine, which is similar to the TOWN CRIER. In solidity, it is very simple to inherit the oraclize contract. This provide us functions such as `oraclize_query`, which leverages this technology straight away. Oraclize is integrated natively with the most widely used public blockchain protocols, such as Ethereum and Bitcoin. Privately, Ethereum-based chains can currently integrate with oraclize by using the Ethereum-bridge. A valid request for data to oraclize, done via the native blockchain integration or via the HTTP API, should specify the following arguments, as quoted in the oraclize documentation:

- **A data source type**: A data source is a trusted provider of data. It can be a website or web API, such as Reuters, Weather.com, BBC.com, or a secure application running on a hardware-enforced **trusted execution environment** (**TEE**), or an auditable, locked-down virtual machine instance running in a cloud provider.

- **A query**: A query is an array of parameters that needs to be evaluated in order to complete a specific data source type request. The intermediate result of a query may need to be parsed.
- **An authenticity proof type (optional)**: Oraclize is designed to act as an untrusted intermediary. Optionally, a request to oraclize can specify an authenticity proof. Not all proofs are compatible with all data source types.

The interaction between oraclize and an Ethereum smart contract is asynchronous. As illustrated in *Figure 5.7*, any request for data is composed of two steps, as quoted in the oraclize documentation:

1. Firstly, in the most common case, a transaction executing a function of a smart contract is broadcast by a user. The function contains a special instruction that manifests it to oraclize, which is constantly monitoring the Ethereum blockchain for such instructions and requests for data.

2. Secondly, according to the parameters of such requests, oraclize will fetch or compute a result, build, sign, and broadcast the transaction carrying the result. In the default configuration, such transactions will execute the `_callback` function, which should be placed in the smart contract by its developer.

One of the fundamental characteristics of oraclize is the capability of returning data to a smart contract together with one or more proofs of authenticity of the data. But for that, token compliance plays a major role.

ERC20 is one such token compliance that is followed in the Ethereum blockchain. Whenever we create a coin, we implement a smart contract. All of the coins that are running on the Ethereum blockchain network are actually just smart contracts. And when we are writing a smart contract, we implement a set of functions. In smart contracts, we have this concept of a contract that is similar to a class. So, when I am implementing my coin, I am exposing a set of functions that other people can use in order to interact with my coin. So what are those functions? For example, one function could be fetching the total amount of coins in circulation. This is a very useful function that all of the coins require. Now to implement such a function, I need to give the function a name. Now, if I follow the ERC20 standard, I would give it the name `totalSupply()`. There is a whole list of such functions that are recommended as an ERC20 token standard. We will discuss them in later chapters where we create our own cryptocurrency token. The point is, the ERC20 compliance standard is a set of recommendations to which Ethereum-based tokens need to adhere so that they are accepted by the public wallets with minimal customization.

You might still be wondering what ERC20 stands for. Well, it stands for Ethereum Request for Comment-Issue #20. Largely led by developer, Fabian Vogelsteller's efforts, the idea of ERC20 was conceived on the GitHub archives. Having a common set of standard APIs between tokens makes it easier for developers to build advanced functionality, such as an oraclize or multi-sig wallet that can handle any external datafeeds or ERC20-compatible tokens without any special update or support. And no, all Ethereum-based tokens might not follow this standard strictly, but its popularity is catching up fast due to ease of compatibility:

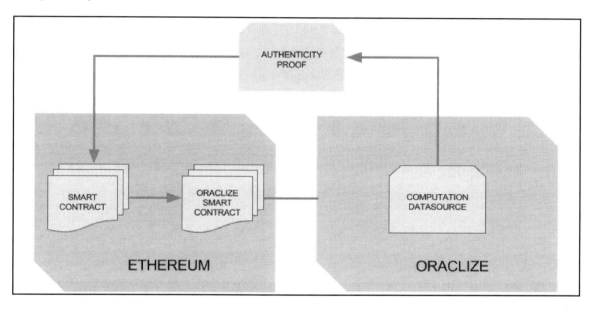

Figure 5.7: Ethereum-oraclize data interaction. Source: Oraclize blog

Designing a voting DApp

Decentralized voting on a blockchain has many perks. It is extremely hard to tamper with once a candidate is voted for. In this section, we try to design a simple voting DApp using both the private blockchain (also known as a private testnet) and remix platform that was introduced in Chapter 3, *Hello World of Smart Contracts*.

At this point, it will be good to recap the difference between an EthereumJS-based testrpc and Geth-based testnet from `Chapter 2`, *Grokking Ethereum* . A test RPC is a third-party client implementation used for testing. It is basically a Node.js-based Ethereum client. It simulates a full client. Whereas Geth-based testnet is an official full client implementation in the Go language, having a command-line interface, which can be used to connect to the real blockchain or on public testnet blockchains, such as Ropsten, or on a private testnet blockchain like ours.

The voting DApp we will develop has three basic functions:

- It initializes a list of candidates
- It lets anyone vote for the candidate
- It displays the total vote of each candidate

We are using the solidity programming language to write our voting DApp smart contract. The contract has been named the simple voting Dapp. It has a constructor function to initialize an array of candidates. We also have two methods, one to return the total number of votes received by a candidate and another one to increment the vote count of a candidate. To instantiate this smart contract after deploying on the blockchain, we need to pass the input parameter as an array of candidate names, who will be assigned specific addresses. In our example input, we have used three candidates [`Tom`, `Dick`, and `Harry`].

What is more interesting about this DApp is that the constructor can be invoked once and only once when we deploy it on the blockchain. Unlike a normal web application, where every new deployment with the same name overwrites the old code, the deployed code in a blockchain is immutable. That is, if we modify our contract and deploy again, the old contract will still survive in the blockchain untouched, along with all the store data. The new deployment will just create a separate new instance of the original contract.

A corporate version of the voting app has also been provided in the code archives with the name `corporateVotingDapp.sol` with detailed comments of each function. This version combines the coin buying capability of a DAO along with the voting functionality. In this smart contract, we pass two more parameters along with the array of candidate names. These are the amount of total coins available for the voters or electorates, and the unit of each token in ether.

For example an input of `10000,1, [Tom, Dick, and Harry]` means we have a voting contract that has at maximum, 10,000 tokens for the voters of 1 ether per token and voters can vote for three candidates. If Tom is voted for using 100 coins by one voter then the other voters can vote for any one of the three candidates using the remaining 9,900 tokens.

Figure 5.8 depicts the solidity smart contract of the voting DApp with necessary comments. *Figure 5.9*, *Figure 5.10*, *Figure 5.11*, *Figure 5.12*, and *Figure 5.13* depict the voting Dapp on the private blockchain. *Figure 5.14* and *Figure 5.15* represent the same simple version and corporate version of the voting DApp in the remix browser with the vote count output of candidates:

```solidity
browser/simpleVotingDapp.sol
1  pragma solidity ^0.4.11;
2  contract simpleVotingDapp {
3    /*
4    The key of the mapping is candidate name stored as type bytes32 and value is
5    an unsigned integer to store the vote count
6    */
7    mapping (bytes32 => uint8) public votesReceived;
8    /*
9    We use an array of bytes32 instead to store the list of candidates
10   */
11   bytes32[] public candidateList;
12   /* This is the constructor which will be called once when we
13   deploy the contract to the blockchain. When we deploy the contract,
14   we will pass an array of candidates who will be contesting in the election
15   e.g.["Tom","Dick","Harry"]
16   */
17
18   function simpleVotingDapp(bytes32[] candidateNames) {
19     candidateList = candidateNames;
20   }
21
22   // This function returns the total votes a candidate has received so far
23   function totalVotesFor(bytes32 candidate) returns (uint8) {
24     if (validCandidate(candidate) == false) revert();
25     return votesReceived[candidate];
26   }
27
28   // This function increments the vote count for the specified candidate. This
29   // is equivalent to casting a vote
30   function voteForCandidate(bytes32 candidate) {
31     if (validCandidate(candidate) == false) revert();
32     votesReceived[candidate] += 1;
33   }
34
35   function validCandidate(bytes32 candidate) returns (bool) {
36     for(uint i = 0; i < candidateList.length; i++) {
37       if (candidateList[i] == candidate) {
38         return true;
39       }
40     }
41     return false;
42   }
43 }
```

Figure 5.8: Simple votingDapp.sol

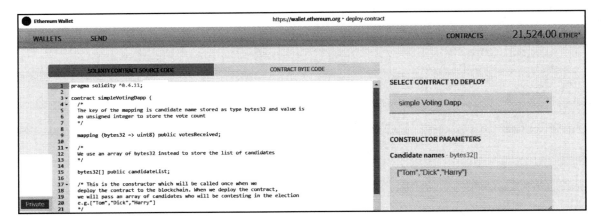

Figure 5.9: VotingDapp on private blockchain with candidate array as a constructor parameter

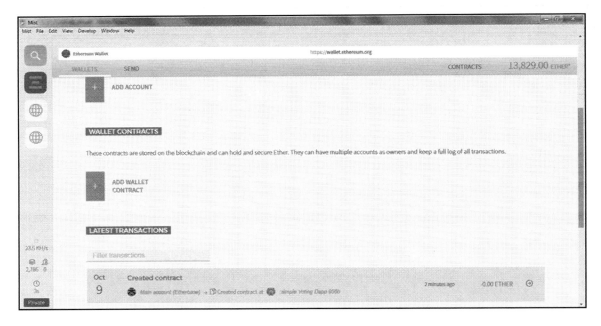

Figure 5.10: Contract deployment by miners on a private blockchain

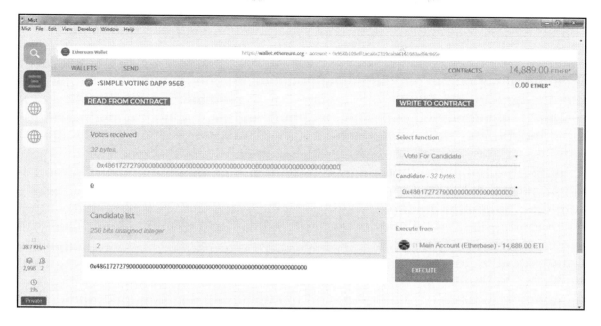

Figure 5.11: Voting candidate 2

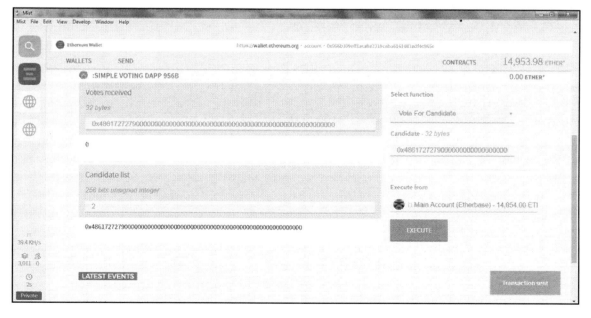

Figure 5.12: Voting transaction completed for candidate 2

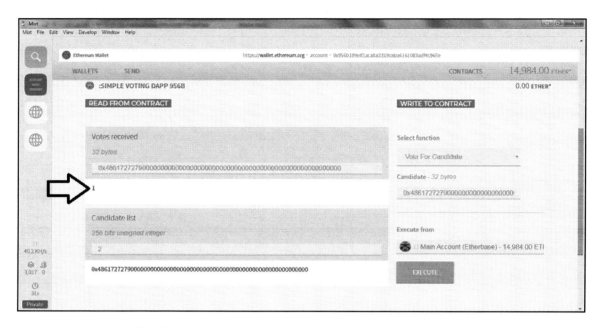

Figure 5.13: Change in vote-receive count from 0 to 1 after successful voting transaction for candidate 2

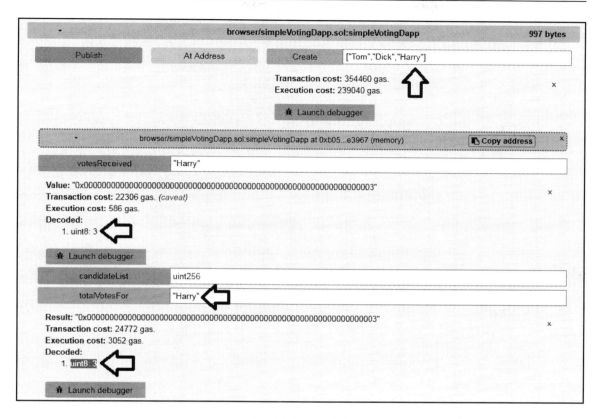

Figure 5.14: VotingDapp on remix browser

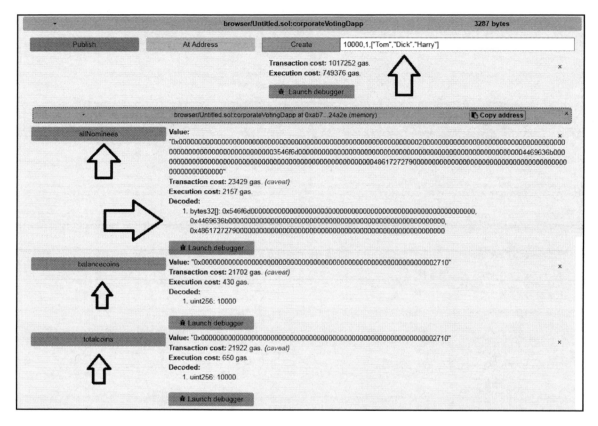

Figure 5.15: Corporate votingDapp on remix browser

This brings us to the end of this chapter. That said, smart contracts are still a rapidly evolving subject. In `Chapter 6`, *Solidity in Depth*, we will discuss the solidity programming language and how it helps in creating complex smart contracts.

Summary

We started this chapter by busting the myths about smart contracts. We realized that smart contracts cannot make decisions on their own and need an algorithmic trigger to accomplish such a feat. We also studied the original definition of a smart contract and realized the smart contract models lie on a spectrum ranging from encoded natural language to full automation. We learned that the role of code in a smart contract consists of a judicious mix of optimization, auditing, and adhering to compliance. We discussed gas-costly code patterns that remained unoptimized by the solidity compiler and categorized them into useless code and expensive loops. Then, we took a quick look at how oraaclization is used to feed authentic data and how an issue on the GitHub archive gave rise to the ERC20 standard. We concluded the chapter by deploying a decentralized voting application on a private blockchain. In Chapter 6, *Solidity in Depth*, we will look into the Turing complete solidity programming language in depth.

6

Solidity in Depth

This chapter is all about the Turing-complete solidity language on the Ethereum blockchain. We will start by peeking into the design decisions and why we really need a new language such as solidity at all. The next sections will cover the nuances of the solidity language and basic syntax used in it. Specifically, we will cover the contract-oriented features, functions, events, inheritance, libraries, expressions, control structures, units, and variables. Then we will peek into the optimizer and debugging options. We will conclude this chapter by analyzing the code flaw that led to the recent Parity wallet hack in the Ethereum blockchain that stole around $30 million worth of ethers.

After studying this chapter, you will be able to:

- Appreciate the need for solidity over other high-level languages
- Understand the nuances, syntax, and features of solidity
- Peek into the solidity optimizer and debugging options
- Analyze the flaw behind the $30 million Parity wallet hack

Need for solidity

Let me tell you a dirty secret about programmers. We are the laziest lot of technicians in the entire community of engineering. We work really hard to remain lazy. We abide by the oath:

"If necessity is the mother of all inventions, laziness is their father."

No wonder we love the open source movement so much. Reusing another lazy programmer's code is what we fantasize about. And to add a little sprinkle of hypocrisy, we never ever forget to complain or criticize how messy the original code was, and how heroically we drove away the bugs and documented it to make it 2.0 or higher. It is just in our blood.

But, sometimes, in this land of lazy nerds, there comes an outlier, one who writes something entirely original from scratch. The entire lazy community then laughs at this scratchy code. Slowly this outlier removes the bugs from the new stuff, and starts getting traction. Still, we keep ignoring it. By now the outlier has already moved out to do yet another new thing and some of his ardent followers from the period of traction are building on top of the core code. Then our lazy community starts fighting against it. The critics launch the famous X versus Y war, the ones that ask, *"Which language should I prefer as a fresh college dropout-without-a-job, should it be X that my grandma used at her university, or Y, which my grandkid, I wrongly think, would be using?"* on online forums. By this time, half a decade has passed by, and the new stuff is flying high on the IEEE list of the most-wanted programming languages, world-class universities are encouraging us to learn it, and the industry is trying to develop de facto standards and frameworks revolving around its usage. While us, the lazy lords, are searching frantically for its free copy, to install and "master" it.

And no, it is not Python (though your guess was close enough) that I was referring to, in our chapters context. It is good old JavaScript (with the de facto standard as ECMAScript) and the outlier is Brendan Eich.

A programming language design is done with a particular operating environment in mind and a list of target tasks it needs to complete. All design decisions, features that are to be supported, and ones that need to be dropped, are driven by these two distinct factors. In the case of Ethereum, the operating environment was the **Ethereum virtual machine** (**EVM**), which would take care of the second factor, to perform the entire assigned task over the Ethereum blockchain.

But who would pass the instructions to the EVM? We need some sort of human machine interface. Hence, the **application binary interface** (**ABI**) was introduced. The sole aim of this interface was to make machine code portable across the blockchain. It is analogous to an **application programming interface** (**API**), where we make the source code portable across various high-level languages.

But the ABI was not enough to make complex abstractions such as a wallet or an oracle. The ABI is static, strongly typed, and known at compilation time. The need for a Turing-complete programming language that could totally adapt with the EVM and seamlessly couple with the ABI was obvious. It needed to have the user-rich features of JavaScript bundled with the assembly level, high performance of C++. Gavin Wood proposed a design of such a language and code-named it solidity. This language, along with the capability of writing a smart contract, also included properties such as safe language subsets, static analysis, in-built test-generations, executing environments, named components, contracts as class entities, and the ability of a contract to map segment information to storage.

The EVM is just a very different beast. The decision to make a language specifically tailored to the EVM execution environment has helped the Ethereum community to prevent the problem of highly sub-optimal code execution. But a new language comes with its own set of grammar rules and features, which we will be discussing in the next section.

Nuances, syntax, and features of solidity

The most striking feature of solidity lies in its resemblance to ECMA Script standards (ES6 Harmony). To begin with, a solidity source file layout contains an arbitrary number of contract definitions along with pragma directives and optional imports at a global scope along with comments.

Pragma, import, and comments

A pragma directive of solidity always has versions in the form 0.x.0 or x .0.0, as shown in *Figure 6.1*. This ensures that any future version of the solidity compiler is ignored that might introduce incompatibility:

```
pragma solidity ^0.4.0;
```

Figure 6.1: Pragma directives

Although solidity does not have the ability to export or spool-out results yet, it supports import statements, which are very similar to JavaScript. This keyword is used at contract compile time in our local build environment. Once a contract gets deployed on a blockchain using EVM, it can neither read nor write files. *Figure 6.2*, lists down a few uses of the import statement at the global scope:

```
import "filename";
import * as symbolName from "filename";
import {symbol1 as alias, symbol2} from "filename";
import "github.com/ethereum/dapp-bin/library/iterable_mapping.sol" as it_mapping
```

Figure 6.2: Import syntax with global scope

Comments in solidity are of three types. These are single-line comments, multi-line comments, and the undocumented `natspec` comment, as depicted in *Figure 6.3*. Natspec comments are used directly above a function definition and the @ tags provide a confirmation to the user during static code analysis of whether a variable described in the comment is actually used in the code or not:

```
// This is a single-line comment.

/*
This is
multi-line comment.
*/

/** @title natspec comments */
```

Figure 6.3: Comments in solidity

Class properties of a contract

Solidity is often called a contract-oriented language, as every operation that can occur on the blockchain must reside inside the scope of a contract. A contract serves as a template definition for the functions and variables, very similar to the definition inside a class for an object-oriented language. Like a class, contracts can inherit from other contracts.

A contract can contain declarations ranging from functions and function modifiers, state variables, events, enum, and struct types. *Figure 6.4* summarizes these declarations in a tabular representation.

For further details and nuances, solidity has a freely available public documentation site. The document is generated using the sphinx package of the Python language and can be accessed at `http://Solidity.readthedocs.io/en/develop/index.html`:

Declaration	Description	Example
State Variables	Permanently stored values in contract storage	`uint32,bool, ufixed,address`

Functions	Executable code units inside a contract	`contract SampleContract {`
		`    function newfunction() payable {// Function`
		`      // code`
		`    }`
		`}`

Function Modifiers	Used as a declarative way of amending semantics of functions	`contract newContract {`
		`    address public bidder;`
		
		`    modifier onlyBidder() {// Modifier`
		`      require(msg.sender == bidder);`
		`      _;`
		`    }`
		
		`    function abort() onlyBidder {// Modifier usage`
		`      // code`
		`    }`
		`}`

Events	Used for EVM logging facility and Convenience Interface	`contract NewAuction {`
		`    event HighBidIncrease(address bidder, uint amount); // Event`
		
		`    function bid() payable {`
		`      // code`
		`      HighBidIncrease(msg.sender, msg.value); // Triggering event`
		`    }`
		`}`

Structs Types	Customized type to group several variables	`contract VotApp {`
		`    struct Electorate {// Struct`
		`      uint identity;`
		`      bool voted;`
		`      address delegate;`
		`      uint vote;`
		`    }`
		`}`

Enum Types	Customized type with a finite set of values	`contract Volcano {`
		`    enum State { Active, Extinct, Dormant }// Enum`
		`}`

Figure 6.4: Summarized declarations of solidity

Functions

Solidity has basically two types of function calls. One is the internal, also called a message call, which does not make an actual call to the EVM. Another is the external function call, which is part of the contract interface and can be called from other contracts via transactions. These functions are mostly efficient when the contract is receiving large arrays of data. An external function cannot make internal calls.

Function visibility has classified solidity into four types, namely `external`, `internal`, `public`, and `private`. The private visibility only prevents other contracts from accessing or modifying information residing in the contract, but it is still visible to the whole world on the live public blockchain.

During this entire book, we have been trying to build contracts and deploy them over a blockchain. A contract, once deployed on the blockchain, continues to run forever. But real life has some constraints; we might not want certain contracts to continue after a certain period of time. For example, we might not want to renew our car insurance contract as we plan to sell the car. That is why we need some mechanism to terminate or kill a contract.

Figure 6.5 represents a killer contract that has a function, which when executed, kills a live contract, and takes it off the blockchain. Actually it is done by an in-built EVM operation, `selfdestruct`. It needs an input parameter in terms of the address to send the remaining ethers and the killing occurs, which takes away the contract from the blockchain:

```solidity
1   pragma solidity ^0.4.11;
2
3   contract MyKillerContract {
4       address owner;
5
6       function MyKillerContract() public {
7           owner = msg.sender;
8       }
9
10      function getCreator() public constant returns(address) {
11          return owner;
12      }
13
14      function kill() public {
15          if(msg.sender == owner) {
16              selfdestruct(msg.sender);
17          }
18      }
19  }
```

Figure 6.5: Killer contract using selfdestruct operation

Apart from `selfdestruct`, a function can be declared as a `view`, `pure`, `getter`, and `fallback` function. A `view` declaration ensures that the state of a function is not modified. A `pure` declaration ensures the function is not read and does not modify the state of a function. The compiler automatically creates a `getter` function for all state variables, hence they have external visibility. Fallbacks are basically nameless functions that generally do not have arguments and cannot return anything. This chapter's last section on Parity hack will discuss fallback function in greater details.

Events

EVM logging facilities can be conveniently used by a smart contract via events. How is this done using events? Well, JavaScript comes to the rescue here. While developing DApps, the frontend is almost always a JavaScript page, mostly using Node.js or web3.js. These pages listen for events and, in turn, initiate JavaScript calls in the DApp's user interface.

When such event calls happen, they cause arguments to get stored in transaction logs. These logs are a special data structure in the blockchain and are associated with the address of the contract. These logs stay as long as a block is accessible. We cannot access the event or log data within a contract. This requires PoW. Events are inheritable and a great tool for debugging smart contracts.

Inheritance

Solidity imitates the Python language, in the context of inheritance. It supports general inheritance, multiple inheritance, and polymorphism. In simple words, inheritance is the property where a contract copies properties from a parent contract. In the case of multiple inheritance, a contract copies properties from more than one contract. Polymorphism denotes a general contract that can be reused by many other contracts.

For example, a contract, `eat()`, can be used by both `human()` contract and `birds()`, as well as `animal()` contracts. In solidity, IS is the keyword used for inheritance of contracts.

Multiple inheritances sometimes lead to deadlock problems. *Figure 6.6* illustrates this problem in terms of solidity, which gives the peculiar error, **Linearization of inheritance graph impossible**. This happens because C requests Y to override D. This is done by specifying D and Y in the order D, Y at line 6. But D itself has requested to override Y at line 5. This results in a contradiction that cannot be resolved. Hence, solidity follows Python standards and forces only specific orders to be followed, or else gives rise to such an error:

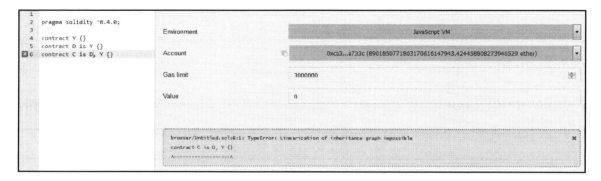

Figure 6.6: Deadlock problem in solidity

Libraries

I used to be a British council library member (the card expired this year, but haven't renewed it yet). These libraries are quite good. They give us a membership card, and we can go and pick books, videos, and movie disks (I was lucky enough to meet my spouse, but that's a different story).

These libraries have racks stacked with books and are very organized. All I needed was just one card and when I placed a request, they gave out books for three weeks. If I used them for a longer period, I would be subject to penalties. Better to return them on time, you see.

Well, solidity has a similar concept. They are basically a fat and thickly-loaded smart contract full of interesting functions that can be called from outside the contract by a different contract and are made by a delegate call operation to it. These library contracts just sit on the EVM without consuming any sort of gas on their own. If a foreign contract wants to reuse some of its functions, they do so using a delegate call and the gas cost is on the foreign contract. The same as renting a book from the library to get my college assignments done.

Technically speaking, these are very analogous to API classes we import in Java, packages we import in Python, or header files we include in C++. In solidity, there are a few ground rules for a library contract, which differentiates it from a normal contract. These are:

- A library cannot have a state variable
- A library cannot inherit or be inherited
- A library cannot receive ether

More on the pitfalls of a library call in the Parity hack section at the end of this chapter. Hold your horses until then.

Expression and control structures

Expression and control structures are summarized in the following 10 pointers. For more details, jump into the solidity documentation or ask a question at the Ethereum stack exchange forum:

- Input parameters of a contract are declared in the same way as variables. Output parameters are declared similar to input parameters just after the `return` keyword. Both can be used as an expression in the function body. Functions can return multiple outputs but must be the same as the number of output parameters.
- Like JavaScript, solidity has most of the familiar control structures, except `go to` and `switch`. Unlike C and JavaScript, solidity does not have a non-Boolean to Boolean type conversion yet.
- Recursive function calls are allowed internally in solidity. That is a function call to itself. These calls are translated to a single `JUMP` operation in the EVM. External calls to a contract are possible using this keyword but are potentially very dangerous due to its ability to change internal function states of other contracts leading to hacks. So, careful coding and testing for loopholes is mandatory.
- A contract can create a new contract using the new keyword. But a recursive call using `new` is not possible as the body of a new contract needs to be known in advance of creation. (Thinking about how a blockchain worm malware would be using recursion? Nasty mind!!).

- The order of precedence for evaluating expressions has not been formalized yet for solidity but taking the default precedence of JavaScript is safe and, according to the documentation, is safest (`http://Solidity.readthedocs.io/en/develop/miscellaneous.html#order`).

- Interestingly, using a `unit8` consumes more gas than `unit32`. This is because the state variable has to do the extra padding operations for `unit8`. So, to use under-utilized variables, it is recommended to have a `struct` type, where the spaces are utilized, efficiently leading to lower gas consumption.

- Irrespective of the state, the default value of a variable is typically the zero state. For a `bool` type, it is `false`. For unsigned integers, such as `unit`, `unit8`, and `unit32`, it is 0. For statically declared arrays, all the array elements by default hold the zero state value of that type. For dynamically declared arrays, such as bytes and strings, the fields are empty.

- Solidity inherits the scoping rules of JavaScript. Hence, a variable declared inside a function remains in the scope of the entire function regardless of where it is declared.

- The `throw` keyword has been deprecated since solidity version 0.4.13. For exception handling and triggering exceptions, `revert ()` is used. Checking conditions can be done using the `assert` and `require` keywords. Catching exceptions is not possible in solidity yet.

- Low-level assembly opcodes, such as `call`, `delegatecall`, and `callcode`, return `success` if the calling account does not exist. The onus is on the developer to check the existence of a contract prior to calling using these operations.

Units and variables

Figure 6.7 illustrates the category of units and variables available in the global workspace. These parameters are basically used to define various properties of the blockchain that are embedded into the smart contracts:

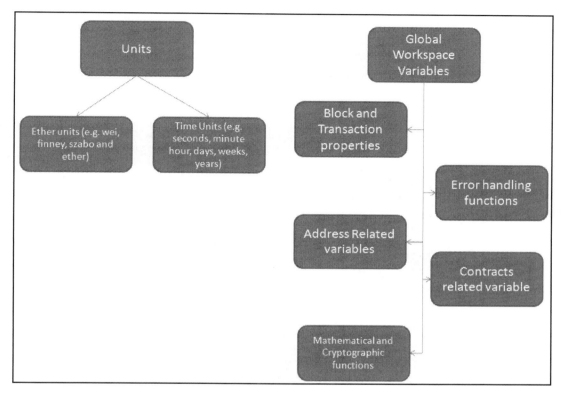

Figure 6.7: Unit and globally available variable classification for solidity

Optimizer and debugging options

In the previous chapter, we studied how gas-costly coding patterns are classified into two categories in terms of smart contract optimization. In this section, we will try to understand how the internal optimizer of the solidity compiler works. The sole aim of this optimizer is to generate assembly opcodes and, subsequently, machine code from high-level programming constructs in a way that reduces the gas cost during runtime.

We will go through a high-level view of the optimizer, take on a simple contract, and see how our assembly opcodes are generated in the presence and absence of an optimizer. This will also serve as an option to debugging a solidity smart contract for better performance in terms of gas-cost.

So what happens in a solidity optimizer when it is fed with a piece of code? It basically splits the sequence of instructions into blocks of atomic instructions at JUMPs and JUMPDESTs opcodes. It operates on the assembly so that it can be used by other languages as well.

What actually happens inside these atomic blocks of instructions? These blocks are analyzed and every modification to memory, the stack, or storage is recorded as an expression. These expressions consist of an instruction and a list of arguments that are basically pointers to another expression.

The main motive is to find equivalent expressions and club them into an expression class. This is a recursive activity and, at the end of this process, we know which expression has to be on the EVM stack and have a list of storage and memory modifications. This metadata about a block of instructions is stored together with the atomic block linking them together.

Apart from this, information about the memory, storage, and the stack configuration is forwarded to the next block. We can even build a **control flow graph** (**CFG**) of the entire program if we know the targets of all JUMP and JUMPI instructions.

At last, the code in each block is completely regenerated and a dependency graph is developed from such expressions. These expressions are then placed on the stack at the end of the block. Any operation that is not part of this dependency graph is essentially removed. The code is now generated in the order they were present in the original solidity code. This applies to the modifications to memory and storage as well. Finally, all these values that are generated need to be on the stack in the correct place. *Figure 6.8* illustrates an optimizer output to the EVM after doing all the preceding steps in the background to reduce the overall gas-cost at runtime:

```
1   // code snippet fed to optimizer
2   var x = 8;
3   data[8] = 10;
4   if (data[x] != x + 2)   //data[8] != 8+2 is false condition
5       return 3;
6   else
7       return 1;
8
9   // optimizer returns to assembly to reduce gas-cost
10  data[8] = 10;
11  return 1;
```

Figure 6.8: Illustration of solidity optimizer output to EVM

Now that we have a high-level view of how the solidity optimizer works when fed with a solidity code snippet, let us go through the assembly instructions that get generated in the presence, as well as in the absence, of a code optimizer. *Figure 6.9* represents the solidity contract along with the assembly opcode that is getting generated. As you can see, a lot of changes to the assembly opcodes are generated due to `optimizer-off`. Along with the events described in the last section, this is also an effective debugging option:

```
pragma solidity ^0.4.0;          //Optimizer off
                                 PUSH1 0x60
                                 PUSH1 0x40
contract dummy                   MSTORE
{                                PUSH1 0xA
    uint32 value = 10;           PUSH1 0x0
}                                PUSH1 0x0
                                 PUSH2 0x100
         //Optimizer on          EXP
         PUSH1 0x60              DUP2
         PUSH1 0x40              SLOAD
         MSTORE                  DUP2
         PUSH1 0x0               PUSH4 0xFFFFFFFF
         DUP1                    MUL
         SLOAD                   NOT
         PUSH4 0xFFFFFFFF        AND
         NOT                     SWAP1
         AND                     DUP4
         PUSH1 0xA               PUSH4 0xFFFFFFFF
         OR                      AND
         SWAP1                   MUL
         SSTORE                  OR
         CALLVALUE               SWAP1
         PUSH1 0x0               SSTORE
         JUMPI                   POP
```

Figure 6.9: Opcode generation with and without optimizer

Parity hack demystified

Parity (`https://parity.io/`) is a UK-based, venture capitalist-funded, tech start-up company. They provide an Ethereum client, also called Parity, which has an extensive Ethereum wallet and DApp environment for contract deployment. The entire application is written and compiled in the RUST language. The wallets are multi-sig. Multi-sig wallets, in simple words, are wallets that require at least two separate agreements to spend a token from the wallet. These wallets are supposed to be more secure than normal single-sig wallets.

Unfortunately, on July 19, 2017, three multi-sig wallets were exploited from a total of 596 wallets with similar vulnerabilities. *Figure 6.10* shows these compromised accounts in Etherscan, the public Ethereum block explorer. When the Parity team got alerted of this hack, they tackled this situation by forming a "White Hat Group" and used the same vulnerability to siphon all the tokens from the remaining 593 wallets into a safe repository so that the hacker could not lay their hands on these wallets. Even then, the damage done by exploiting the three wallets was around 83,017 ETH (~ $30 million on July 2017):

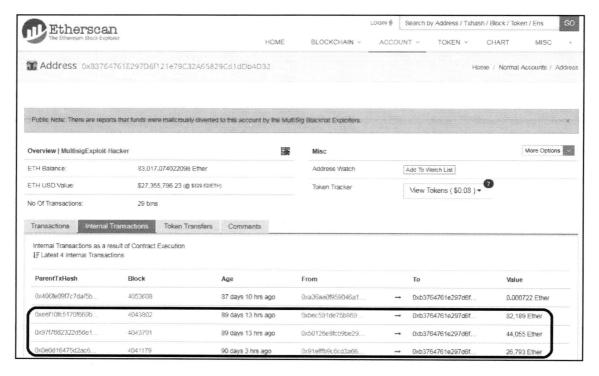

Figure 6.10: Parity Multi-Sig Hacker account on Etherscan (https://goo.gl/CZCEji)

To become a professional smart contract developer, especially in solidity, it is very important to learn from the previous mistakes of senior developers. So let us walk through the solidity code snippet of the Parity wallet to understand the vulnerability that led to this hack. We are going to learn what actually happened in the source code, step-by-step, and at the end we will see how the Parity team fixed this issue. We will refer to the original source file present in the GitHub archives and take a look at the fixes that were made in the code in order to prevent such hacks in the future. And we will study that by looking at the history of GitHub commits to this project. Sounds like a post-mortem analysis from a Sherlock Holmes' crime scene, doesn't it? Bring on the magnifying glass, my dear Watson!!

First of all, we need to understand how this hack happened because this hack was not a flaw in the Ethereum blockchain or Ethereum virtual machine. This hack did not happen because Ethereum itself had some technical loophole or vulnerability. Neither was the hack due to a flaw in the solidity language. The Parity client did not have any vulnerabilities either. (Now you might be thinking, *"Then who let the dogs out!? Who? Who? Who?!"*). My dear Watson, the flaw was actually in the piece of source code the Parity team gave to the users who wanted to create their own multi-sig wallet smart contracts. Being open source software, they are bound to give such source code to anyone under the creative commons license of the open source coding practice.

For example, I want to use the Parity client but I want to use my own multi-sig wallet. Then, the Parity team would give me a snippet or rather a template of source code with some pre-defined function calls and library calls already written inside the code template in which I can code my own logic of multi-sig functionality, yet remain compatible to interact with the Parity client over the Ethereum blockchain to transfer and store ethers. The flaw was in that snippet of source code. A villainous hacker could manipulate it to exploit the main Parity client deployed over the live Ethereum blockchain.

For instance, imagine you have installed CCTV cameras in each of your rooms for extra security. You lock every door and gate, and keep the duplicate keys under your favorite flowerpot in case of an emergency. Somehow, you totally forget to switch on privacy mode for your YouTube account, and all your home-locking activity is getting live fed into your normally "private" YouTube channel, which you think is still secure. Now, if a random thief, living nearby, was watching some random videos on YouTube and accidentally stumbled on your live feed channel, he will know where you keep the extra pair of keys. And it is just a matter of time; the thief will enter your home without even breaking or raising any alarms, and steal your valuables.

At this stage, you might be thinking that this is going to be a complex code debugging operation, with many senior developers such as Gavin Wood himself involved in fixing the code, even though he had not developed it. I also thought the same when the news hit the media channels. But we will see in a short while, how simple the flaw was and how easily such flaws can get overlooked even after many rounds of peer review.

Let us now get inside the code logic. Firstly, we will locate the actual code in GitHub. The path of the code (also depicted in *Figure 6.11*) is:

- `https://github.com/mayukhdifferent/parity/blob/master/js/src/contracts`
  `/snippets/enhanced-wallet.sol`

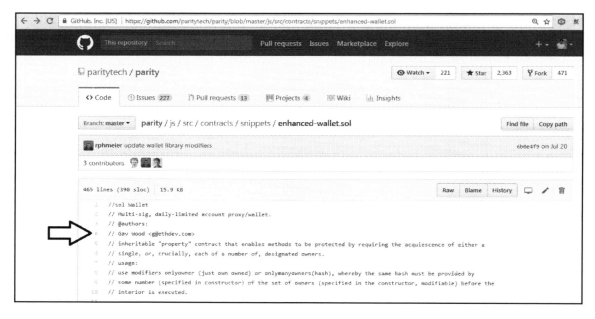

Figure 6.11: enhanced-wallet.sol at Parity GitHub archives

Here, you will notice that the author is Gavin Wood himself. Actually, this is the post-hack enhanced version, where the crucial bug fix was provided by Gavin Wood himself, as shown in *Figure 6.11*. The funny thing about viral media is that even though it spreads catastrophic news like wild fire, it also suppresses many parts of credible news that also deserves applause. The strategy and fix employed by the Parity team to stop the Parity hack midway actually saved 593 equally vulnerable wallets valued at around $179 million, approximately six times greater than the $30 million loss. Gavin Wood and the entire Parity team deserves applause for this on-the-feet thinking and risk mitigation strategy. It is very easy to act clever and wise once a theft has happened, but it takes real presence of mind to stop a heist from happening mid-way, which the team of developers at Parity has shown.

Let us now study the enhanced-wallet.sol file. This wallet code consists of four contracts, namely `WalletEvents`, `WalletAbi`, `WalletLibrary`, and `Wallet`. Each contract consists of several functions. For ease of understanding, a simpler version of the wallet has been shown in *Figure 6.12*, which concentrates only on the bare minimum code snippet required to understand the vulnerability.

Before we start talking about the workings of this simplified contract, we need to understand what libraries are. When we're deploying our smart contracts on the Ethereum blockchain to build a decentralized application, we'll need to use certain functionalities that many other DApps will have used as well. Instead of coding these common functionalities from scratch, we bundle up such functionalities into a library. Now, this bundled-up library package can not only be used by me but also by several other developers who want to have this common set of functionalities in their decentralized applications. In this way, we are creating reusable coding assets.

When we develop multi-sig wallets for Parity, our code basically uses a helper library. *Figure 6.12* has one such helper library named `WalletLibrary`. This has a function called `initWallet`. So, one thing this library contract could do is initialize a wallet. If we are building our own wallet contract code, we can call this library function from our contract to initialize the wallet.

Also, we can check whether an address is the owner of a wallet by calling the `isOwner` function instead of implementing it in our wallet contract. So, the library contract is basically a bundled product of standard helper functions:

```
1   contract WalletLibrary{
2
3       function initWallet(){
4           //coding logic
5       }
6
7       function addOwner(address owner){
8           //coding logic
9       }
10
11      function isOwner(address _adr) constant returns (bool){
12          //coding logic
13      }
14
15  }
16
17  contract Wallet{
18
19      function isOwner(address _adr) constant returns (bool){
20          return _walletLibrary.delegatecall(msg.data);
21      }
22
23      function() payable{
24          // gets called when no other function matches
25          _walletLibrary.delegatecall(msg.data);
26          //delegatecall is a pre-defined identifier for inline assembly opcode
27      }
28
29      address constant _walletLibrary = 0xcafecafecafecafecafecafecafecafecafecafe;
30  }
```

Figure 6.12: Simplified code snippet wallet.sol to understand the Parity hack

Now, if we observe the code in the `Wallet` contract, we see that it also has an `isOwner` function. But, instead of implementing any functionality itself it just delegates a call to the `isOwner` function of the `WalletLibrary` contract.

Basically the `Wallet` contract is saying to the `WalletLibrary` contract, *"Big bro, I am just a tiny little wallet but you are loaded with all those cute little functions running around doing the paper work for you. Please do some for me too. See, I don't have so many servant functions. Would you rent me some of yours? Don't worry about the gas. I got that covered. My user just loaded me with a bunch of ethers."*

Apart from helper functions in `Library` contracts, we have a special type of function definition existing in the `Wallet` contract. Peculiarly, it has no name. The word payable is a solidity keyword to denote an action performed by the function, but the function is essentially nameless. These functions are called the fallback functions. Ideally, it gets called when we do not have any matching function name present in the `Wallet` contract itself.

Hmm, sounds a bit tricky, right? Let us approach this concept in a simpler manner. We have a contract named `Wallet`. This `Wallet` has two functions. One is a nameless function. Another one is a "named" function with the name `isOwner`. Now, a novice user calls a function, `donateEther`, using our `Wallet` contract. As this alien function, `donateEther`, does not match with any of the functions present in our `Wallet` contract, the nameless fallback function gets called by default, which has a `delegatecall` operation inside it.

So, the nameless `fallbackfunction()` basically says, *"Big bro* `WalletLibrary`*, see my user have called this god-knows-what* `donateEther` *function. I have no idea what this function is. I do not have any definition of it inside me. Can you please check whether this is one of your cute little helper functions."*

`WalletLibrary` replies, *"Sorry man, none found. I also do not has this* `donateEther` *function. Throw some exception to the user, buddy. They will understand that something went wrong."*

Fallback functions are deceptively elegant in such cases. Not only did it elegantly delegate back to the helper library but also performed some error handling. But this is where the deception creeps in. What if, as a hacker, we call to execute a function named `initWallet` from my `Wallet` contract? By the rules, this function does not exist inside the `Wallet` contract. So, the `fallback` function delegates the call to the helper `WalletLibrary` contract. Interestingly, the `initWallet` function does exist in the `WalletLibrary`. Note, these calls are now happening using EVM automatically. The hacker just had to pass the function name parameter to his own `Wallet` contract and deploy it over EVM. And once the function `initWallet` got initialized using the hacker's `Wallet` contract, the hacker was able to take ownership of the `Library` contract and change the owner address to his own wallet address, which helped to drain all the ether funds of some other user address into the hacker's wallet, as already shown in *Figure 6.11*.

So, the vulnerability was in the `fallback` function call of the client's wallet, which is delegated without any security checks. This was really disastrous because the Parity team would not have any control over the user wallet. As a tactical measure, they used the same vulnerability to literally steal from every remaining wallet, amounting to $179 million, and deposit into a safe-haven, as they did with the $30 million-worth of ethers.

As a strategic solution, they had to modify their `WalletLibrary`, whose code was under their control. The changes are depicted in *Figure 6.13* from GitHub, which shows a before and after scenario of the Parity hack:

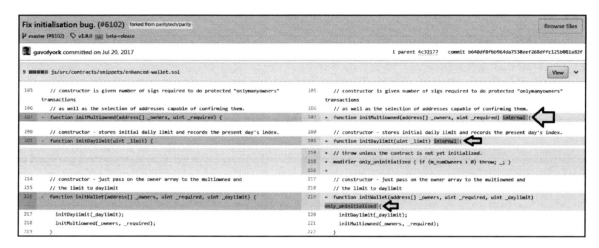

Figure 6.13: Code comparison of Parity wallet SOL file before and after hack

As we can see in *Figure 6.13*, the Parity team has added the keyword `only_uninitialized` to the `initWallet` function, which ensures that the `walletLibrary` can be executed only when it has not been initialized. If a foreign wallet tries to execute `initWallet` using `delegatecall` then the execution will be halted because the live wallet is already initialized and hence cannot be re-initialized by some other function call.

Similarly, the `internal` keyword has been used to restrict the scope of crucial functions and prevent them from getting executed by outside function calls. `initWallet` cannot be made internal because it has to remain a public function and it still needs to be called from the `Wallet` contract in the constructor.

So, you can see how the lack of a single keyword such as `internal` and `only_uninitialized` led to a multi-million dollar loss. Hence, as we stated in previous chapters, smart contract auditing is a very significant area where we will require subject matter experts, or else we might face such perils quite frequently. Until now, we have mostly concentrated on the backend of smart contract development. In the next chapter, we will look into the wonderful world of frontend web development using web3.js and how it helps in capturing a large user base for blockchain-related products and services.

Summary

Solidity is a work-in-progress yet well-documented language, being gradually developed as users face various problems while implementing smart contracts on the blockchain. In this chapter, we have covered a few fundamental aspects of this new language. We started off with praising JavaScript and how it has evolved as a robust language for web development. Solidity has been chosen for the blockchain on this legacy. Then we moved on to see various nuances this language has to offer us with its new concept of contract-oriented programming. We then nose-dived into the solidity optimizer's inner workings, and explored debugging options using events and bare-bone assembly opcodes. We closed the chapter by discussing and analyzing the Parity wallet hack, which helped in gaining deeper insights into how libraries and fallback functions play a crucial yet vulnerable role in ensuring the future of the smart contract industry. To be honest, it is just the beginning and we have barely scratched the surface of the iceberg of technology.

In `Chapter 7`, *Primer on Web3.js*, we will introduce web3.js and explore its potential as a user interface for blockchains.

7

Primer on Web3.js

In this chapter, we introduce Web3.js, which is a special application programming interface library written in JavaScript. This interface connects our web browser with the Ethereum blockchain node. We will begin this chapter by looking at the differences between geth, Web3.js, and Mist. Then we will learn how to import this API library and get connected with geth. We will then explore the API structure inside the Web3.js library. We conclude the chapter by studying the design of an ownership contract.

After studying this chapter, you will be able to do the following:

- Differentiate between Mist, geth, and Web3.js
- Realize how Web3.js interacts with the Ethereum blockchain
- Use Web3.js to run a basic smart contract
- Know the API structure of Web3.js library
- Understand the design of an ownership contract

Web3.js in the Ethereum ecosystem

Dale Carnegie, the famous self-improvement trainer, said that financial success is due to 15 percent technical skill, the remaining 85 percent being due to the ability to express ideas and arouse enthusiasm among people. Blockchain might be a cutting-edge technology backed by sound computing principles, but to make it a financial success we need to have mass adoption among people. For this, we need an interface to which everyone can relate.

Web3.js is one technology that can help us in this area of concern. Web3.js provides JavaScript bindings to Ethereum, which can then be used to build intuitive user interfaces using the web stack.

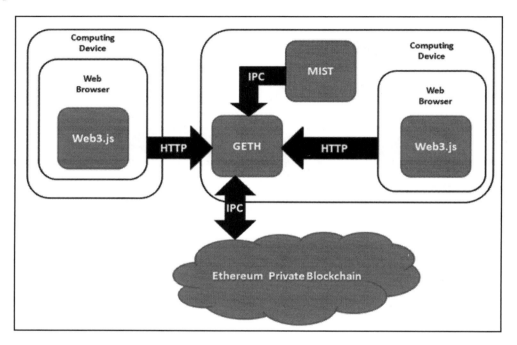

Figure 7.1: Web3.js interacting with a private blockchain via geth

It provides an abstraction to hide the complex internal works of smart contracts on the blockchain. In simple words, a web application implemented in JavaScript communicates with an Ethereum node or transacts with a smart contract on the blockchain using the Web3.js library.

Figure 7.1 illustrates this interaction. *Figure 7.2* differentiates clearly between Mist, geth, and Web3.js. In this table, we can see that Mist and geth use IPC, whereas Web3.js uses **Remote procedure calls (RPC)**.

In the Ethereum ecosystem, IPC generally works locally on a computer. IPC normally involves geth creating an IPC pipe on our computer's local filesystem, named `geth.ipc`. This pipe can now be used by different processes in the same computer to create bi-directional communication with the geth console. RPC, on the other hand, work across different computers, unless we strictly specify to connect with a localhost by using RPC endpoints as localhost: `8545` or `127.0.0.1:8545`:

Mist	Geth	Web3.js
It is a browser	It is a command line interface	It is an API Library
Mainly implemented using JavaScript	Mainly implemented in Golang	Mainly implemented using JavaScript
It is used as a wallet and can run Dapps over Blockchain	It is a tool for running full ethereum Node or a Private Blockchain	It interacts with Ethereum node using User triggered Events
Uses Inter-Process Communication (IPC)	Uses Inter-Process Communication (IPC)	Uses Remote Procedure Calling (RPC)

Figure 7.2: Mist versus geth versus Web3.js

Interestingly, both IPC and RPC with geth and Web3.js use a common protocol called JSON-RPC. **JavaScript Object Notation (JSON)** is a lightweight data-interchange format for human-machine interaction. Humans find this format easy to read and write. Machines find this format easy to parse and generate. This data format is completely language independent and basically consists of two structures: a name-value pair and an ordered list of values.

JSON-RPC is a stateless, lightweight RPC protocol that uses RFC 4627 as the data format. **Request for Comments (RFC)** was released by IETF (refer to `Chapter 2`, *Grokking Ethereum*).

A typical example of a JSON-RPC request is as follows:

```
{"jsonrpc":"2.0","method":"eth_coinbase","params":[],"id": 67}
```

In the preceding example we have a list of four properties:

- `jsonrpc`: This is a string specifying the version of the JSON-RPC protocol. Here, the version is `"2.0."`
- `method`: This is a string that contains the method to be invoked.

- `params`: This contains the parameter values to be used during the invocation of the method.
- `id`: This is an identifier established by the client. If it is specified, we let the server know that we are expecting a response. Otherwise, the server assumes the message to be a notification.

At the time of writing, the working version of Web3.js is 0.x.x; the 1.0 version is still unreleased. Once Web3.js version 1.0 is released, its library will support a collection of modules, as shown in *Figure 7.3*.

Each module contributes specific functionalities to the Ethereum ecosystem:

- The `web3-eth` module is for developing smart contracts on the Ethereum blockchain
- The `web3-shh` module is for peer-to-peer communication using the whisper protocol
- The `web3-bzz` module is for decentralized file storage using the swarm protocol
- The `web3-utils` module is for DApp development and contains useful helper functions

This is visualized in the following figure:

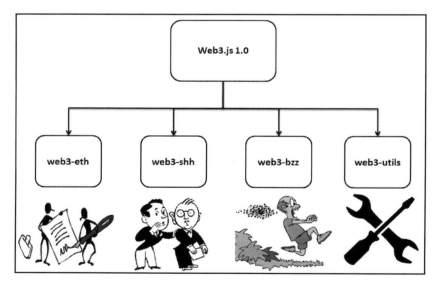

Figure 7.3: Modules of Web3.js for Ethereum ecosystem

Running a smart contract using Web3.js

In this section, we will do a hands-on tutorial. So put on your lab coats! We will do the following right now:

1. Install Web3.js from GitHub.
2. Install an HTTP server and get it up and running.
3. Write a quick-and-dirty JavaScript smart contract using Web3.js.
4. Open geth and attach our private blockchain with Web3.js.
5. Open a web browser to launch our smart contract using Web3.js.
6. Open Mist to validate the outcome of our smart contract.

To install Web3.js from GitHub on Windows, we require the git bash kernel. Once we have installed the git bash kernel, we can clone the Web3.js GitHub path and download the HTTP server using the following command:

```
> git clone https://github.com/ethereum/web3.js.git
> install -g http-server
```

The outcome is as follows:

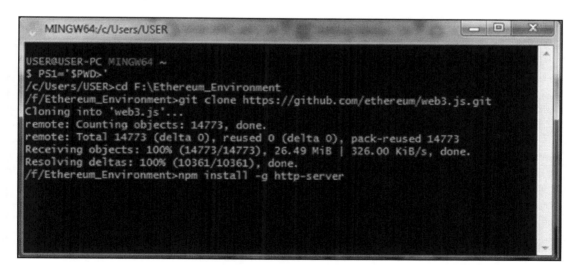

Figure 7.4: Web3.js and http-server installation from GitHub

Once the HTTP server is installed, we can kick-start the server with the `http-server` command. To kill the server instance, we need to press *Ctrl + C*. Now we open our geth node using Cygwin, using the following geth command:

```
> geth -datadir=./chaindata/ --rpc --rpccorsdomain "*"
```

This is **Cross-Origin Resourcesharing (CORS)**. For example, say you want to send and receive data to and from multiple servers using a single web-page application, this is where CORS comes in. For example, say you want to send and receive data to and from multiple servers using a single web-page application, this is where CORS comes in. It acts as a work-around to browser's same-origin security policy. It acts as a work-around to browser's same-origin security policy. After the private blockchain is set up with Web3.js, we write a basic contract named `myDapp` that fetches my wallet balance. This file is named `index.html` and is placed just outside the `Web3.js` folder.

Figure 7.5 shows the HTML script that calls the Web3.js library using a JavaScript code:

```html
1    <!doctype html>
2        <html>
3    <head>
4        <title>myDapp</title>
5        <script src="web3.js/dist/web3.min.js"></script>
6        <script type="text/javascript">
7
8        if (typeof web3 !== 'undefined') {
9            web3 = new Web3(web3.currentProvider);
10       } else {
11           // set the provider you want from Web3.providers
12           web3 = new Web3(new Web3.providers.HttpProvider("http://localhost:8545"));
13       }
14
15       function getBalance() {
16           document.getElementById("myBalance").innerText =
17           web3.fromWei(web3.eth.getBalance(web3.eth.accounts[0]), "ether");
18       }
19       </script>
20   </head>
21   <body>
22   <h1>This is my balance</h1>
23   <button onclick="getBalance()">Update my balance</button>
24   <span id="myBalance"></span> in Ether
25   </body>
26   </html>
```

Figure 7.5: Web3.js library in index.html

When we open this `index.html` file on a web browser and press the balance button, it returns the amount of ethers present in my private blockchain, which in turn can be verified by opening the Mist browser. This comparison is illustrated in *Figure 7.6*. In the next section, we will have a high-level view of the API structures in Web3.js:

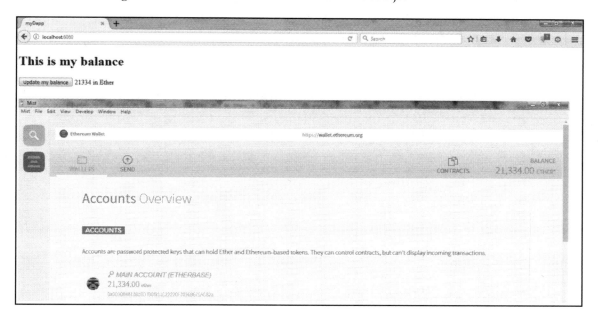

Figure 7.6: Ether balance comparison of Mist and a Web3.js-based Dapp

API structure of Web3.js

Let me be very honest with you, going through the Web3.js library to find the suitable function required for our contract can be mind-boggling. This is the reason we need to consider the Web3.js 1.0 documentation as our perfect tour-guide brochure. The entire documentation is freely available at `https://web3js.readthedocs.io/en/1.0/index.html`.

In this section, we will visualize a map of the important APIs so that when we are actually coding our contracts, we can directly jump to the sections of the Web3.js documentation for specifications and parameter usage patterns.

As depicted in *Figure 7.3*, we have four sub-modules, namely `web3-eth`, `web3-shh`, `web3-bzz`, and `web3-utils`. In *Figure 7.4*, we have subdivided the `web3-eth` module into important sub-API modules. Each sub-module has several helper functions that can be called by a smart contract.

To complete any generic task available via helper function, the calling smart contract must spend ethers necessary for the operation.

```
web3.eth.personal.sign(dataToSign, address, password, [callback])
```

Here's an example that calls this function and prints the output to the console:

```
web3.eth.personal.sign("Dear Lord",
"0x11f4d0A3c12e86D4D5F39D213F9E19D048296DAe", "test
passphrase").then(console.log);
>"0x30955ed65396facf86c53e6219c52D4daeDe92aa4941d89635409de4c9c9f9466d4e9aa
ec9999f05e923889D33c0d0dd29d9226D6e6f56ce939465c5cfd04De400"
```

Here are the API sub-modules of `web3.eth`:

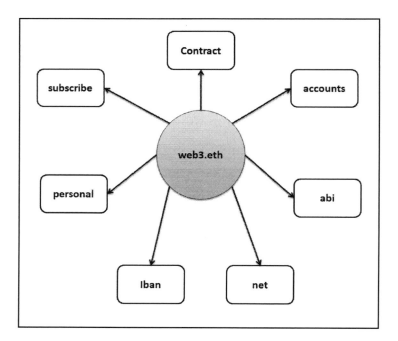

Figure 7.7: API sub-modules of web3.eth

In a nutshell, the functions inside the API sub-modules of the `web3.eth` module help to accomplish the following tasks:

- `web3.eth.subscribe`: This lets us subscribe specific events happening on the blockchain.
- `web3.eth.Contract`: This makes it easy to interact with smart contracts on the blockchain, as if they are JavaScript objects.
- `web3.eth.accounts`: This helps to generate data, Ethereum accounts, and sign transactions.
- `web3.eth.personal`: This allows our contract to interact with the Ethereum node accounts.
- `web3.eth.Iban`: This lets us convert Ethereum addresses from and to **International Banking Account Number (IBAN)** and **Basic Banking Account Number (BBAN)**.
- `web3.eth.abi`: This allows the contract to decode and encode parameters to the **Application Binary Interface (ABI)** for function calls to the **Ethereum Virtual Machine (EVM)**.
- `web3.eth.net`: This helps our contract to interact with the network properties of Ethereum nodes. This sub-module is common to all the web3 modules except utils; hence, it is denoted by `web3.*.net`, where `*` can be `eth`, `shh`, or `buzz`.

In similar fashion, *Figure 7.8* depicts the 33 API sub-modules of the `web3.shh` module. Ignoring the `web3.shh.net` module, each of the 32 sub-modules is a function with a distinct input and output argument definition that utilizes the whisper protocol for peer-to-peer communication:

- `setProvider`: Changes the provider for its module
- `providers`: Contains current available providers
- `givenProvider`: Returns current native provider by the browser
- `currentProvider`: Returns current set provider or null
- `batchRequest`: Creates and executes batch requests
- `extend`: Allows the extension of web3 modules
- `getId`: Gets the current network ID

- `isListening`: Checks whether a node is listening for peers
- `getPeerCount`: Gets the number of connected peers
- `getVersion`: Gets the version of the running whisper
- `getInfo`: Gets information about the current whisper node
- `setMaxMessageSize`: Sets the maximum message size allowed for a whisper node
- `setMinPoW`: Sets the minimal PoW required by a node
- `markTrustedPeer`: Marks specific trusted peers to allow it to send expired or historic messages
- `newKeyPair`: Generates a new public and private key pair for message encryption and decryption
- `addPrivateKey`: Stores a key pair derived from a private key to return its ID
- `deleteKeyPair`: Deletes specific keys if they exist
- `hasKeyPair`: Checks for the private key of a key pair in a whisper node matching a given ID
- `getPublicKey`: Returns the public key for a key pair ID
- `getPrivateKey`: Returns the private key for a key pair ID
- `newSymKey`: Generates a random symmetric key to store under an ID
- `addSymKey`: Stores a key and returns an ID
- `generateSymKeyFromPassword`: Generates a key from a password and stores it to return its ID
- `hasSymKey`: Checks the symmetric key stored with a given ID
- `getSymKey`: Returns the symmetric key associated with a given ID
- `deleteSymKey`: Deletes the symmetric key associated with a given ID
- `post`: Posts a whisper message to the network
- `subscribe` : Subscribes to the incoming whisper message
- `clearSubscriptions`: Clears the subscription to whisper nodes
- `newMessageFilter`: Creates a new filter within a node

- `deleteMessageFilter`: Deletes a message filter in a node
- `getFilterMessages`: Retrieves messages received between the last time this function was called and and that match the new filter criteria

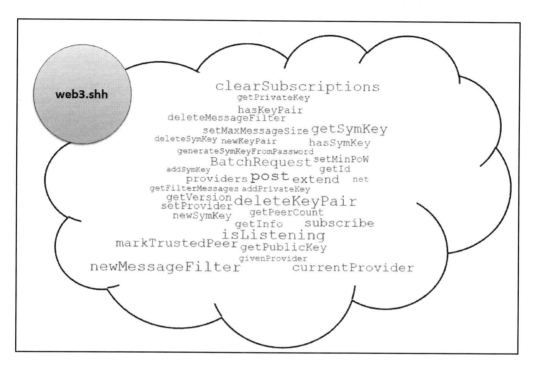

Figure 7.8: API sub-modules of web3.shh

Figure 7.9 lists the API sub-modules of the `web3.bzz` module. These functions interact with the swarm:

- `setProvider` : This changes the provider for its module
- `givenProvider` : This returns the native current provider of the Ethereum-compatible browser
- `currentProvider` : This returns the current provider's URL or NULL
- `upload` : This uploads files, folders, or raw data to a swarm
- `download` : This downloads files and folders as buffer or to a disk from a swarm

- `pick`: This opens a file picker to aid in selecting files in the browser
- `net`: This allows us to interact with Ethereum node network properties

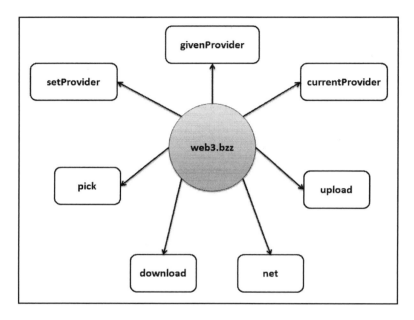

Figure 7.9: API sub-modules of web3.bzz

Figure 7.10 models the 28 API sub-modules of the web3.utils module. These are common functions used when a contract conducts basic node-related operations. For example, `web3.utils.sha3()` generates the hash for a string literal passed as an input to the function. This function has an alias named `web3.utils.keccak256()`. Another peculiar function exists that provides a useful helper function, without extending any built-in objects. It is called the underscore function and is normally defined as `web3.utils._()`. The functions have been listed here for convenience:

- `randomHex` : Generates cryptographically strong pseudo-random HEX strings from a given byte size
- `_`: Provides workaday functional helpers such as `map`, `filter`, and `invoke` as well as more specialized goodies such as function binding, JavaScript templating, creating quick indexes, and deep equality testing
- `BN`: Calculates big number operations in JavaScript

- isBN: Checks whether a given value is a BN.js instance
- isBigNumber : Checks whether a given value is a BigNumber.js instance
- sha3: Calculates the sha3 of the input
- soliditySha3: Calculates the sha3 of the given input parameters by ABI conversion and tightly packing them before being hashed
- isHex: Checks whether a given string is a HEX string
- isHexStrict: Checks whether a string prefixed with 0x is a HEX string
- isAddress: Checks whether a given string is a valid Ethereum address
- toChecksumAddress: Converts an upper or lowercase Ethereum address to a checksum address
- checkAddressChecksum: Checks the checksum of a given address
- toHex: Auto converts any given value to HEX
- toBN: Converts a value to a BN.js instance for big number operations in JavaScript
- hexToNumberString: Returns the number representation of a given HEX value as a string
- hexToNumber: Returns the number representation of a given HEX value
- numberToHex: Returns the HEX representation of a given number value
- hexToUtf8: Returns the UTF-8 string representation of a given HEX value
- hexToAscii: Returns the ASCII string representation of a given HEX value
- utf8ToHex: Returns the HEX representation of a given UTF-8 string
- asciiToHex: Returns the HEX representation of a given ASCII string
- hexToBytes: Returns a byte array from the given HEX string
- bytesToHex: Returns a HEX string from a byte array
- toWei: Converts any ether value value into wei
- fromWei: Converts any wei value into an ether value
- unitMap: Shows all possible ether values and their amount in wei

- `padLeft`: Adds a padding on the left of a string, useful for adding paddings to HEX strings
- `padRight`: Adds a padding on the right of a string, useful for adding paddings to HEX strings
- `toTwosComplement`: Converts a negative number into a two's complement:

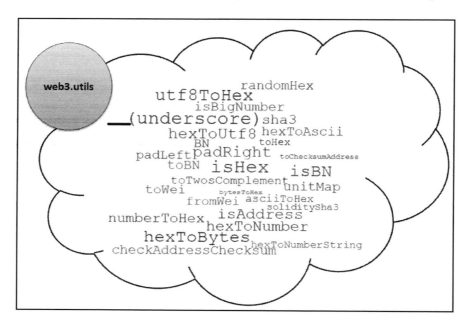

Figure 7.10: API sub-modules of web3.utils

Designing an ownership contract

Ownership contracts have a wide number of real-life applications. But what is an ownership contract? Basically, these are smart contracts that can prove the ownership of a file without revealing the content of the file. As the contracts run on a blockchain, they can prove that a contract existed at a particular timestamp and check the document's integrity.

The integrity of a file is achieved by storing a hash of the file along with the file owner's name in the form of a key-value pair. The hash helps us to prevent fraud of ownership because any tampering with the file's content will give rise to a completely new hash value. *Figure 7.11* shows a solidity implementation of the ownership contract:

```solidity
1   pragma solidity ^0.4.19;
2   contract OwnershipContract
3   {
4       struct FileMapping
5       {
6           uint timestamp;
7           string owner;
8       }
9
10      mapping (string => FileMapping) files;
11
12      event FileLogStatus(bool status, uint timestamp, string owner, string fileHash);
13
14      //Used to store the owner of file at the block timestamp
15      function set(string owner, string fileHash) public
16      {
17          //Here we are checking for default value i.e., all bits are 0
18          if(files[fileHash].timestamp == 0)
19          {
20              files[fileHash] = FileMapping(block.timestamp, owner);
21
22              //triggering an event to notify the frontend
23              FileLogStatus(true, block.timestamp, owner, fileHash);
24          }
25          else
26          {
27              //returning out a false status to the frontend
28              FileLogStatus(false, block.timestamp, owner, fileHash);
29          }
30      }
31
32      //this is used to get file information
33      function get(string fileHash) internal view returns (uint timestamp, string owner)
34      {
35          return (files[fileHash].timestamp, files[fileHash].owner);
36      }
37  }
```

Figure 7.11: Ownership smart contract

The corresponding `web3.js` file shown in *Figure 7.12* can be embedded inside a JavaScript file:

```
var browser_untitled_sol_ownershipcontractContract = web3.eth.contract([{"constant":false,"inputs":[{"name":"fileHash","type":"string"}],"name":"get","outputs":
[{"name":"timestamp","type":"uint256"},{"name":"owner","type":"string"}],"payable":false,"stateMutability":"nonpayable","type":"function"},{"constant":false,"inputs":
[{"name":"owner","type":"string"},{"name":"fileHash","type":"string"}],"name":"set","outputs":[],"payable":false,"stateMutability":"nonpayable","type":"function"},
{"anonymous":false,"inputs":[{"indexed":false,"name":"status","type":"bool"},{"indexed":false,"name":"timestamp","type":"uint256"},
{"indexed":false,"name":"owner","type":"string"},{"indexed":false,"name":"fileHash","type":"string"}],"name":"FileLogStatus","type":"event"}]);
var browser_untitled_sol_ownershipcontract = browser_untitled_sol_ownershipcontractContract.new(
  {
    from: web3.eth.accounts[0],
    data:
'0x606064052341561000f57600080fd5b61079c8061001e6000396000f30060606040526004000357c010000000000000000000000000000000000000000000000000000463ffffffff168063693ec85e
1461004857806e942b516146101255760080fd5b341561005357600080fd5b341561005357600080fd5b341561005357600080f...'
...
    gas: '4300000'
  }, function (e, contract){
    console.log(e, contract);
    if (typeof contract.address !== 'undefined') {
      console.log('Contract mined! address: ' + contract.address + ' transactionHash: ' + contract.transactionHash);
    }
})
```

Figure 7.12: Web3.js equivalent of a solidity contract

As you can see, we have not gone into the details of implementing this Web3.js equivalent of an ownership contract in the JavaScript code to develop a frontend application.

In `Chapter 8`, *Developing a Cryptocurrency from Scratch*, we will take a closer look at implementations where we would develop a cryptocurrency token from scratch.

Summary

This chapter began with a clear distinction between geth, Mist, and Web3.js, and how they come together to operate over the Ethereum blockchain using IPC and HTTP. Both were seen to use the JSON-RPC protocol. Then we moved on to categorize the Web3.js library into four main modules, namely eth, shh, bzz, and utils. We also saw how we can call the Web3.js library on plain JavaScript to run smart contracts over private blockchains. We learned how to explore various API sub-modules and functions of the Web3.js library. We concluded this chapter with a solidity implementation of an ownership contract along with its Web3.js equivalent code generation.

In `Chapter 8`, *Developing a Cryptocurrency from Scratch*, we will develop a cryptocurrency token from scratch and learn about **initial coin offering (ICO)**.

8

Developing a Cryptocurrency from Scratch

In this chapter, we will discuss one of the wide-spread applications of Ethereum, that is, crypto tokens. We will begin with a short introduction to the Truffle framework and create an ERC20-compatible token using it. Then, we will discuss **initial coin offerings (ICOs)** and how they can be identified as scam, Ponzi, faucet-like, or legit. We will then introduce the concept of arbitrage with respect to cryptocurrencies. We will also learn about **Fiat2Crypto (F2C)** and **Crypto2Crypto (C2C)** exchange. Then, we conclude the chapter with yet another parity hack case study.

After studying this chapter, you will be able to:

- Use Truffle to develop ERC20-compatible tokens
- Identify Ponzi, scams, faucets, and legit ICOs
- Understand arbitrage trading using cryptocurrencies.
- Know about Fiat2Crypto and Crypto2Crypto exchange
- Case study another parity hack and learn the importance of token safekeeping

Token versus coin

The title of this chapter is misleading. It has been made misleading on purpose. This has been chosen to make you realize the subtle difference between a cryptocurrency and a token in the perspective of Ethereum. When you explore the web to gain knowledge about cryptocurrency, you will observe that the terms cryptocurrency, coins, and tokens are often used interchangeably.

Figure 8.1 represents a classification that brings out the subtle differences between them:

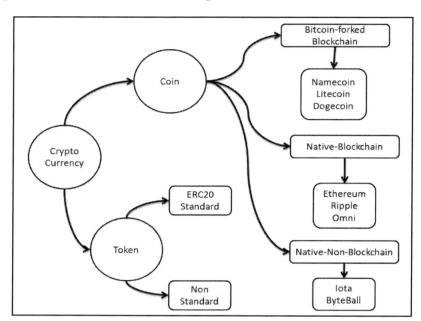

Figure 8.1: Token versus coin

In simple words, the following four points summarize the difference between coins and tokens:

- Coins are separate currencies on their own blockchain, while tokens are mainly based on a single blockchain variant.
- Coins generally have a limited functionality, store-of-value, while tokens can store a complex, multi-faceted level of values.
- Coins are mostly generated by mining a blockchain, while tokens are generated by executing smart contracts on the blockchain.
- So, when we say cryptocurrency in this chapter, we actually mean tokens because the book is about Ethereum smart contracts. With this tiny yet crucial piece of information, we will explore the next section on how to develop an Ethereum token from scratch by following ERC20 compatibility.

ERC20 token development using Truffle

Truffle is a framework for development, testing, and asset pipelining for Ethereum. It also has an incorporated package specification using the ERC190 standard. ERC190 is a request for comments, which lays down a set of rules about package specifications for Ethereum smart contracts.

Asset pipelining for Ethereum is a concept that has been borrowed from Ruby on Rails. This is a feature that provides a framework to concatenate, minify, or compress JavaScript, Solidity, and CSS assets in the required sequence of execution. This feature helps the developer to create compressed and pre-processed library-like modules that can be reused by other coding modules, which helps in improving productivity.

Let's start by installing the Truffle framework. The installation is pretty straightforward and can be accomplished in the Git Bash window with the following command, as shown in *Figure 8.2*:

```
$ npm install -g truffle
```

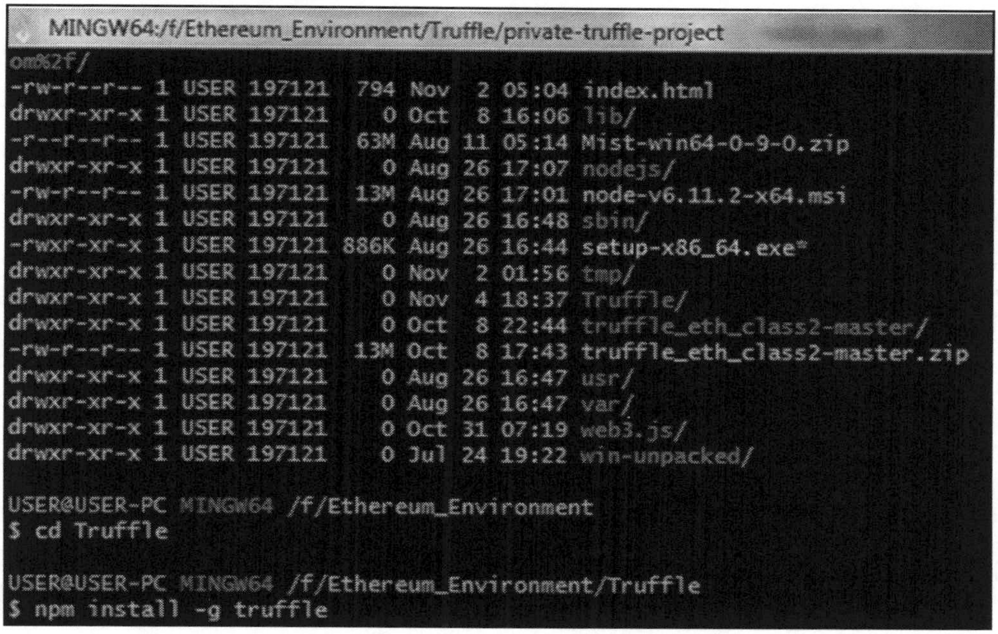

Figure 8.2: Installation inside a new folder named Truffle

After the installation, we need to initiate the framework, which can be done as shown in *Figure 8.3*. If you run into any trouble during installation or initiation, please refer to the Ethereum stack exchange or Truffle documentation for the known troubleshooting issues.

 It is to be noted that, to initiate Truffle for a new project, we must always use the `Truffle init` command in a new folder with a custom project name. We cannot initiate Truffle in a project folder where the Truffle framework is already initiated, as this then throws an exception.

This is how it works:

```
USER@USER-PC MINGW64 /f/Ethereum_Environment/Truffle
$ mkdir private-truffle-project

USER@USER-PC MINGW64 /f/Ethereum_Environment/Truffle
$ cd private-truffle-project

USER@USER-PC MINGW64 /f/Ethereum_Environment/Truffle/private-truffle-project
$ truffle init
Downloading...
Unpacking...
Setting up...
Unbox successful. Sweet!

Commands:

  Compile:        truffle compile
  Migrate:        truffle migrate
  Test contracts: truffle test

USER@USER-PC MINGW64 /f/Ethereum_Environment/Truffle/private-truffle-project
$ truffle.cmd version
Truffle v4.0.1 (core: 4.0.1)
Solidity v0.4.18 (solc-js)
```

Figure 8.3: Initiation of Truffle framework

Let's now create a simple ERC20-compatible token. For that, we create a new folder, ERC20_token, inside the `private-truffle-project` folder and write a solidity file, `ScratchToken.sol`, inside it.

We place this solidity file, along with the `Migration.sol` file, inside the `contract` folder.

Now, we open another Git Bash window and type in `testrpc` to start the `testnet`, as shown in *Figure 8.4*:

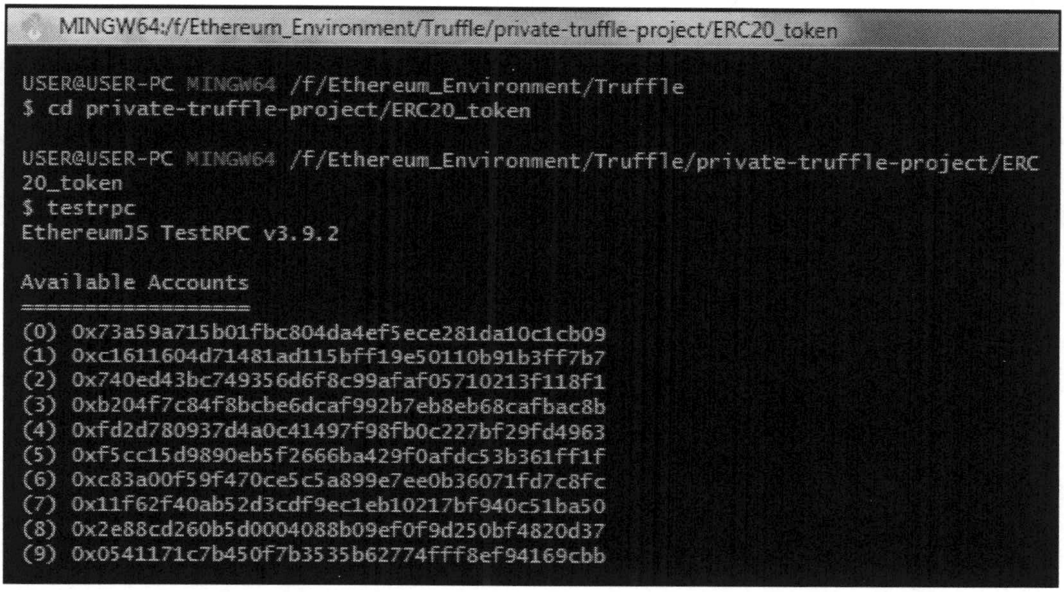

```
MINGW64:/f/Ethereum_Environment/Truffle/private-truffle-project/ERC20_token

USER@USER-PC MINGW64 /f/Ethereum_Environment/Truffle
$ cd private-truffle-project/ERC20_token

USER@USER-PC MINGW64 /f/Ethereum_Environment/Truffle/private-truffle-project/ERC
20_token
$ testrpc
EthereumJS TestRPC v3.9.2

Available Accounts
==================
(0) 0x73a59a715b01fbc804da4ef5ece281da10c1cb09
(1) 0xc1611604d71481ad115bff19e50110b91b3ff7b7
(2) 0x740ed43bc749356d6f8c99afaf05710213f118f1
(3) 0xb204f7c84f8bcbe6dcaf992b7eb8eb68cafbac8b
(4) 0xfd2d780937d4a0c41497f98fb0c227bf29fd4963
(5) 0xf5cc15d9890eb5f2666ba429f0afdc53b361ff1f
(6) 0xc83a00f59f470ce5c5a899e7ee0b36071fd7c8fc
(7) 0x11f62f40ab52d3cdf9ec1eb10217bf940c51ba50
(8) 0x2e88cd260b5d0004088b09ef0f9d250bf4820d37
(9) 0x0541171c7b450f7b3535b62774fff8ef94169cbb
```

Figure 8.4: Starting testrpc

In the old Git Bash window, we change the `truffle.js` file to point to our localhost, as shown in *Figure 8.5*:

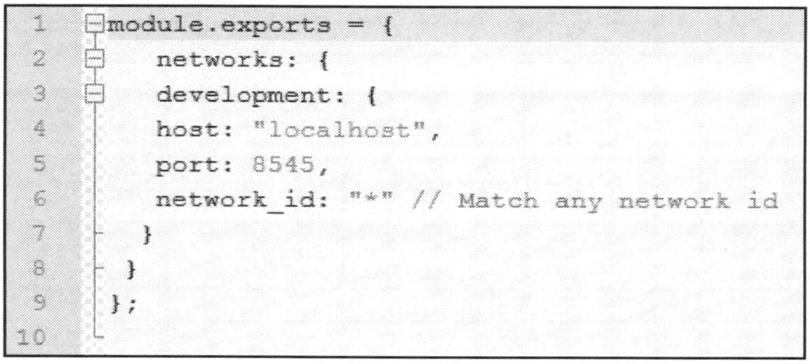

```
1   module.exports = {
2       networks: {
3       development: {
4       host: "localhost",
5       port: 8545,
6       network_id: "*" // Match any network id
7       }
8       }
9   };
10
```

Figure 8.5: Truffle.js configuration changes

Then, we compile the `.sol` files, as shown in *Figure 8.6*; they can now be deployed using the command `truffle.cmd deploy` in the `testnet`:

```
USER@USER-PC MINGW64 /f/Ethereum_Environment/Truffle/private-truffle-project/ERC20_token
$ truffle.cmd compile
Compiling .\contracts\Migrations.sol...
Compiling .\contracts\ScratchToken.sol...

Writing artifacts to .\build\contracts

USER@USER-PC MINGW64 /f/Ethereum_Environment/Truffle/private-truffle-project/ERC20_token
```

Figure8. 6: Compiling ScratchToken.sol

This is how we deploy a basic ERC20-compliant token using the Truffle framework. We can add more functionality for incorporating other ERC20-compliant functions that are required for a full-fledged token with security enhancements.

In the chapter on smart contracts, we have discussed why we need a compliance such as ERC20 and promised to list the various functions mandated in an ERC20 token.

An ERC20-compliant token must have the following list of functions with the same naming convention:

```
totalSupply ()
```

This function has no arguments and gets back the total supply of tokens that is in circulation.

For example, if we create an ERC20 token that imitates the bitcoin ideology, then the `totalSupply()` would fetch 21 million as a number:

```
balanceOf (owner)
```

The preceding function has an argument inside the parenthesis, which is the address of the owner. Hence, this `balanceOf` function need the address of the owner to return back the balance value.

```
transfer (to,value)
```

The preceding function has two arguments, namely, the address of the `to`, that is, the recipient's address, and the value of how many tokens needs to be sent to that address.

```
transferFrom (from,to,value)
```

The preceding function has three arguments, namely, the sender's address, the recipient's address, and the value of the token that needs to be transferred.

```
approve (spender,value)
```

The preceding function empowers the owner to approve a third-party entity to spend tokens up to a designated maximum value.

```
allowance (owner, spender)
```

The preceding function allows the owner to empower a third-party entity to spend tokens on their behalf, without enforcing any spending limit.

In addition to the previous functions, such a token has two events:

```
event Transfer(from, to, tokens)
event Approval(tokenOwner, spender, tokens)
```

For example, if there is a token that has a `totalSupplyInCirculation()` function, which has the same functionality as `totalSupply()`, the token is ERC20-non-compliant, because the function name has changed.

Events, on the other hand, are broadcast throughout the network. For example, when a transfer occurs, a transfer event is broadcast throughout the network so that the network is aware of the transaction and the blocks are updated accordingly in the blockchain. Approval events are also broadcast in a similar manner to make the network aware of the change of authority of the spender's address.

Arbitrage trading for cryptocurrencies

Ajay was an orphan. We were high school friends. To support his studies, he used to do odd jobs. Early in the morning, he used to sell vegetables; at night, he sold bangles. He could not complete his studies and graduate due to the excessive commute time. Fast forward 20 years: he runs an event management business and owns two bungalows and three sedans, all of which are rented for event functions. He still lives in the one-story apartment from his childhood days. He does not pay rent anymore, as he has bought it from the owner and paid in cash

We met a few days ago in one of his bungalows where a third-party was hosting a dinner party. I casually asked him what made him tick. He told me that, firstly, he never took any loans. He does not have a credit card, even now. Secondly, the railway tracks.

You see, our house is very near to a train station. We could literally hear the whistles of the trains every night. Ajay told me he made the bulk of his money during school days. The station has two-way rail tracks, and local trains commuted every half an hour from the city junction to remote villages.

He used to buy vegetables from train vendors who sat on the right platform and sold them to morning walkers and joggers on the left platform.

Our school was on the left side. When the school bell rang he used to go to buy bangles and then return home. Once twilight began to set in, he came out with bangles near a temple just beside the right platform.

Ajay, without any formal business training, knew exactly what arbitrage was. It is an opportunity in which an investor can make a riskless profit by exploiting price differences in different markets for identical goods. For Ajay, the two markets were on either side of the rail platform.

Arbitrage trading is an old trade practice used to make quick profit. It is also known as pair trading.

In the case of cryptocurrency, cross-border, cross-exchange arbitrage is a possibility due to a highly volatile conversion rate at different geographical localities. The ETH/INR or BTC/INR rates are much higher than ETH/USD or BTC/USD. Even with a 1% commission for the miners, the net profit is good enough for high-volume cryptocurrency trading.

The ICO story

A video log exists on YouTube at the following link:

```
https://www.youtube.com/watch?v=4bMf4xZg_4U&feature=youtu.be&t=4m19s
```

At the time of writing, it has gathered only 285 views. This is a clip from the Bitcoin 2013 conference in San Jose. At 4:19 in the clip, a panelist posed an idea he about developing a new protocol on top of the bitcoin blockchain protocol with some new X, Y, and Z features, using a group of trustworthy software developers. He also emphasized that he wanted to create this start-up without going to any venture capital firms. Rather, he would release a few tokens that the mass crowd could buy as an investment, which will act as the kick-starter fund. The value of these tokens will increase as the start-up grows, which in turn will reward the early adopters of such tokens.

"I'll take them," someone shouts, and the video ends.

This person in the video is J.R. Willet and the idea he pioneered in this video is the concept of **initial coin offering** (**ICO**). Sadly, this idea never took off on the bitcoin blockchain as there were no early adopters. A few years later, Vitalik Buterin used this concept to pitch the ICO on the Ethereum blockchain and has bagged around USD 2 billion worth of ether in terms of funding within the first nine months of 2017.

An ICO is an unregulated way of offering investors some units of a new cryptocurrency or crypto token in exchange for market-established cryptocurrencies, such as bitcoin and Ethereum, via smart contracts.

The good news is that a legitimate ICO, such as Ethereum, Augur, and Golem, is an amalgamation of a kick-starter model and an **initial public offering** (**IPO**). The bad news is that most of the ICOs that come out in today's market do not have the proof-of-concept to start with, which is the core of any kick-starter model, nor are they regulated by the Securities and Exchange Commission, which is the backbone of all securities offered in IPOs. *Figure 8.7* represents this dilemma. Such dilemmas give rise to scams, Ponzi schemes, and faucets that we need to identify.

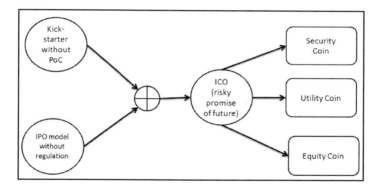

Figure 8.7: ICO dilemma

Now, you might be wondering why I would even consider Ethereum as a legitimate ICO, after so many hacks have happened in the past few months. To answer this, we need to understand that all the hacks that have happened on Ethereum were due to bad coding practices on smart contracts, rather than the infrastructure itself, that is, the Ethereum blockchain or the Ethereum virtual machine and solidity.

Most importantly, in terms of ICO, the tokens on sale were ethers, which are the same tokens that are being used for running smart contracts on gas over the Ethereum blockchain.

This brings us to the point where we can identify a scam ICO. The important pointer of a scam ICO would be that the smart contracts running on the blockchain would not be using the tokens that were on the ICO.

Imagine this: would you buy or invest in a company that says it is a diamond merchant but offers you roasted almonds as a token or receipt of your investment? Either it provides you with legal paper contracts equivalent to your amount invested on the tokens, or some sort of valuable stone.

Ponzi ICOs are a different kind of financial fraud. In fact, the concept of Ponzi originated offline 150 years ago, where an investor is promised to recover their investments with interest, only if they can dupe in other investors to participate in this scheme. An affiliate business without any products is a form of Ponzi business. The world of Ethereum has, unfortunately, become a breeding ground for new Ponzi ICOs.

Figure 8.8 represents the classification of an Ethereum-based Ponzi, which has been identified by Massimo Bartoletti et al. from the Department of Mathematics and Informatics at the University of Cagliari, Sardinia, Italy (arXiv:1703.03779v5):

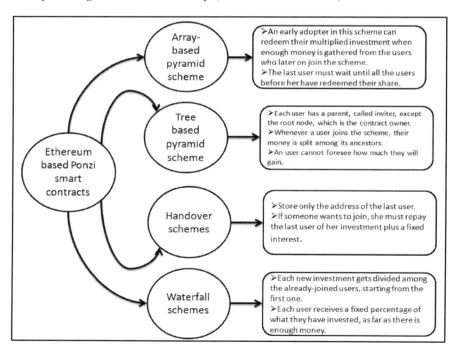

Figure 8.8: Ethereum-based Ponzi smart-contracts

Faucets are not related to ICOs. They are basically websites where the user has to do certain menial tasks to earn ethers. The tasks can be as simple as clicking a web page, participating in a survey, playing games, writing reviews, or simply copy-pasting affiliate links. The ether earned per task is extremely low, while the watermark eligible for ether transfer into the user's wallet from the faucet can be extremely high or can take an enormous amount of time. Faucets are borderline cases of fraud, because some do pay the users who have grown due to affiliation and persistence. Yet, these are not legitimate miners who are mining ethers; rather, they are user-turned-slaves lured in by free ethers.

Fiat2Crypto and Crypto2Crypto exchange

Cryptocurrencies are not yet the financial instrument of choice for paying even the most routine purchases.

For example, to use a bitcoin wallet to buy a cup of coffee, we have to send BTC to the exchange for conversion, wait while the confirmations are processed, sell the bitcoins at a substantial loss, and then transfer the Fiat funds to our card. In some cases, the movement of our money would be the responsibility of an actual person acting as a courier. In the case of Ethereum, this is even more cumbersome.

There are many mushrooming exchange portals, but these carry a high risk. A couple of time-tested exchanges are poloniex.com and cex.io.

Estonia has adopted cryptocurrencies with open arms. The country has plans to open up a crypto bank by 2018 named Crypterium.

Figure 8.9 depicts the ICO sale for Crypterium. The crypto bank Crypterium, will be a basic DApp with the following exchange facilities:

- **Fiat2Crypto**: The DApp withdraws Fiat money from the user and stores the cryptocurrency in the user's account
- **Crypto2Crypto**: The DApp withdraws cryptocurrency from the other user's wallet and sends the cryptocurrency of the same or different variant to the user's account (for example, BTC/ETH, ETH/BTC, BCH/BTC)

- **Crypto2Fiat**: The DApp withdraws cryptocurrency from the user's wallet or account and sends the equivalent Fiat currency (USD/EUR/GBP and so on) to the user's bank account.

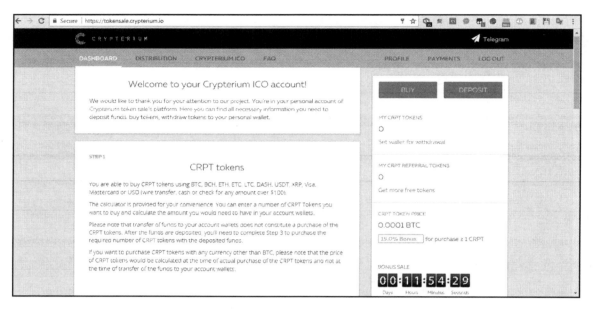

Figure 8.9: Crypterium ICO sale

Parity hack returns

In the previous chapter on solidity, we discussed the parity hack by the multi-signature wallet in the library contract. After that hack, the parity team had changed the library contract with the necessary fix. However, in doing so, they forgot to audit the other sections of the library smart contract, which had a new vulnerability.

Figure 8.10 shows the portion of the self-destruct code, which was available to outside users. A rookie developer with the alias name devops199 accessed this function and accidentally executed it. Hence, the entire library contract self-destructed and took itself off the blockchain.

The impact was realized much later when the wallets calling this library became meaningless and the tokens worth multimillion USD remained trapped forever in these dangling wallet contracts. Such hack stories make us realize the importance of peer review on any open source code and demonstrate why we should use hard wallets in place of a hot wallet.

```
// kills the contract sending everything to `_to`.
function kill(address _to) onlymanyowners(sha3(msg.data)) external {
    suicide(_to);
}
```

Figure 8.10: Suicide function of parity wallet library smart contract

Summary

We began this chapter by making a clear distinction between a token and a coin. Then, we discussed how to use the Truffle framework to develop ERC20-compliant tokens. We then explored the concept of arbitrage trading of cryptocurrencies and how to distinguish legitimate ICOs from scams and Ponzi schemes.

We spoke about the Crypterium ICO and how it can revolutionize C2C and F2C exchange. We concluded the chapter by analyzing yet another parity hack, which froze multimillion dollar ethers forever in a suicidal smart contract library.

In Chapter 9, *Enterprise Use Cases*, we will look into some enterprise usecases of Ethereum smart contracts.

9
Enterprise Use Cases

This chapter focuses on how blockchain and smart contracts have penetrated the industry. We start this chapter by introducing the concept of the Internet of Money, and explore how smart contracts have started affecting technology, society, and economics in various industries. Specifically, we will explore 18 use cases for blockchains and 12 use cases for smart contracts. We conclude this chapter by designing various modules of a command-line interface-based, decentralized, microblogging platform and deploy it over a private blockchain.

After studying this chapter, you will be able to:

- Appreciate the concept of the Internet of Money
- Know about various use cases for smart contracts and blockchains
- Understand the building blocks of a microblogging DApp
- Explore the security and administrative properties of a DApp

"What you seek is seeking you"
- Rumi

Before we start this chapter, I want you to take a step back and ponder on the preceding quote, which was said by the famous 13th-century, Persian, Sunni Muslim poet, Jalal ad-Din Muhammad Rumi. This notoriously simple six-word quote carries a mystic yet deep philosophy within it.

For instance, if you are seeking a life partner, there is someone out there in this world who is seeking a person exactly like you.

Let us take one of the simplest technical examples now. We all search on the web, right? We normally Google it (never heard anyone say, let's Bing it, or let's duck duck go it, though that is perfectly normal), and that too, is free. But in this web economy, when we are getting something for free, we must understand that we are a product. You might ask, for whom? The advertisers, the market researchers, the product designers—for them, we are the product. The links we click, the products we view, the transactions we make, the quotes we like, the songs we hear—literally every action we make on the web is being recorded. Even the tiniest message we type in our favorite chat apps to send to our friends, and then delete to send a more formal one, that too gets recorded. These are sold to companies, data giants, and product makers who get a glimpse of our truly private psychology. They use our psychology as a product to create products or ads for those products, which we will eventually click and generate revenue for the search engine companies. So, the more we seek on the web, the more it seeks us.

For a privacy-sensitive human being, this is certainly alarming. An obvious question will arise in our mind, *"Why would my individuality profit someone else other than me?"* Of course, we are taking a service from a platform, but that does not have to be at the expense of our individuality or privacy. This is the very idea that planted the seed of decentralization and decentralized applications, where our individuality is our responsibility and no middleman/machine should profit from it without our explicit permission.

Seeking love and knowledge is fine, but we have a bigger monster within us to feed. It is the hunger to be recognized, to be respected in society, to be someone in power, and in control of the internal workings of the society we live in. And somehow, it has transpired, through generations of human civilization, that seeking and earning money brings us this recognition. Although the other two, knowledge and love, can accumulate and provide much more recognition, most ordinary mortals feel that money can bring us fame in our own lifetime. And so our symbiosis with the banks began, because somehow it made us believe that our money is safe with them and can grow if we keep it there for a long time. Then came the stock markets, a type of legalized and regulated gambling, which can sometimes multiple our money, provided we are willing to risk it all. Then came the derivatives, the bonds, the futures, and the regulations and compliances; the financial police who would guard us from going astray with so many lucrative, yet risky, offers.

But on the ill-fated day of September 15, 2008, when a 150-year-old investment bank named Lehman Brothers filed for bankruptcy, the entire world realized that banks are not as safe as they claim to be. However, people still needed money, and banks had to stay. On January 3, 2009, an anonymous entity, Satoshi Nakamoto, introduced the concept of bitcoin, which started a power struggle between common people and the so-called regulated institution of finance.

These financial institutions first thought that if they just ignored this revolution, this crypto-economy would soon die a natural death. Like a tortoise retreating back into its shell, the financial world started to ignore this on-going revolution. But cryptocurrency, over the last eight years, has grown. The blockchain technology has not only brought money to the internet, but the introduction of smart contracts has made money programmable.

Our seeking of money has brought us to a new paradigm, the Internet of Money. Here, money is not just a medium of exchange but also a medium of expression. In the previous chapter, we discussed ICOs, which were basically human ideas converted into cryptocurrency tokens. We are at a juncture of technology where money is seeking us. It is seeking us by transforming our ideas into tokens that people can buy. If our idea triumphs, so do our tokens.

This newfound freedom in the Internet of Money, without any widely accepted framework or guidelines, has resulted in a very volatile situation in the tech industry. Programmable money is not equivalent to some new web app or software. The very concept of immutability on a blockchain makes the design of the Internet of Money a nightmare for enterprise architects. They can no longer think as data scientists or software developers. They must think more like firmware developers or construction workers. It is like making a customized home for a living. We can propose whatever changes we want during the floor planning, but once it is approved and the home is built, it is extremely difficult to modify a room without making changes to the original floor plan.

Again, if the original floor plan has some weak points and vulnerable blind spots, a burglar can barge in and steal all the valuables, as we saw in the Ethereum hacks of DAO and Parity. For this technology, we need to take a step backward and encourage monolith architectures, rather than modular ones, as the former are compact and less vulnerable to hacks:

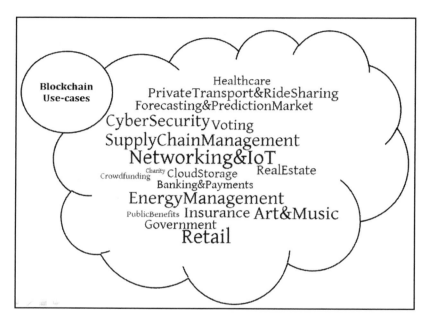

Figure 9.1: Blockchain use cases

Banking and payments

The blockchain is going to disrupt the banking industry the way the World Wide Web did the media industry. It is destroying regulations and compliances arising due to borders, as cryptocurrencies such as bitcoin and Ethereum are making cross border transactions in seconds, with substantially lower transfer fees. This is connecting the investors of developed countries to the innovators of developing countries. Banks such as Barclays are implementing blockchains to strengthen their operational capabilities. Banks are also seed-funding and investing in blockchain-based start-ups.

Insurance

The global market of insurance is based on trust. A blockchain is a new way of managing trust. It can be used to verify the insured person's identity, as well as interact with real-time data using frameworks such as oraclize to make amendments on the sum assured during payouts. Smart contracts for automobile and crop insurance can be powerful in determining a payout, without any significant human intervention.

Fizzy.axa is an Ethereum-based insurance product launched by the French insurance giant, AXA. These are smart contracts that self-trigger payouts for flight delays lasting more than two hours.

Supply chain management

By documenting cost, labor, waste, and emission monitoring on a blockchain at every supply chain point, management can be disrupted. We can even track the source of a product to ensure the entire supply chain is conflict free and adheres to fair-trade policies. Blockchains can also be used to check the quantum effects a product has on the environment, by recording its ecological and carbon footprints in a continuous manner.

Tech giant Microsoft has teamed up with Mojix, a **radio frequency identification (RFID)** start-up company, to develop product identification and track from the origin to delivery, using an Ethereum blockchain called project manifest. The primary research is done by a team of professors and students from Auburn University's RFID lab.

Forecasting and prediction market

Blockchain is about to revolutionize the prediction industry. We can place bets using smart contracts and the winning amount will be automatically transferred to our account. Any challenging event such as election results, superbowl match results, and world cup finalist predictions can be converted into an automated yet legalized game of gambling.

App.Augur.net is an Ethereum-based prediction market platform where we can place bets and do money trading in terms of ether. It is completely decentralized.

Charity

Corruption due to middlemen and the inefficiency of escrows is a common problem in the charity space. These issues prevent money from reaching those who actually need it. Blockchain is disrupting the charity space by providing donation tracking features, which makes sure our money is reaching the right person.

In the Ethereum space, `giveth.io` has introduced a concept called liquid pledging, which is basically a smart contract that can transfer ether funds directly, or pledge to transfer funds through an automated delegate, to a person, with transparent tracking on the distributed ledger. Whenever the funds are moved, the donor is notified and can veto any action.

It also provides a platform to develop decentralized altruistic communities, which can allocate funds to campaigns and track the donations as they deliver on predefined goals.

Their source code and development status can be tracked at the following GitHub link: `https://github.com/Giveth`.

Public benefits

The blockchain is a good framework to allocate social welfare funds in a transparent manner. Pensions, army benefits, scholarships, and unemployment benefits can be distributed without suffering slowness, corruption, and bureaucracy.

GovCoin Systems Limited has partnered with Barclays and University College London to develop a social welfare distribution system using blockchain and smart contracts, which will be trialed by the Department for Work and Pensions of the UK government.

Energy management

Energy grids and utility industries are highly centralized. To buy gas, fuel, and electricity, we have to go through public grids or authorized private corporations. Even the producers have to go through highly regulated channels to sell basic utilities. The blockchain can disrupt this monopoly as well, by bringing peer-to-peer utility share frameworks.

RWE, a German power company, has partnered with Ethereum-based blockchain start-up, Slock.it, to develop decentralized car charging stations for electric cars.

Art and music

Illegal art auctions and music piracy has always been a challenge to the entertainment industry. Coupled with manager and record company commissions, a serious percentage of money has been stolen from artists. The blockchain provides a transparent system of direct payment to the artist from the consumer, and the use of unique signatures to store the identity of an art piece.

Maecenas is an open blockchain platform for accessing and auctioning fine art in a decentralized manner. Mycelia is an online music platform that pays artists directly from consumers.

Retail

When we buy our monthly consumables from Spencers or a food bazaar, we trust the retail system to pay the actual producer of the goods. The blockchain can connect the producer with the consumers without the middle entities. This can lead to a sharp drop in the retail price.

`https://www.openbazaar.org/` is a bitcoin, blockchain-based, online, peer-to-peer store that allows everyone to set up their eShop and sell their product without any middle-entity commission. The platform accepts transactions in bitcoins.

Real estate

Buying and selling real estate can involve a lack of transparency, bureaucracy, mistakes in public records, and fraud. The blockchain can reduce paper-based record keeping and speed up transactions.

Smart contracts can help to automate tracking, transferring property deeds, verifying ownership, and ensuring document accuracy.

The state government of Andhra Pradesh, India, has partnered with a Swedish start-up, ChromaWay, to build a blockchain-based solution for land registry. It is estimated that $700 million is paid in the form of bribes to land registrars across India.

Cyber security

Cyber security and the blockchain have a symbiotic relationship. Both need each other to grow and disrupt each other. The basic foundation of the blockchain is based on a cryptographic hash function, and as the blockchain is in a nascent stage, cyber security is of prime importance.

Quantum computing is a real threat to modern asymmetric cryptography. Iota.org is a next-generation, graph-based, distributed ledger technology that claims to overcome this quantum threat and enhance the security of DLTs.

Crowdfunding

The blockchain has leveraged crowdfunding to a whole new level, by introducing the concept of initial coin offering. As we discussed in the introduction and previous chapter, we have a long way to go before we have a consensus regulated ICO framework with proper audits. Currently, the ICO arena can be considered a "wild-wild-west" situation for crypto-equity tokens.

Networking and the Internet of Things

Blockchains can enable communication and micro payments between machines, without human intervention. The economy of machines is an emerging field that will prove crucial in steering innovation in automation.

Project Oaken is an award-winning, Ethereum-based, smart contract project that uses the IoT to pay automated tolls to tolling booths for self-drive and manual cars. The prototype was tested successfully using Tesla, resulting in a $100K win at the Dubai Blockchain Hackathon. Currently, Oaken Innovations have teamed up with Toyota research and MIT Media Labs to research such prototypes for an autonomous drive future.

Voting

"It is enough that the people know there was an election. The people who cast the votes decide nothing. The people who count the votes decide everything."

- Joseph Stalin

Data scientist might be the sexiest job according to the Harvard Business Review, but it miserably failed to predict the 2016 US general election. Rigging of the voting system might be a conspiracy theory to divert from the major data science failure, but cannot be entirely ruled out. Blockchain technology can work wonders for such democratic processes due to its immutable property.

`https://www.democracy.earth/` and `https://followmyvote.com/` are blockchain-based voting apps that are funded by venture capitalist firms. They also have plans and road maps to incorporate smart contracts in the near future.

Government

Government systems are often prone to corruption, slow, and not transparent. Implementing blockchain-based systems can significantly increase security, transparency, and efficiency by reducing bureaucratic overheads of government operations.

Estonia is planning to open crypto-banks. Dubai is aiming to upload government documents on the blockchain by 2020.

Private transport and ride sharing

It is a fact that Uber and Ola have disrupted the taxi and public transportation industry. The blockchain can take this a notch higher by providing a decentralization and peer-to-peer sharing paradigm. This will help the driver community to earn more without the unnecessary middlemen commission.

Oaken Innovations and MIT Media Labs has tied up with Toyota for yet another project on toll-fee collection for developing a peer-to-peer ride sharing DApp. `Lazooz.org`, based in Tel-Aviv, Israel, has launched a decentralized, community-owned transportation system with ride-sharing facilities.

Cloud storage

The blockchain allows cloud storage to be encrypted and highly distributed, making it more robust against attacks. Data on a centralized server is vulnerable to data loss, hacks, and human error.

Storj.io is an encrypted cloud storage network using blockchain. But the pricing of the storage and retrieval is still a challenge. Swarm and IPFS also have the potential to evolve into a mature cloud storage with the fee structure at a minimum.

Healthcare

Technologies such as the blockchain can be a boon to the health record industry, for tamper-proof personal health records, which relies a lot on government authorities and legacy storage systems. It can empower the general public to fight against meaningless politics. Ledgers are open to the public with anonymized patient data, right from admission to discharge. No modification is possible. No tampering allowed.

MedRec is one such project incubated within MIT Media Labs that has developed a medical record-keeping prototype on an Ethereum-based, private blockchain. This decentralized application can connect the patient record along with external data sources, like Fitbit (real-time physical activity tracking app using IoT) and 23andMe (DNA tree determining app from saliva samples). MedRec also allows patients to securely grant access to different doctors as well as healthcare providers, researchers, and even the patient's children and grandchildren to their personal health information.

Smart contract use cases

In this section, we will be discussing how smart contracts as a technology can disrupt every aspect of society and its economy.

Figure 9.2 depicts 12 use cases for smart contracts:

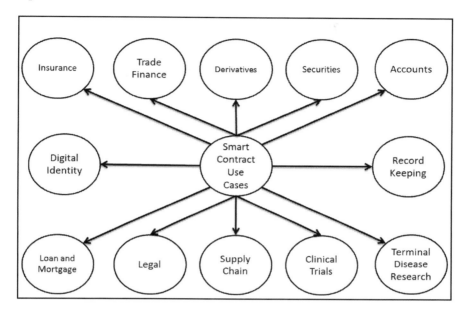

Figure 9.2: Smart contract use cases

Insurance

Most of the insurance processes are disjointed by nature with many human interventions. Smart contracts along with the IoT can make self-aware decisions for automated insurance payouts.

It increases savings by reducing duplicated work in verifying reports and policies.

Trade finance

Smart contracts facilitate faster letters of credit and payment initiations, leading to streamlined international transfers. This increases the liquidity of assets, improves efficiency in creating contract agreements, and promotes faster approval of payments.

Derivatives

Smart contracts eliminate duplicate processes during a trading life cycle by streamlining post-trade processes. It supports real-time valuation of promotions, automated external event processing, and automated settlement of obligations while processing triggered trade events.

Securities

Smart contracts can facilitate automated dividend payouts, stock splits, and management of liabilities.

It also reduces operational risk by circumventing intermediaries and managing capitalization.

It provides a digitized transparent and traceable end-to-end workflow due to securities on a distributed ledger.

Accounts

Decentralized financial record-keeping using smart contracts improves transparency and data integrity, which leads to market stability. Insight into the capital amount gets improved owing to increased accessibility to financial data.

Digital identity

Smart contracts can enable individuals to control and own their digital identity. Every individual can then choose which personal data they would expose to third parties as KYC information.

This will lead to lower data leakage by counterparties and increase compliance and interoperability.

Record-keeping

Automated compliance, auto renewal, auto release, and automated commercial code filing are some of the major advantages of a smart contract.

This in turn reduces legal bills, tracks loans and collateral values, and archives automatically.

Loans and mortgages

A mortgage is currently a very confusing and manual process. Smart contracts can automate this by connecting different parties involved in mortgage transaction, enabling a less error-prone process.

It increases the visibility of the service records and automates the release of control from mortgaged property when it is paid off.

Legal

Legal services such as property transfer can be made fraud free and seamless using smart contracts. The transactions are efficient and transparent. The audit and assurance costs are also reduced.

Supply chain

Smart contracts simplify complex multi-party delivery systems and achieve granularity on product tracking; traceability and verification get enhanced and reduce fraud and theft. Oracles play an important role in the supply chain to provide external data to smart contracts.

Clinical trials

Smart contracts increase cross-institutional visibility, defying geographical borders, which can immensely benefit clinical trials. It enables consent tracking of patient data, increases data privacy, streamlines trials, and processes setups by enhancing reproducibility of trial results by independent groups of researchers.

Terminal disease research

Terminal diseases such as cancer have their share of research challenges through collaboration due to data privacy concerns and misaligned incentives. Smart contracts can unleash the power of data by providing efficient data sharing across many sectors yet preserve patient privacy. It also helps in real-time visibility and policy enforcement, while maintaining regulatory requirements and patient consent.

Decentralized microblogging

In this section, we are going to explore the design of a basic Ethereum-based microblogging platform. Using these platforms, new users can register to get a personal microblogging account, which they can you to send anonymous tweets to a decentralized Ethereum-based private blockchain, with comments disabled by default.

But why do we need a decentralized blockchain for tweeting, and more importantly why are the users anonymous? To answer this question we need to understand the administrative and security constraints of a normal centralized microblogging platform, which we discuss in the next section.

Administrative and security constraints

Popular microblogging platforms such as Twitter, Tumblr, and Weibo (the Chinese variant of microblog, dominated by Sina and Tencent) are basically centralized social network services that are prone to problems.

The problems are mainly in two separate dimensions. One is technical, another one is social. In the technical dimension, the rapid popularity of such services results in an increasing cost of infrastructure management. This gives rise to many administrative problems while doing scalability deployments in production.

For example, recently, US President Trump's Twitter handle @POTUS auto-blocked many followers due to a technical glitch. Such glitches can be quite severe as automated trade-bots constantly monitor tweet sentiments and decide various stock prices on the worldwide stock exchanges, which can lead to multibillion dollar wipe-outs from the market capitalization in the blink of an eye.

In the social dimension, we see a growth of trolls and online abuse to legitimate microblogging accounts. There have been instances where people have lost their employment, politicians had to resign, celebrities were fined because of their own race, gender, or religion.

Even in our lives, we feel quite a pressure to microblog in the open, if our immediate supervisor or people from human resource are following our microblogging handles. So, in the social dimension, individual freedom and security becomes a big issue.

A decentralized, microblogging platform can prevent problems in both technical and social dimensions, by providing a decentralized platform and anonymity respectively. However, it is important to note that anonymity is a choice rather than a mandate while using decentralized technologies like a blockchain. In simple terms, using a blockchain does not make us anonymous automatically; rather, it is an add-on feature that needs to be separately implemented on top of a blockchain.

The idea of this decentralized platform under discussion was originally conceived by a software developer named **Jahn Bertsch**. The entire functional logic was implemented in the Solidity programming language. It has two main smart contracts. An account related smart contract (`TwtAccount.sol`) and a user-registration related smart contract (`TwtRegistry.sol`). When these two smart contracts are deployed on the private blockchain, they interact with each other to form a command-line interface-based, decentralized, microblogging platform.

In the subsequent sections, we will dive into the individual Solidity file, set up the service on the private blockchain, and check how these smart contracts perform in CLI and remix browser mode.

TwtAccount.sol

This solidity file models a single Twitter account on a blockchain. *Figure 9.3* summarizes the important functions present in this tweeter account contract:

```
contract TwtAccount{

    function TwtAccount()

    function getOwnerAddress()constant returns(address adminAddress)
    function adminDeleteAccount()
    function adminRetrieveDonations(address receiver)

    function getLatestTweet()constant
    returns(string tweetString,uint256 timestamp,uint256 numberOfTweets)

    function isAdmin()constant returns(bool isAdmin)

    function getTweet(uint256 tweetId)constant
    returns(string tweetString,uint256 timestamp)

    function getNumberOfTweets()constant returns(uint256 numberOfTweets)
    function tweet(string tweetString)constant returns(int256 result)
}
```

Figure 9.3: TwtAccount contract summary

Now, let us understand explicitly what each function in this smart contract does. *Figure 9.4* denotes the start of the account contract where `TwtAccount()` is a constructor function. Tweet denotes the data structure of a single tweet. The mapping denotes an array of all tweets to a particular tweet, account, which helps in retrieving each tweet by their `tweetID`. The other two variables denote the owner of the account and the total count of tweets by the particular owner:

```
pragma solidity ^0.4.0;
contract TwtAccount {

    struct Tweet {
        uint timestamp;
        string tweetString;
    }
    mapping (uint => Tweet) _tweets;
    uint _numberOfTweets;
    address _adminAddress;

    function TwtAccount() {
        _numberOfTweets = 0;
        _adminAddress = msg.sender;
    }
```

Figure 9.4: Struct and constructor function

Figure 9.5 denotes the function `isAdmin()`, which checks whether a tweeter is the real owner of the tweeter account or not. The function returns a true or false:

```
function isAdmin() constant returns (bool isAdmin) {
    return msg.sender == _adminAddress;
}
```

Figure 9.5: Account owner-check function

Figure 9.6 depicts the main tweet function, which allows a legitimate tweeter account owner to create a new tweet within 160 characters, if the tweets are greater than 160 characters they are rejected by this function:

```
function tweet(string tweetString) returns (int result) {
    if (!isAdmin()) {
        // only owner is allowed to create tweets for this account
        result = -1;
    } else if (bytes(tweetString).length > 160) {
        // tweet contains more than 160 bytes
        result = -2;
    } else {
        _tweets[_numberOfTweets].timestamp = now;
        _tweets[_numberOfTweets].tweetString = tweetString;
        _numberOfTweets++;
        result = 0; // success
    }
}
```

Figure 9.6: tweet() function

Figure 9.7 denotes two important functions, `getTweet()` and `getLatestTweet()`. The first one retrieves the actual tweet message along with the time of the post using the `tweetID`. The second function retrieves the details of the last tweet message posted by the account owner:

```
function getTweet(uint tweetId) constant returns (string tweetString, uint timestamp) {
    // returns two values
    tweetString = _tweets[tweetId].tweetString;
    timestamp = _tweets[tweetId].timestamp;
}

function getLatestTweet() constant returns (string tweetString, uint timestamp, uint numberOfTweets)
{
    // returns three values
    tweetString = _tweets[_numberOfTweets - 1].tweetString;
    timestamp = _tweets[_numberOfTweets - 1].timestamp;
    numberOfTweets = _numberOfTweets;
}
```

Figure 9.7: Important tweet retrieval functions

The following *Figure 9.8* summarizes the remaining functions of the account contract. `getNumberofTweets()` returns the count of tweets by the account owner. `getOwnerAddress()` returns the account owner's blockchain address. The function `adminRetrieveDonations()` can be further developed to allow the account owner to retrieve any donations they have received from other users. So, this contract can then behave as a donation wallet that can tweet messages. We have muted this functionality to keep the contract simple. The function `adminDeleteAccount()` kills his tweeter account and retrieves all donations received:

```
function getNumberOfTweets() constant returns (uint numberOfTweets) {
    return _numberOfTweets;
}

function getOwnerAddress() constant returns (address adminAddress) {
    return _adminAddress;
}

function adminRetrieveDonations(address receiver) {
    if (isAdmin()) {
        receiver.transfer(this.balance);
    }
}
        function adminDeleteAccount() {
            if (isAdmin()) {
            selfdestruct(_adminAddress);
            }
```

Figure 9.8: Miscellaneous functions

But to have a new tweeter account, we need user registration. This action is achieved by the TwtRegistry smart contract that is described in the next section.

TwtRegistry.sol

This contract is used to register a new user with a tweeter account. *Figure 9.9* summarizes the functions available in this registry contract:

```
contract TwtRegistry{
  function TwtRegistry()
  function adminUnregister(string name)
  function register(string name,address accountAddress)returns(int256 result)
  function getNumberOfAccounts()constant returns(uint256 numberOfAccounts)
  function adminRetrieveDonations()
  function getAddressOfName(string name)constant returns(address addr)
  function adminDeleteRegistry()
  function adminSetAccountAdministrator(address accountAdmin)
  function adminSetRegistrationDisabled(bool registrationDisabled)
  function getNameOfAddress(address addr)constant returns(string name)
  function unregister()returns(string unregisteredAccountName)
  function getAddressOfId(uint256 id)constant returns(address addr)
}
```

Figure 9.9: TwtRegistry contract summary

Similar to an account contract, `TwtRegistry()` is a constructor function, and different variables and mappings have been used to see the number of users, force them to use a newer version of registration updates, and administrate accounts using bool `_registrationDisabled` as shown in *Figure 9.10*:

```solidity
pragma solidity ^0.4.0;
contract TwtRegistry {

    mapping (address => string) _addressToAccountName;
    mapping (uint => address) _accountIdToAccountAddress;
    mapping (string => address) _accountNameToAddress;

    uint _numberOfAccounts;
    address _registryAdmin;
    address _accountAdmin;
    bool _registrationDisabled;

    function TwtRegistry() {
        _registryAdmin = msg.sender;
        _accountAdmin = msg.sender;
        _numberOfAccounts = 0;
        _registrationDisabled = false;
    }
```

Figure 9.10: Constructor, variables, and mapping

The `register()` function, as shown in *Figure 9.11*, is used to create new unique user accounts. The admin can force users to use the upgraded version of registration if available:

```solidity
function register(string name, address accountAddress) returns
(int result)
{
    if (_accountNameToAddress[name] != address(0)) {
        // name already taken
        result = -1;
    } else if (bytes(_addressToAccountName[accountAddress]).length != 0) {
        // account address is already registered
        result = -2;
    } else if (bytes(name).length >= 64) {
        // name too long
        result = -3;
    } else if (_registrationDisabled){
        // registry is disabled because a newer version is available
        result = -4;
    } else {
        _addressToAccountName[accountAddress] = name;
        _accountNameToAddress[name] = accountAddress;
        _accountIdToAccountAddress[_numberOfAccounts] = accountAddress;
        _numberOfAccounts++;
        result = 0; // success
    }
}
```

Figure 9.11: register() function definition

Different account related information can be retrieved using the self-explanatory functions shown in *Figure 9.12*:

```
function getNumberOfAccounts() constant returns (uint numberOfAccounts) {
    numberOfAccounts = _numberOfAccounts;
}

function getAddressOfName(string name) constant returns (address addr) {
    addr = _accountNameToAddress[name];
}

function getNameOfAddress(address addr) constant returns (string name) {
    name = _addressToAccountName[addr];
}

function getAddressOfId(uint id) constant returns (address addr) {
    addr = _accountIdToAccountAddress[id];
}
```

Figure 9.12: Account related functions

Registration and deregistration of accounts can be done using the following functions shown in *Figure 9.13*. The address, once registered, is not removed on purpose, to maintain the history on the blockchain. The deregistration removes the user but keeps the address intact in an unused state:

```
function unregister() returns (string unregisteredAccountName) {
    unregisteredAccountName = _addressToAccountName[msg.sender];
    _addressToAccountName[msg.sender] = "";
    _accountNameToAddress[unregisteredAccountName] = address(0);
    // _accountIdToAccountAddress is never deleted on purpose
}

function adminUnregister(string name) {
    if (msg.sender == _registryAdmin || msg.sender == _accountAdmin) {
        address addr = _accountNameToAddress[name];
        _addressToAccountName[addr] = "";
        _accountNameToAddress[name] = address(0);
        // _accountIdToAccountAddress is never deleted on purpose
    }
}

function adminSetRegistrationDisabled(bool registrationDisabled) {
    // currently, the code of the registry can not be updated once it is
    // deployed. if a newer version of the registry is available, account
    // registration can be disabled
    if (msg.sender == _registryAdmin) {
        _registrationDisabled = registrationDisabled;
    }
}
```

Figure 9.13: Registration related functions

Lastly, we have the miscellaneous functions similar to those discussed in the accounts smart contracts, as shown in *Figure 9.14*:

```
function adminSetAccountAdministrator(address accountAdmin) {
    if (msg.sender == _registryAdmin) {
        _accountAdmin = accountAdmin;
    }
}

function adminRetrieveDonations() {
    if (msg.sender == _registryAdmin) {
        _registryAdmin.transfer(this.balance);
    }
}

function adminDeleteRegistry() {
    if (msg.sender == _registryAdmin) {
        selfdestruct(_registryAdmin);

    }
}
```

Figure 9.14: Misc functions of TwtRegistry contract

Service setup on the private blockchain

Setting up the tweet service on our private blockchain is quite simple. First we need to initiate our **inter protocol communication (IPC)** using the geth command line inside our project folder, as discussed in Chapter 3, *Hello World of Smart Contracts*.

```
$ geth –datadir=./chaindata/
```

Then we open the Mist browser and go to the new contract option. *Figure 9.15* denotes an smart contract account deployment on our private blockchain:

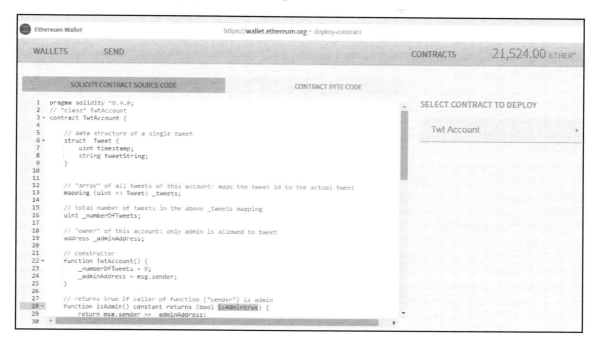

Figure 9.15: Compiling TwtAccount in Mist

We compile the registry smart contract in a similar fashion as shown in *Figure 9.16*. Before clicking the deploy button, we need to start the private miner in the geth command line, using the $ `miner.start(1)` command. We can stop the miner, using the $ `miner.stop(0)` command:

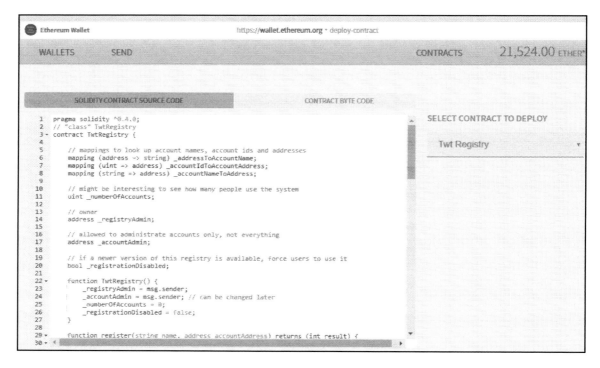

Figure 9.16: Compiling TwtRegistry in Mist

To deploy these contracts, we need to denote the gas amount and give the passcode, `new123456`, as done in `Chapter 3`, *Hello World of Smart Contracts*. Then these contracts are set up in the private blockchain post-miner confirmation, as shown in *Figure 9.17*:

Figure 9.17: Tweet contracts getting mined

Please note, we need to upgrade the Mist browser to `0.9.2` or higher, or else the source code will not compile, owing to certain bugs in the older compiler. Also, there is an ongoing bug in this compiler, which shadows existing overridden declarations. A work-around is not to use the same name for a function and variable. Here, we have used the variable name, `isAdminTrue` in place of `isAdmin`.

Reading tweets

By post-mining the smart contracts, the functions can be used from smart contract accounts to read the tweets posted by users on the private blockchain. Here, we are showing a different variant by using the remix browser in *Figure 9.18*. We deploy three tweets on the blockchain as a test:

Tweet0: "Hello Blockchain."

Tweet1: "Hello Ethereum."

Tweet2: "This is a junk tweet which contains spurious characters in order to exceed the 160 character limit which is being used as a negative test case and check the correctness of the smart contract operation."

We can see in *Figure 9.18* the number of tweets returns only two because the third tweet gets rejected:

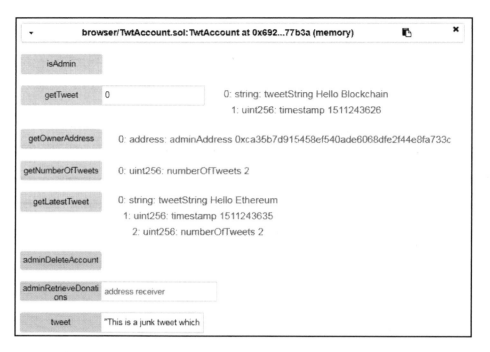

Figure 9.18: Tweeter smart contract testing using remix browser

Summary

We began this chapter by understanding the concept behind the Internet of Money. We saw how programmable money is like building a concrete house that requires a lot of prior planning. Then we discussed various use cases of smart contracts and the blockchain. We listed almost every aspect of society and the economy that has a chance of getting disrupted by this revolutionary technology. We concluded this chapter by designing a decentralized microblogging application and deployed it into our private blockchain.

In Chapter 10, *BaaS and the Dark Web Market*, we will discuss certain enterprise-level frameworks that are using Ethereum blockchain to set up a development platform. We also have a glimpse of the dark web marketplace and how to explore it safely.

10
BaaS and the Dark Web Market

This chapter introduces you to various platforms specific to smart contract and blockchain development. We will begin with a discussion about private, consortium, and public blockchains on the permission spectrum. Then we will dive into the concept of **blockchain-as-a-service** (**BaaS**) and introduce enterprise platforms, such as Hyperledger, Azure, and AWS. We conclude this chapter by exploring the mysterious dark web marketplaces with notes on money laundering.

After studying this chapter, you will be able to:

- Identify different types of blockchain
- Understand the concept of blockchain-as-a-service
- Understand Hyperledger, Azure, and AWS
- Explore the dark web marketplaces

Playful privacy

You might have noticed that throughout the previous chapters, all of the examples were coded over a private blockchain, which we created using a genesis block in `Chapter 3`, *Hello World of Smart Contracts*. This was done because private blockchains are what industries prefer; apart from making things much easier to play around with, there is no need to wait for blocks or spend real money. Cryptocurrency such as ETH and ETC are on top of the Ethereum blockchain, which are completely different chain-types compared to our private chain. Confused?

Let us look into the different types of blockchains to understand this classification.

Types of blockchain

Before we dive into the types of blockchain, we must get familiar with the concept of the permission spectrum of distributed ledger technology aka DLT. A blockchain is a DLT and exists throughout the permission spectrum.

To understand the permission spectrum, we need to identify the two extreme ends of this spectrum. At one end, we have to seek complete permission from an entity to participate in a consensus, and at the other extreme, we do not have to seek any permissions whatsoever from any entity to participate in a consensus.

The interesting thing about the permissionless extreme is that we have no obligation to reveal our identity to anyone participating in the consensus. As we move toward complete permission, somewhere in the mid-spectrum of permission, this identity aspect needs to be revealed in order to participate in a consensus, just to validate our stakes in a consensus. As we arrive at the complete permission, we need to identify ourselves as well as take permission from an authority to participate in a consensus.

This very ideology of any entity or authority for seeking permission endangers the ideas of decentralization and is a topic of serious and often heated debate in the blockchain community and traditional enterprise.

Coming back to DLT, a blockchain is called a permissioned blockchain if:

- It restricts the participants who can contribute to the consensus of the system state
- Only a restricted set of identified users have rights to validate the block transactions
- An authority can restrict access to approved actors who can create smart contracts
- Permission is required from an authority to send/receive transactions

A permissioned blockchain ends up using consensus algorithms such as RAFT or Paxos (refer to `Chapter 1`, *Blockchain Basics*) because all of its participants have their identities revealed. The effort spent to verify blocks is not rewarded by the system and participants end up charging the end users for this by behaving as intermediaries.

Enterprise-level financial institutions love this concept of a permissioned blockchain because they can enjoy the borderless transaction facility that bitcoin or other cryptocurrencies provide, but within their private high-speed network comes fine-grained access control, privacy within the approved group of participating institutions, and scalability on their intranet.

Permissionless blockchains, on the other hand, are those in which:

- Anyone can join the network
- Anyone can participate in the process of block verification
- Anyone can create a smart contract

Ethereum and the bitcoin blockchain are great examples of a permissionless blockchains. The block verification process is similar to mining and is highly incentivized by the system. These blockchains use consensus algorithms such as PoW and may be PoS in the near future, where the participants might have to reveal their ownership to claim their stake. But participation essentially remains permissionless and irrespective of ownership revelation.

Figure 10.1 summarizes the key characteristics that differentiate the two extremes of the permission spectrum:

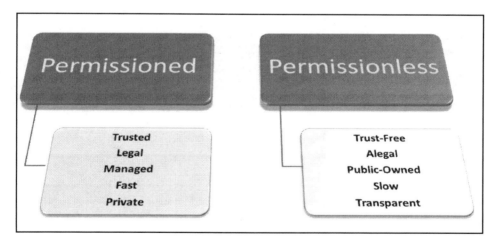

Figure 10.1: Permissioned versus permissionless

Bitcoin and Ethereum blockchains are hardened blockchain platforms. They have stood the test of time even after many hacks and occasional market crashes. Andreas Antonopoulos wrote the following about bitcoin, which is almost entirely applicable for Ethereum:

> *".....is a sewer rat. It's missing a leg. Its snout was badly mangled in an accident in the last year. It's not allergic to anything. In fact, it's probably got a couple of strains of bubonic plague on it which it treats like a common cold. You have a system that is antifragile and dynamic and robust.*
> *Let's take it, cut off its beard, take away its piercings, put it in a suit, call it blockchain, and present it to the board. It's safe. It's got borders. We can apply the same regulations. We can put barriers to entry and create an anti-competitive environment to control who has access. It will be more efficient than our existing banking system."*

At this point, we can introduce the three broad types of blockchain, namely public, private, and consortium. The consortium blockchains are sometimes referred to as federated blockchains. *Figure 10.2* illustrates these three types along the permission spectrum:

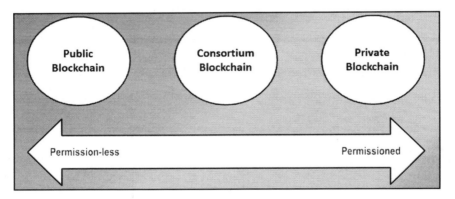

Figure 10.2: Types of blockchain on permission spectrum

Private blockchains

Private blockchains take advantage of blockchain technology by setting up private groups that can verify transactions internally. Write permissions are centralized, like traditional database management systems. Read permissions may be restricted or public to a certain extent. These blockchains have their niche use cases because of their scalability, compliance to data privacy rules, and other regulatory guidelines. Such blockchains can reduce cost but are not disruptive. MONAX and multichain are prominent players in the private blockchain space.

Public blockchains

Public blockchains are based on state-of-the-art consensus algorithms, are open source, permissionless, and provide incentives to transaction validating effort:

- Anyone can start running a public node by downloading the free code on their local device
- Anyone can participate in the consensus by validating transactions in the network, thus determining what block gets added to the chain along with the current state
- Anyone in the world can do valid transactions and reflect them on a blockchain

Using a public block explorer, anyone can read transactions, making it transparent yet pseudonymous. Bitcoin, namecoin, Ethereum, bitcoin cash, Ethereum classic, and litecoin are just few of the hundreds of examples of public blockchain protocols.

Consortium blockchains

Consortium blockchains operate within a group of stakeholders. Unlike public blockchains, they don't allow any random person with access to to the internet to participate in the process of transaction verification. Consortium blockchains are highly scalable and provide transaction privacy. These blockchains are mostly used in the banking and corporate sector, where various banks form a consortium to interact in their own intra-network to replace legacy systems, reduce transaction costs and data redundancies, and simplify document handling using smart compliance mechanisms.

Bankchain is a consortium that has come together for building and exploring blockchain solutions. The member list can be retrieved from the following link where it is listed in a chronological manner: http://www.bankchain.org.in/members.php.

Some prominent names in these lists include State Bank of India, Deutsche Bank, Dubai Islamic bank, and even tech corporations such as Intel. This consortium has tied up a blockchain start-up called Primechain Technologies to roll out various beta version DApps by the end of 2017. One of the DApps is Primechain-KYC, which is a smart contract-based solution deployed on a permissioned consortium blockchain to share **Know-Your-Customer (KYC)**, **Anti-Money-Laundering (AML)**, and **Countering the Financing of Terrorism (CFT)** data.

Primechain Technologies has, in turn, partnered with Microsoft to provide a blockchain-as-a-service model to the consortium members using the Azure developmental platform. Other prominent consortium blockchains are R3 (Banking), EWF (Energy), B3i (Insurance), and Corda(legal).

In the following sections, we will try to understand what blockchain-as-a-service implies, and how various enterprises are providing different platforms for this BaaS model.

Blockchain-as-a-service

There is a diverse landscape of solutions and approaches to implement a blockchain. *Figure 10.3* represents a broad classification of such approaches. Blockchain-as-a-service is an industry practice that merges the *development platform approach* with the *IT services approach* to provide tangible blockchain-based solutions to clients:

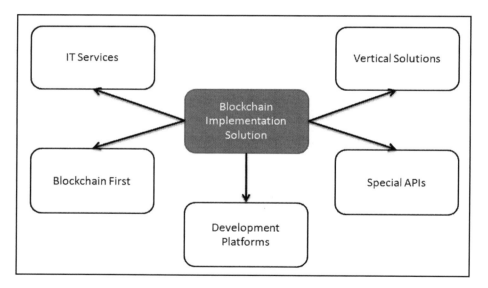

Figure 10.3: Blockchain implementation solution

We have seen in the previous chapters that we need several software components, such as geth, node.js, and Java runtime environments along with programming tools, such as, Solidity and web.js, on top of an operating system to develop a complete end-to-end, blockchain-based, decentralized application from scratch.

This is fine for making a new and highly customized product to a certain extent, but to implement a repeatable and scalable service, coding from scratch is equivalent to reinventing the wheel.

The big players in the cloud computing industry, such as IBM (Bluemix), Microsoft (Azure), and Amazon (AWS), have realized this gap and have come up with this BaaS model. They have seen the potential benefits of offering blockchain services in the cloud, where clients and users benefit from avoiding the overhead of hardware investment, as well as the problem of configuring and setting up a working blockchain network.

Using BaaS, developers have access to single-click, drag-and-drop, cloud-based blockchain environments, that allow for rapid prototyping and deployment of DApps and smart contracts.

Enterprise platforms for BaaS

In this section, we will introduce a few enterprise platforms with BaaS offerings using three pointers. All these platforms provide a freemium version of the development platform to develop consortium blockchain-based applications.

IBM Hyperledger

Hyperledger was introduced in 2015 by the Linux foundation as an umbrella project to advance cross-industry blockchain technologies. Hyperledger Fabric is one of the blockchain projects that provides permissioned consortium blockchains, where users on the network must enroll through a membership service provider. IBM (BlueMix) has partnered with Hyperledger to offer BaaS to its customers. It has also been leveraged with the cognitive capabilities of IBM Watson to provide IoT-based solutions.

Microsoft Azure EBaaS

Initially, Microsoft collaborated with ConsenSys to offer **Ethereum blockchain-as-a-service (EBaaS)** on the Microsoft Azure cloud platform. Then they announced project Bletchley to provide consortium, blockchain-based solutions to their clients. Now they are building an enterprise smart contract framework on top of the existing infrastructure that follows a multi-trust model, which will allow their clients to harness their DApp development skills.

Amazon Eris

Amazon announced they would be offering the BaaS in collaboration with the digital currency group. They developed Eris on top of the Amazon cloud, which is a platform for building, testing, maintaining, and operating distributed applications with a blockchain backend to wrangle complex smart contracts.

Unfortunately, this service is currently unavailable to new users and is provided to old cloud-based clients of Amazon.

Dark web marketplace

To really understand the dark web, we need to differentiate it from the normal web. By normal web, we imply the surface web that we browse using a web page address, or search using natural language typed into search engines, such as Google or Bing. There is yet another type of web called the deep web. *Figure 10.4* depicts the three strata of the web using an iceberg analogy:

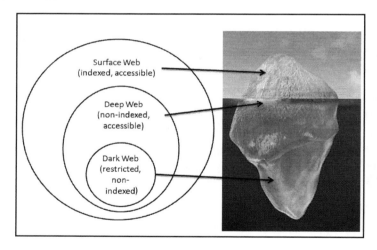

Figure 10.4: Web kernel diagram and iceberg analogy

In simple words, the surface web is anything on the internet that a search engine can find and index. The deep web is something a search engine cannot find. To understand intuitively how search engines find a page, we can do a manual exercise by going to any news channel website and then keep clicking on the articles as they come up.

So, we navigate throughout the article by clicking on some web links, which lands us to a new page of articles. This is what, in search engine parlance, is called web crawling. Now, there are many other sites such as Expedia or Airbnb, which cannot be fully explored just by crawling. We need to provide inputs such as flight date, departure city, arrival city, economy or business class, and number of hotel rooms required in order to move through such pages. They even ask for our name, email, and contacts, which then takes us to new web content. Such websites cannot be explored using a search engine alone. These are parts of the deep web.

The dark web can be considered as a subset of the deep web that has been intentionally hidden and is inaccessible through standard web browsers. So, even though both the surface web and deep web can be explored using a standard browser such as Chrome, Firefox, IE, Opera, or Safari, to navigate through the dark web we need a totally new browser called the Tor browser (there is also I2P and others, but Tor is more prominent). The website address ends with `.onion` suggesting the file type.

Figure 10.5 shows such an `.onion` site called hidden wiki using the Tor browser. Note that, the opposite is true; that is, Tor can be used to browse the surface web pages:

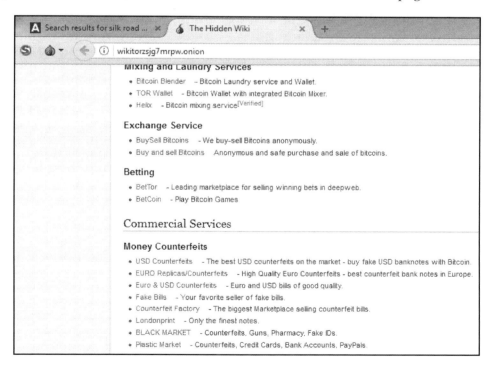

Figure 10.5: Hidden Wiki on the dark web

As you can observe in the hidden wiki, the dark web is full of illegal ongoing activities, ranging from drug dealing and counterfeiting, to hired assassination and illegal arms purchase.

Figure 10.6 represents one such site for fake UK passports. Also, you can notice the payment is strictly using cryptocurrencies, such as bitcoin. For many sites, Ethereum is also accepted. This is because of the anonymity of the source that cryptocurrencies enjoy:

Figure 10.6: Fake ID offering UK passport

Unfortunately, such sites are pretty short-lived and keep changing domain names. A study by Virgil Griffith et al. a team of researchers at MIT, has revealed that more than 87% `.onion` web pages that they traced while crawling get lost. They also suggested that the word "web" in dark web is a misnomer and it is apparently a set of largely isolated dark silos.

Such an isolated setup makes the dark web a safe haven for money launderers. Money laundering looks complex but can be broken down into three stages, as quoted in the **Association of Certified Anti-Money Laundering Specialists (ACAMS)** guide:

1. **Stage one**.
   Placement: The physical disposal of cash or other assets derived from criminal activity
2. **Stage two**.
   Layering: The separation of illicit proceeds from their source by layers of financial transactions intended to conceal the origin of the proceeds
3. **Stage three**.
   Integration: Supplying apparent legitimacy to illicit wealth through the re-entry of the funds into the economy, in what appears to be normal business or personal transactions

For example, a drug dealer can sell their products anonymously using a flash sale on the dark web to their customers worldwide by charging them in Ethereum or bitcoins. Then these coins can be used in cryptocurrency trading or you can just get them converted into some other cryptocurrency in the exchanges. Later these "white" currencies from the exchanges can be converted back to fiat money.

This brings us to the end of this chapter. By now you will have realized that the properties that keep cryptocurrencies and blockchains a state-of-the-art technology and boon to humanity, can also be used for many illegal activities. It is our onus to treat this Pandora's box as the benefit of mankind.

Project smartCV

In this section, we are going to develop smart-contract-based curriculum vitae. Originally designed by *Ryan Hendricks,* a New-York based smart contract developer, this basic contract has two crucial modules:

- Library (cvSection)
- Contract (cvContract)

The contract can be further subdivided into three parts:

1. *Contract definition and constructors*
2. *New profile data module*
3. *Edit profile data module*

Figure 10.7 depicts the `library` function, which is made up of various Struct datatypes:

```
library cvSections {

    struct Profile {
        string _name; string _title; string _summary; string _website; string _phone; string _email;string _description;
    }
    struct Role {
        string _company; string _Role; string _startDate; string _endDate; string _summary; string _highlights;
    }
    struct Education {
        string _institution; string _focusArea; int32 _startYear; int32 _finishYear;
    }
    struct Project {
        string name; string link; string description;
    }
    struct Publication {
        string name; string link; string language;
    }
    struct Skill {
        string name; int32 level;
    }
}
```

Figure 10.7: Library definition

Each structure definition inside the `library` has different set of arguments. Next, we see *Figure 10.8*, which depicts the contract definition:

```
contract cvContract {
    mapping (string => string) Profile;
    address owner;

    cvSections.Project[] public projects;
    cvSections.Education[] public educations;
    cvSections.Skill[] public skills;
    cvSections.Publication[] public publications;


    // =============================
    // ==== CONSTRUCTOR ====
    // =============================
    function cvContract() public{
        owner = msg.sender;
    }

    modifier onlyOwner {
        require(msg.sender == owner);
        _;
    }
}
```

Figure 10.8: cvContract definition

This contract is capable of managing multiple CVs from different persons. This is accomplished by the `setProfile` and `getProfile` modules. *Figure 10.9* depicts the `setProfile` module:

```
// ==============================
// ===== ADD NEW PROFILE =====
// ==============================
function setProfileData (string key, string value) public onlyOwner() {
    Profile[key] = value;
}

function editProfileData (string key, string value) public onlyOwner() {
    Profile[key] = value;
}

function editProject ( bool operation, string name, string link, string description ) public onlyOwner() {
    if (operation) {
        projects.push(cvSections.Project(name, description, link));
    } else {
        delete projects[projects.length - 1];
    }
}

function editEducation ( bool operation, string name, string speciality, int32 year_start, int32 year_finish ) public onlyOwner() {
    // == similar logic goes here
}

function editSkill(bool operation, string name, int32 level) public onlyOwner() {
    // == similar logic goes here
}

function editPublication (bool operation, string name, string link, string language) public onlyOwner() {
    // == similar logic goes here
}
```

Figure 10.9: New profile add module

In a similar fashion, *Figure 10.10* depicts the get profile data, which is used to check after any append on updates to the main cv contract:

```
// ==============================================
// ======= Retriving Profile data =======
// ==============================================
function getProfileData (string arg) public constant returns (string) {
    return Profile[arg];
}

function getSize(string arg) public view returns (uint) {
    if (keccak256(arg) == keccak256("projects")) { return projects.length; }
    if (keccak256(arg) == keccak256("educations")) { return educations.length; }
    if (keccak256(arg) == keccak256("publications")) { return publications.length; }
    if (keccak256(arg) == keccak256("skills")) { return skills.length; }
    revert();
}
```

Figure 10.10: The get profile module

Once the entire contract is compiled, the remix output looks like *Figure 10.11*:

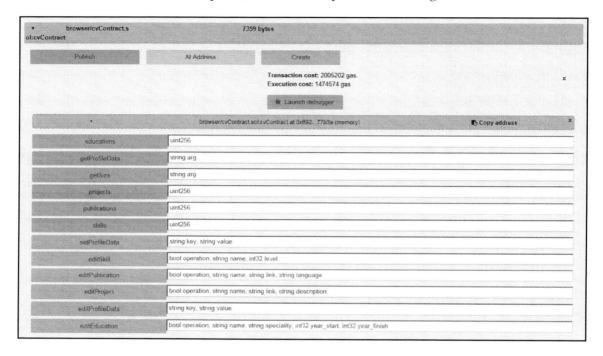

Figure 10.11: cvContract

The blue icons in the preceding screenshot are used to fetch the data and the pink icons are used to input the data.

We can add multiple profile and other attributes such as publication and skills, as shown in *Figure 10.12*:

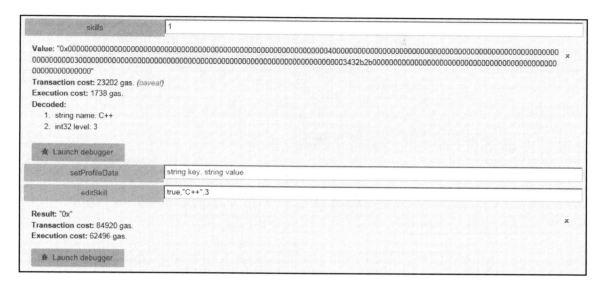

Figure 10.12: Get_Set skills

Moreover, we can submit the codes of this smart contract on GitHub and then introduce it to ethercast as shown in *Figure 10.13*:

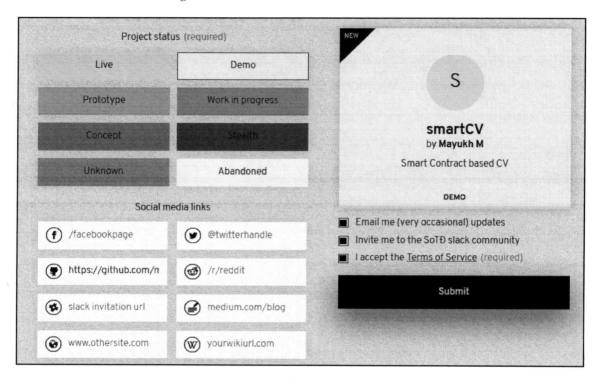

Figure 10.13: Ethercast

This way, we can develop and publish a demo/prototype smart-contract-based CV, which can be finally published on public Ethereum chain or private chain.

Summary

The chapter started with a concept-enhancing discussion on private, consortium, and public blockchains. We saw that public blockchains are mostly permissionless by nature, while private blockchains are strictly permissioned. Hence, industries prefer the middle way of consortium blockchaining, to achieve a democracy among stakeholders. We then listed a few developmental platforms that help us in setting up such consortium blockchains. Hyperledger from IBM, Azure from Microsoft, and AWS Cloud promised us an exciting road map for consortium blockchains. We then explored the concepts of money laundering, and how dark web marketplaces have been used since the beginning of the cryptocurrency evolution to fuel this ever-increasing economic plague. We ended the chapter with a balanced note about how the concepts of smart contracts and blockchains have opened up a new set of Pandora's boxes, and how we as technologists, have the onus of squeezing out the goodness from them.

In Chapter 11, *Advanced Topics and the Road Ahead*, we will discuss some advanced topics in the ever-growing field of blockchains and smart contracts, and wrap up our chunk of learning in this book.

11

Advanced Topics and the Road Ahead

This chapter deals with select advanced topics related to Ethereum and blockchains. We discuss five broad topics to further your research interests and academic pursuits. We begin with a section on common design patterns that can be applied during smart contract development at enterprise level. Then we move on to the topic of decentralized, autonomous corporations and societies. We devote an entire section to the **Ethereum improvement proposal (EIP)**, where we discuss the life cycle of a proposal. Consortium blockchain concepts are revisited with case studies. We conclude the chapter with a unique topic called Tangle and provide indicators to explore the emerging field of graph-based, distributed ledger technology with special emphasis on Iota.

After studying this chapter, you will be able to:

- Identify different design patterns
- Understand the concept of DACs and DAS
- Understand the Ethereum improvement proposal life cycle
- Discuss consortium blockchains using case studies
- Appreciate the concepts behind Tangle and Iota

Common design patterns

Recently, my dad retired and found comfort in his passion of cooking. He has his own set of spices that he does not even share with my mom. From chicken to chickpeas, whatever dishes he prepares have a typical hint of his signature masala mix. He argues that the flavor is not about the spices he uses, but the pattern he applies to mix his spices while designing his recipes.

So, what is a design pattern? In software engineering parlance, it is generally a piece of pseudo-code that represents a generic solution that can be reused while developing applications to avoid reinventing-wheel scenarios. A common example would be the functionality of passcode-based user-authentication. Most applications require this basic functionality and they are almost similar in design. A user has to first register with the application. The application then sends an OTP or confirmation link to set up up a new passcode and registers a new user. Once a registered user has to log in, they have to provide a username and password to the application. The application then checks its registry database for this username and password and permits or blocks the user accordingly.

Software design patterns are broadly classified into three categories, as shown in *Figure 11.1*:

- **Structural**: Such patterns deal with relationships between entities, making it easier for these entities to work together
- **Creational**: Such patterns make it easier to create objects in a way that suits a given situation

- **Behavioral**: Such patterns are used to communicate flexibly between two or more entities:

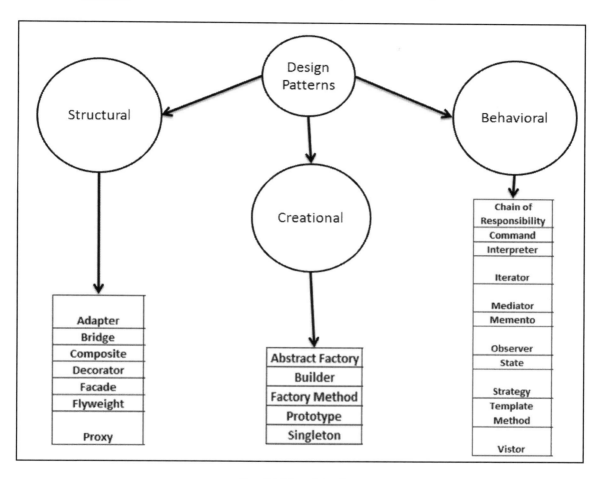

Figure 11.1: Software design patterns

These three categories are also called the **Gang of Four (GoF)** design patterns, which refers to its four authors, namely Erich Gamma, Richard Helm, Ralph Johnson, and John Vlissides. *Figure 11.2* briefly explains each GoF design pattern.

In the following section, we will discuss some frequently used design patterns by smart contract developers on the Ethereum blockchain:

Abstract Factory	Allows for the creation of objects without specifying their concrete type
Builder	Used to create complex objects
Factory Method	Creates objects without specifying the exact class to create
Prototype	Creates a new object from an existing object
Singleton	Ensures only one instance of an object is created

Adapter	Allows for two incompatible classes to work together by wrapping an interface around one of the existing classes
Bridge	Decouples an abstraction so two classes can vary independently
Composite	Takes a group of objects into a single object
Decorator	Allows for an object's behavior to be extended dynamically at run time
Facade	Provides a simple interface to a more complex underlying object
Flyweight	Reduces the cost of complex object models
Proxy	Provides a placeholder interface to an underlying object to control access, reduce cost, or reduce complexity

Chain of Responsibility	Delegates commands to a chain of processing objects
Command	Creates objects which encapsulate actions and parameters
Interpreter	Implements a specialized language
Iterator	Accesses the elements of an object sequentially without exposing its underlying representation
Mediator	Allows loose coupling between classes by being the only class that has detailed knowledge of their methods
Memento	Provides the ability to restore an object to its previous state
Observer	Is a publish/subscribe pattern which allows a number of observer objects to see an event
State	Allows an object to alter its behavior when its internal state changes
Strategy	Allows one of a family of algorithms to be selected on-the-fly at run-time
Template Method	Defines the skeleton of an algorithm as an abstract class ,allowing its sub-classes to provide concrete behavior
Vistor	Separates an algorithm from an object structure by moving the hierarchy of methods into one object

Figure 11.2: GoF design pattern summary

Restricting access

Access restriction is a common functionality for smart contracts. In earlier chapters, we discussed how external contracts exploited the access related vulnerability in the Parity library contract to self-destruct the entire wallet library and block $300 million-worth of ethers. We can never restrict any human or computer from reading the contract's state. We can make it a bit difficult by using encryption.

The only viable thing for a developer to keep in mind is that the state of a contract is public, and then design it in a way without problems. We can, however, restrict the number of entities allowed to make modifications to a contract by using function modifiers on the entity addresses. Such addresses can be maintained on an **access control list** (**ACL**), but with a caveat, that the read-only access will be available to anyone for a public blockchain.

Modifiers are used to change the body of a function. If such modifiers are used, they prepend a check that only passes if the function is called from a certain address.

This design implementation is a kind of structural design pattern.

Token systems

These are related to behavioral design patterns. Token systems are analogous to the template method, where the skeleton of an algorithm is defined as an abstract class, allowing the sub-classes to provide concrete behavior.

In the previous chapters, we discussed how the ERC20 standard is implemented for Ethereum-based token systems for compatibility. ERC20 is not a piece of code, software, or technology. It is a technical specification.

Figure 11.3 depicts a sample ERC20 standard contract interface with the recommended function definitions:

```
1  contract ERC20 {
2      function totalSupply() constant returns (uint totalSupply);
3      function balanceOf(address _owner) constant returns (uint balance);
4      function transfer(address _to, uint _value) returns (bool success);
5      function transferFrom(address _from, address _to, uint _value) returns (bool success);
6      function approve(address _spender, uint _value) returns (bool success);
7      function allowance(address _owner, address _spender) constant returns (uint remaining);
8      event Transfer(address indexed _from, address indexed _to, uint _value);
9      event Approval(address indexed _owner, address indexed _spender, uint _value);
10 }
```

Figure 11.3: ERC20 token system

Factory pattern

This design pattern is a kind of creational design pattern. Using this pattern, objects can be created without specifying the exact class of creation.

Figure 11.4 is a simple hub (`Barrel`) that deploys contracts (`Whisky`) from a template and keeps track of the contracts created.

`Whisky` is part of the source file so `Barrel` can "see it" during compilation. `Whisky`'s bytecode will become part of `Barrel` so the `newWhisky()` invocation knows what to do.

It is not necessary to deploy the template (`Whisky`), once the hub (`Barrel`) has been deployed.

We can create as many of the latter as needed by calling a function in the former:

```solidity
pragma solidity ^0.4.11;

contract Barrel {
    address[] public contracts;
    function getContractCount()
        public
        constant
        returns(uint contractCount)
    {
        return contracts.length;
    }
    function newWhisky()
        public
        returns(address newContract)
    {
        Whisky c = new Whisky();
        contracts.push(c);
        return c;
    }
}

contract Whisky {
    function getFlavor()
        public
        constant
        returns (string flavor)
    {
        return "single malt";
    }
}
```

Figure 11.4: Factory pattern for Barrel and Whisky

Registries

Registries are mainly data design patterns. IT helps to refer contracts or addresses in a human-readable form. It typically consists of name-to-address associations. It is analogous to the facade (literally meaning a deceptive outward appearance) design pattern and belongs to the category of structural design patterns.

In the Solidity programming language, the registry pattern can be implemented using the mapping keyword. It is used to structure value types, such as Booleans, integers, addresses, and structs. It consists of two main parts: a _KeyType and a _ValueType. They appear in the following syntax:

```
mapping (_KeyType => _ValueType) mapName
```

Voting systems

Voting systems are complex design patterns that comprise many simpler design patterns, such as factory, proxy, memento, composite, observer, and chain of responsibilities. Such complex design patterns can themselves serve as standalone applications.

Implementing a completely decentralized voting system is still an open challenge, as the following modules are necessary to design any voting system:

- **Voter**: One who casts a vote. They must be identifiable to avoid double voting. Yet their votes must be private.
- **Authenticator**: This module authenticates the voter's identity.
- **User**: They are basically volunteers who assist the voters for correct usage of the voting process but do not influence the voter's decision.
- **Election officer**: This module supervises any discrepancy that may arise during the voting process.
- **Administrator**: This module maintains the authenticator as well as anonymity of a voter's choice.
- **Researcher**: These are basically statistical agents to detect anomalies and maintain counts.
- **Database**: This is the repository where the voting transactions get stored, as well as voter identity.

Such modules fit well with a centralized repository and authority.

Voting systems, as a unified design pattern, are generally used while developing decentralized autonomous corporations or societies, which we will study in the next section.

DACs and DAS

We have devoted an entire chapter to **decentralized autonomous organization (DAO)**. We also discussed at length, the infamous DAO hack and the vulnerabilities associated with its sloppy programming.

In this section, we will try to understand two similar-sounding concepts that are easily confused with a DAO. These are **decentralized autonomous corporations (DACs)** and **decentralized autonomous society (DAS)**.

To fuel our confusion, it is also true that DACs are a subset of DAO. The term DAC was coined by Daniel Larimer. He stated that DACs pay dividends, while DAOs are inherently non-profit. In a DAC, shares are purchasable and tradable in some fashion, and those shares potentially entitle their holders to continual receipts based on the DAC's success. Of course, we can make money from a DAO, but not by investing in it; by participating in its ecosystem.

As stated by Vitalik Buterin, the distinction between DAO and DAC is more of a fluid one and hinges on emphasizing to what extent dividends are the main point, and to what extent it is more about earning tokens by participation. For example, bitcoin can be considered a DAO. Owning some bitcoin does not entitle us to claim any profit or decision-making ability inside the bitcoin ecosystem. But if we hold a few shares of Microsoft or Google, we do have a legal entitlement of a profit-sharing claim.

DAS, on the other hand, is still an emerging concept. J.Z. Garrod, in his insightful paper *"The Real World of the Decentralized Autonomous Society"* has defined DAS as an emerging society, in which humans are freed from centralized forms of power through proliferation of distributed autonomous organizations.

DAS is a parallel reality, where the role of government decreases and the control of all processes passes directly to the participants. DAS is only at the beginning of its development but it is the future. This future is not about chat-bots, self-drive cars, or augmented reality but about the different approaches to the flow of information, inherent biases, and distributed systems. It is going to change our way of communication and interaction with the rest of society.

Ethereum improvement proposal

To become a successful Ethereum smart contract developer, apart from technical and architectural knowledge, we need to possess the ability to understand design documents. Such documentation is the Holy Grail for any developer, and provides the necessary insights into various intricacies and rationales behind any functionality. For a developer in the Ethereum community, such design documentation is maintained by many senior developers worldwide, and is known as the Ethereum improvement proposal.

The Ethereum improvement proposal is a design documentation that provides information to the Ethereum community. It is used to propose a new Ethereum feature, a new process, or a new environment. EIP provides a concise technical specification and rationale for a proposed feature. The authors of an EIP are responsible for building consensus within the community and documenting opinions of critics. Anyone can propose a new implementation using EIP and if the community agrees with it, they become part of the implementation.

The EIP purpose and guidelines have been authored by Martin Becze and Hudson Jameson. They are heavily derived from the **bitcoin improvement proposal (BIP-0001)**, written by Amir Taaki, which in turn was inspired by the **Python enhancement proposal (PEP-0001)**. The copyright on these proposals are waived under CC0 and are freely available to the public at the following GitHub:

```
https://github.com/ethereum/EIPs
```

In the subsequent sections, we will discuss the bare minimum details about EIPs that will equip you to navigate through the EIP GitHub yourself, without getting lost because of information overload.

Rational behind EIPs

EIPs make it convenient to track implementation progress. Each implementation should ideally be listed as an EIP. This allows participants and investors to conveniently know about the current status of a given library or implementation.

Types of EIP

Figure 11.5 illustrates various types of improvement proposals recommended by the Ethereum community. Mainly, the proposals are of three types:

- **Standard track EIP**: These proposals affect the Ethereum implementation. For example, change of block size, transaction validity rules, and interoperability of applications can be part of such proposals.
- **Informational EIP**: These proposals flag any design issue or provide general guidelines. However, such a proposal does not introduce new features.
- **Meta EIP**: These are also called process EIPs. Such proposals suggest changes to guidelines and processes. Unlike informational EIPs, users cannot ignore such EIPs once they are implemented:

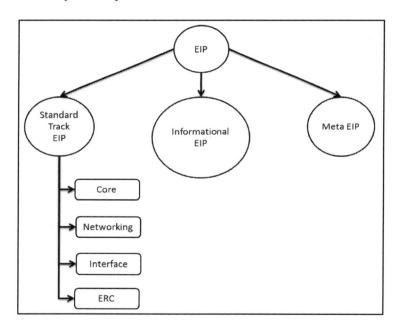

Figure 11.5: Categories of EIPs

Standard track EIPs are further divided into four sub-categories:

- **Core**: These proposals are mainly consensus-critical and involve fundamental changes to the Ethereum protocol and implementation strategies. For example, EIP7 proposed a new opcode, `DELEGATECALL`.

- **Networking**: These proposals primarily deal with changes to swarm, whisper, devp2p, and light sub-protocol implementation. For example, EIP8 proposed devp2p forward compatibility requirements for the homestead edition.
- **Interface**: These proposals provide improvement to the ABI interface or RPC standards. For example, EIP6 proposed renaming suicide opcode.
- **ERC**: These are mainly **request for comments** (**RCs**) and we discussed one such proposal, ERC20, in a previous chapter. These proposals deal with application-level standards and conventions. For example, EIP20 proposed ERC20 token compliance.

EIP life cycle

The life cycle of a proposal life cycle is pretty straightforward. On a typical happy path, a proposal is born with an idea of improvement for Ethereum. Such an idea is formalized by a draft EIP. Once the EIP has gained the confidence of the Ethereum community, the proposal is accepted and assigned an EIP number. Then it is implemented using code, and given a **Final** status, or if it is a guideline, made active on GitHub. The EIP list is eventually updated with the finalized EIP proposal number. The life cycle of a proposal can dramatically change if it is critically opposed by the general community:

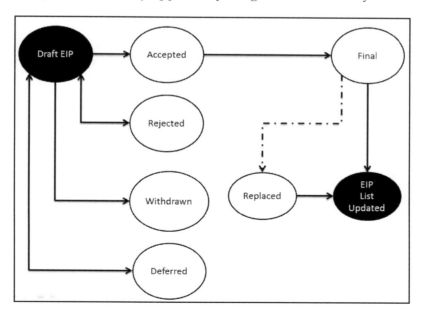

Figure 11.6: EIP workflow

Technically, "life cycle" is a misnomer. We must generally refer to it as a proposal workflow. This is because the proposal does not change its state itself; external human intervention is required to change the status of a proposal. *Figure 11.6* illustrates the different statuses of a proposal, starting from a draft, until it is finalized and updated on the EIP list. Also note that EIPs can be superseded, making the older EIP obsolete. For informational EIPs, making them **Active** is analogous to a final state.

EIP template

A typical improvement proposal template can have the following 10 sections:

- **Preamble**: EIP begins with an RFC 822 style header preamble, as shown in *Figure 11.7*. EIPs may have a `requires` header. This indicates the EIPs on which this current EIP is dependent.
- **Simple summary**: This section provides a layman-approachable explanation of the EIP.
- **Abstract**: This is a short description of approximately 200 words to address the technical issue.
- **Motivation**: This section should clearly explain the present inadequacy of the protocol and how the proposal is going to mitigate or resolve it. Without sufficient motivation, an EIP can be rejected outright.
- **Specification**: This section describes the semantics and syntax of any new feature. The specifications should be detailed enough to support interoperability.
- **Rationale**: This section provides evidence of consensus within the community, important objections, and alternate work considered for this proposal.
- **Backward compatibility**: In this section, any backward incompatibility needs to be discussed and a conclusion reached.
- **Test cases**: This section is mandatory for core EIP changes but optional for other EIP proposals, which lists a few positive and negative test cases.
- **Implementation**: This section's instructions must be completed before the status of an EIP is made "final".
- **Copyrights**: EIPs are always published in the public domain with all copyrights waived.

Figure 11.7 illustrates a sample EIP that has been given a final status number EIP6:

Preamble

EIP: 6
Title: Renaming SUICIDE opcode
Author: Hudson Jameson <hudson@hudsonjameson.com>
Status: Final
Type: Standards Track
Layer: Applications
Created: 2015-11-22

Abstract

The solution proposed in this EIP is to change the name of the SUICIDE opcode in Ethereum programming languages with SELFDESTRUCT.

Motivation

Mental health is a very real issue for many people and small notions can make a difference. Those dealing with loss or depression would benefit from not seeing the word suicide in our programming languages. By some estimates, 350 million people worldwide suffer from depression. The semantics of Ethereum's programming languages need to be reviewed often if we wish to grow our ecosystem to all types of developers.

An Ethereum security audit commissioned by DEVolution, GmbH and performed by Least Authority recommended the following:

Replace the instruction name "suicide" with a less connotative word like "self-destruct", "destroy", "terminate", or "close", especially since that is a term describing the natural conclusion of a contract.

The primary reason for us to change the term suicide is to show that people matter more than code and Ethereum is a mature enough of a project to recognize the need for a change. Suicide is a heavy subject and we should make every effort possible to not affect those in our development community who suffer from depression or who have recently lost someone to suicide. Ethereum is a young platform and it will cause less headaches if we implement this change early on in it's life.

Implementation

SELFDESTRUCT is added as an alias of SUICIDE opcode (rather than replacing it).

Copyright

Copyright and related rights waived via CC0.

Figure 11.7: EIP6 summary

Consortium blockchains

As we discussed in the previous chapter, consortium blockchains lie in between private and public blockchains, and also in the middle of the permission spectrum. In this section, we will do a case study using consortium blockchains adopted by banks.

Banks need blockchains to make money transfers faster, easier, and cheaper. The following are the limitations of a public blockchain if used for this purpose:

- **Speed**: Banks need to do transactions in real time, while Ethereum takes around 12 sec to confirm one transaction.
- **Permission**: Anyone can take part in the consensus for a public blockchain. But banks prefer to remain an authority or hire a regulatory body.
- **Security**: Due to the limited number of participants, proof-of-work is not secure enough.
- **Privacy**: Basically divided into identity privacy and data privacy, it is quite hard to maintain such privacy on a public Ethereum blockchain.

Consortium blockchains generally employ proof of authority, where there is no need for mining. It is a consensus mechanism where the truth is arrived at by referring to a list of validators. Such validators are mainly a group of nodes that are allowed to participate in the consensus.

Case study on R3 Corda

R3 is a distributed ledger company that has developed a blockchain platform, Corda, which can help with a lot of institutional finance services.

Corda has been designed for recording and processing financial agreements and implementing the vision contained in this document.

The Corda platform also supports smart contracts. In Corda, updates are applied using transactions that consume existing state objects and produce new state objects. There are two aspects of consensus: transaction validity and transaction uniqueness.

The smart contracts on Corda are called CorDapp. A CorDapp is generally written in Java or kotlin.

CorDapps are made up of the following key components:

- **States**: This defines the facts over which agreement is reached
- **Contracts**: This defines what constitutes a valid ledger update
- **Services**: This provides long-lived utilities within the node
- **Serialization whitelists**: This restricts what types your node will receive off the wire

The node structure of Corda has the following structure:

```
├── certificates // The node's certificates
├── corda-webserver.jar // The built-in node webserver
├── corda.jar // The core Corda libraries
├── logs // The node logs
├── node.conf // The node's configuration files
├── persistence.mv.db // The node's database
└── plugins // The CorDapps JARs installed on the node
```

A node can have four broad categories of functionality:

- **Network map**: This provides a way to resolve identities to physical node addresses and associated public keys
- **Notary**: This witnesses state spends and has the final say in whether a transaction is a double-spend or not
- **Oracle**: This links the ledger to the outside world by providing facts that affect the validity of transactions
- **Regular mode**: This starts protocols communicating with other nodes, notaries, and oracles and evolves their private ledger

Tangle beyond blockchain

We have devoted the entire book to blockchain-based smart contract development. But there is another ecosystem of cryptocurrencies that are not based on blockchains. These are based on direct acyclic graphs or DAGs. Such systems are called graph-based, distributed ledger technology. Some noteworthy DAG-based DLTs are DagCoin, Byteball, Hashgraph, and Tangle.

DagCoin was the first DAG-based DLT launched in 2012 by Sergio Demian Lerner, pioneer of blockchain-free cryptocurrencies. That was closely followed by Byteball by Anton Churyumov. Hashgraph is currently a private DLT based on DAG, invented by Leemon Baird. Tangle technology was introduced as a whitepaper by Sergey Popov on April 3, 2016. The cryptocurrency on Tangle aims at supporting transactions between **Internet-of-Things** (**IoT**) appliances, hence aptly named Iota.

In the following sections, we will explore the shortcoming of a traditional blockchain, the technology behind Tangle, a GitHub analysis of Iota, and how to purchase and store Iota cryptocurrency.

Shortcomings of a blockchain

Traditional blockchains suffer from two major problems for currency transaction:

- **Mining-pool oligopoly**: Taking into consideration the competitive nature of mining rewards, mining pools with high-end technology make the process profitless for individual miners. Also, with decreasing mining rewards, as we reach the threshold of mining (for example, in bitcoin, currently it is 12.5 BTC; earlier it was 25 BTC, which came down from 50 BTC), miners will be charging high transaction costs to justify the cost of mining and transaction validation using electricity.
- Slow validation processes with no possibility of speed-up.

Tangle demystified

Tangle is a new data structure based on direct acyclic graph. This data structure has no blocks, no chains, and no miners.

So how does a public ledger on Tangle achieve consensus or validate transactions in the absence of miners? This is achieved by involving the user who wants to make a transaction validate and approve two past transactions. This unique way of attesting two past transactions ensures the whole network achieves consensus on the current state of an approved transaction.

An Iota transaction can be broken down into three distinct steps:

1. **Signing**: We sign the transaction inputs with our private keys.
2. **Tip selection: Markov Chain Monte Carlo (MCMC)**: This method of sampling is used to randomly select two tips, which will be validated by our transaction, namely `branchTransaction` and `trunkTransaction`.
3. **Proof-of-Work**: In order to have our transaction accepted by the network, we need to do some PoW, similar to HashCash but not like bitcoin.

An encoded transaction of Iota consists of 2,673 trytes. A tryte is a ternary equivalent of a byte. It is generally represented by alphabet characters starting with 9. The rest of the numbers are denoted from A to Z. Iota uses a balanced trinary system. To make the trinary code human-readable, Iota developers created alphabet mapping to numbers, as shown in *Figure 11.8*:

Tryte	Dec	Char		Tryte	Dec	Char
0, 0, 0	0	9				
1, 0, 0	1	A		-1,-1,-1	-13	N
-1, 1, 0	2	B		0,-1,-1	-12	O
0, 1, 0	3	C		1,-1,-1	-11	P
1, 1, 0	4	D		-1, 0,-1	-10	Q
-1,-1, 1	5	E		0, 0,-1	-9	R
0,-1, 1	6	F		1, 0,-1	-8	S
1,-1, 1	7	G		-1, 1,-1	-7	T
-1, 0, 1	8	H		0, 1,-1	-6	U
0, 0, 1	9	I		1, 1,-1	-5	V
1, 0, 1	10	J		-1,-1, 0	-4	W
-1, 1, 1	11	K		0,-1, 0	-3	Z
0, 1, 1	12	L		1,-1, 0	-2	Y
1, 1, 1	13	M		-1, 0, 0	-1	Z

Figure 11.8: Iota trite alphabets

As there are no miners, the genesis of Iota on Tangle has introduced all the coins into the ecosystem at once, which equals ((3^33-1)/2), equal to 2,779,530,283,277,761 Iota.

Due to the inherent structure of Iota, it possesses the following range of features:

- **Scalability**: Due to the parallelized validation of transactions with no limit to the number of transactions that can be validated in a certain time interval, Iota experiences a very high transaction throughput and it increases with user participation
- **Free from transaction fee**: There is no transaction fees due to the absence of miners to validate transactions
- **Decentralization**: Due to the absence of miners, every user who wants to transact has to actively participate in the consensus, making Iota more de-centralized in nature than blockchain-based protocols
- **Quantum-immunity**: Iota uses the Winternitz one-time signature and utilizes a newly designed trinary hash function called curl, which makes it immune to quantum computing threats to a certain extent, as we cannot use an address more than once after we have sent some Iota from it

Iota GitHub analysis

If you go to GitHub and search for Iota, you will get to a page that links the repositories of Iota cryptocurrency. The GitHub page of Iota consists of three main repositories, namely wallet, **Iota reference implementation (IRI)**, and Iota JavaScript library. *Figure 11.9* depicts these repositories:

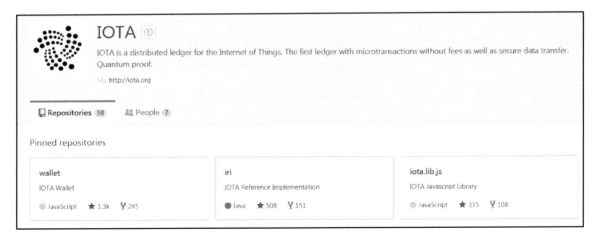

Figure 11.9: Iota GitHub (https://github.com/iotaledger)

Among these three repositories, IRI is the most interesting repository. So what is IRI? It is a reference implementation of the Iota protocol. Much like bitcoin, Iota is also a protocol operating on a DAG-based database called Tangle and not on a blockchain. Now, IRI represents a blueprint of Iota. So, when Iota developers made the reference implementation in Java, they are actually telling the world, *"this is how Iota functions work and using this reference implementation we can use any other Turing complete programming language to set up Iota clients or Iota nodes."*

Now if we step back and think about it for a while, we will realize that using this reference implementation, we can even use Solidity, which is a Turing complete programming language, to develop an Iota client, node, or even a smart contract. The possibility is endless and quite exciting. Isn't it?

Next we have the Iota Wallet. It is written in JavaScript and it is an electron app. So what is electron? It is a tool that programmers can use to package a website as a native application. Basically, when we want to develop native applications for macOS, Windows, or Linux, one way to do it would be to code everything from scratch, which is time consuming and confusing as we have to maintain several different code bases. Instead, what we can do is write a website and package it as a Windows, macOS, or Linux application. Now, if we want to make changes or develop the application further, we just develop this website further and package it once again. Electron is gaining traction on many other cryptocurrency projects as well.

Finally, we have a JavaScript library. It provides coding tools and APIs for other developers. Suppose, as a developer, we want to create a website to interact with the Iota protocol. We can use their JavaScript libraries to invoke various Iota functionalities.

In the next section, we will see how to purchase and store Iota cryptocurrency.

Purchase and storage of Iota

Presently, Iota cannot be purchased directly using fiat currency. It can be bought from crypto-exchanges such as Bitfinex or Binance using ethers or bitcoin.

The following steps need to be followed to buy Iota:

1. Create an account on coinbase.
2. Buy BTC or ETH in coinbase.
3. Open an account on Bitfinex or Binance.

4. Transfer some BTC or ETH to Bitfinex or Binance.

5. Buy Iota by placing an order bid using BTC or ETH. Iota is sold in millions called MIOTA.

Storage of Iota is pretty straightforward by nature. We can store the Iota in the Iota Wallet as provided in the Iota GitHub. Or we can use paper wallets as provided in the following link: `https://arancauchi.github.io/IOTA-Paper-Wallet/`.

To create a paper wallet, we need to pass the 81-digit code and generate a QR code, as show in *Figure 11.10*. We can then take a printout of the wallet and store it in a safe place:

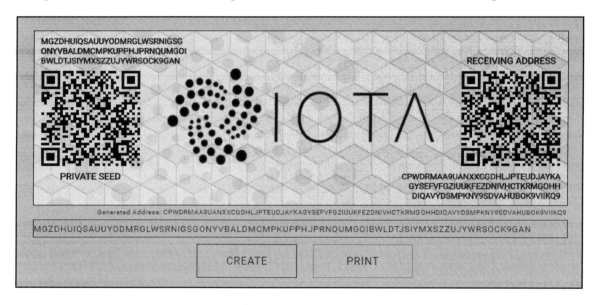

Figure 11.10: Paper wallet for Iota

From Tangle, beyond blockchain, we could end up in an exciting new phase of technological advancement. We will soon be experiencing machine-to-machine economies, which will be facilitated by Internet-of-Things appliances, and Iota might eventually rule the cryptocurrency ranks.

This brings us to the end of this book. But your journey has just began into this exciting world of smart contracts. Consult the wider community spread over YouTube channels, GitHub links, Reddit threads, and stack exchange forums. You now have the power to change the world using this technology in the midst of all the **fear-uncertainty-doubt (FUD)**; all you need is the ability to create some good source code.

Exit 0

Summary

We began this chapter with a quick introduction to design patterns and discussed common patterns, such as restricting access, factory patterns, token systems, registries, and voting systems that are used for smart contract development. Then we moved on to understand the concept of decentralized autonomous corporations and society, and how they are different from DAOs. We explored a few crucial proposals related to Ethereum after understanding the proposal life cycle. Select case studies were picked to understand the future implications of consortium blockchains. We wrapped up the chapter by briefly introducing the world of graph-based distributed ledgers with GitHub analysis of the Iota cryptocurrency, and an introduction to Tangle.

Other Books You May Enjoy

If you enjoyed this book, you may be interested in these other books by Packt:

Building Blockchain Projects
Narayan Prusty

ISBN: 978-1-78712-214-7

- Walk through the basics of the Blockchain technology
- Implement Blockchain's technology and its features, and see what can be achieved using them
- Build DApps using Solidity and Web3.js
- Understand the geth command and cryptography
- Create Ethereum wallets
- Explore consortium blockchain

Mastering Blockchain

Imran Bashir

ISBN: 978-1-78712-544-5

- Master the theoretical and technical foundations of blockchain technology
- Fully comprehend the concept of decentralization, its impact and relationship with blockchain technology
- Experience how cryptography is used to secure data with practical examples
- Grasp the inner workings of blockchain and relevant mechanisms behind Bitcoin and alternative cryptocurrencies
- Understand theoretical foundations of smart contracts
- Identify and examine applications of blockchain technology outside of currencies
- Investigate alternate blockchain solutions including Hyperledger, Corda, and many more
- Explore research topics and future scope of blockchain technology

Leave a review - let other readers know what you think

Please share your thoughts on this book with others by leaving a review on the site that you bought it from. If you purchased the book from Amazon, please leave us an honest review on this book's Amazon page. This is vital so that other potential readers can see and use your unbiased opinion to make purchasing decisions, we can understand what our customers think about our products, and our authors can see your feedback on the title that they have worked with Packt to create. It will only take a few minutes of your time, but is valuable to other potential customers, our authors, and Packt. Thank you!

Index